THE MUSLIM BROTHERS IN PURSUIT OF LEGITIMACY

THE MUSLIM BROTHERS IN PURSUIT OF LEGITIMACY

Power and Political Islam in Egypt under Mubarak

Hesham Al-Awadi

I.B. TAURIS
LONDON · NEW YORK

New paperback edition published in 2014 by I.B.Tauris & Co. Ltd
6 Salem Road, London W2 4BU
175 Fifth Avenue, New York NY 10010
www.ibtauris.com

First published in hardback in 2004 by Tauris Academic Studies,
an imprint of I.B.Tauris & Co. Ltd

ISBN: 978 1 78076 430 6
eISBN: 978 0 85773 564 5

A full CIP record for this book is available from the British Library
A full CIP record is available from the Library of Congress

Library of Congress Catalog Card Number: available

Typeset by Initial Typesetting Services, Edinburgh

CONTENTS

ACKNOWLEDGEMENTS

When I began the research on the Muslim Brothers and Mubarak in October 2000 I was unmarried. Now I am the father of four daughters – Hadil, Sara, Salma and Farah, who bring me all the joy in the world. Throughout the period of my research my wife, May, has provided me with continuous support and encouragement, and without her endless patience and loving understanding of the importance to me of this book, the challenges would have been more difficult.

During the period of the research, I came to regard Egypt as a second home. Despite the various difficulties that I encountered, living in Egypt was an exciting experience, largely because of the support of my family. Despite my mother's worries when I decided to visit 'risky' areas in Egypt, such as Asyut in the 1990s, she never dissuaded me from doing so, being even more determined than I was that the resources of the research should be extended. My utmost gratitude goes to her and to my wonderful father who has been unfailing in his generosity of spirit.

My special thanks to Professor Tim Niblock, who gave me much support and reassurance throughout my research. Without his insights and comments the study would not have come to fruition. I would also like to thank Professor James Piscatori for his support and valuable comments on ways in which the study might be enhanced. I am also grateful to Mrs Lindy Ayubi, who patiently edited the book and gave useful advice on ways to improve it.

Contacts in Egypt were crucial for the research, especially because of the particular sensitivity of the subject of the relationship between the Muslim Brothers and Mubarak's regime, especially before the 2011 Revolution. Various people facilitated contacts with both sides, and thanks are due to Khalid Munir, Hamid Abdul Majid and Sadek Al-Sharkawi for their valuable assistance.

The internal and unpublished documents of the Muslim Brothers were of immense value to my study and greatly influenced my understanding of the subject. Finally, I acknowledge with grateful appreciation my interviewees who, despite personal engagements and the potential risks involved, agreed to discuss the subject with me. Their valuable input provided the main contribution to the book.

LIST OF FIGURES AND TABLES

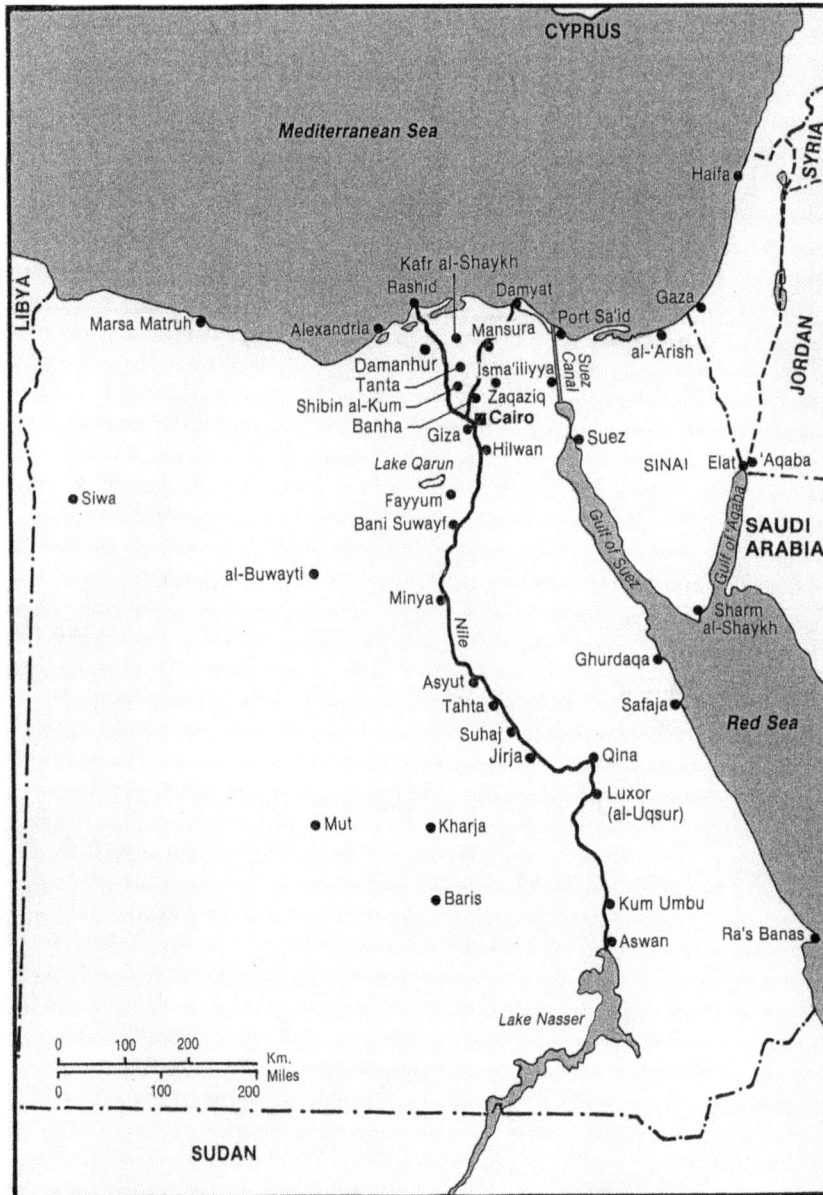

CYPRUS

Mediterranean Sea

Haifa

LIBYA

Marsa Matruh

Kafr al-Shaykh
Rashid
Damyat
Gaza
Port Sa'id
Alexandria
Mansura
al-'Arish

SYRIA
JORDAN

Damanhur
Tanta
Shibin al-Kum
Banha
Giza
Isma'iliyya
Zaqaziq
Suez Canal
Cairo
Hilwan
Suez

Lake Qarun

Siwa

Fayyum
Bani Suwayf

SINAI
Elat
'Aqaba

Gulf of Suez
Gulf of Aqaba

**SAUDI
ARABIA**

al-Buwayti

Minya

Nile

Sharm
al-Shaykh

Ghurdaqa

Asyut
Tahta
Suhaj
Jirja
Qina

Safaja

Red Sea

Mut
Kharja

Luxor
(al-Uqsur)

Baris

Kum Umbu
Aswan

Ra's Banas

Lake Nasser

0   100   200
                    Km.
                    Miles
0   100   200

SUDAN

Egypt

1

INTRODUCTION

Perhaps no one expected that the revolution of 25 January 2011 would topple President Mubarak in 18 days, after having ruled Egypt for 30 years. The authoritarian and brutal regime could not have imagined that a spontaneous, youth-led demonstration could morph into a popular revolution forcing the army to deploy in the streets and impose a curfew, and that chants of 'Bread, freedom, and human dignity' would soon change into the Tunisian slogan of 'The people want to overthrow the regime'. But even more dramatic was the Muslim Brothers' unexpected ascension to power, after winning Egypt's first free presidential elections in May 2012. Their sudden rise to power, after years of exclusion and oppression, was as surprising as the end of the military regime that had ruled the country since 1952. The Muslim Brothers' candidate, Mohammad Morsi, won by a narrow margin (51 per cent) over Ahmed Shafiq, the last prime minister under Mubarak. Remnants of the old regime, the state's apparatuses, including the media, as well as many Copts preferred Shafiq, while the majority who voted for Morsi did so because they identified Shafiq with the old regime, and realised that if he came to power the revolution would be doomed.

But to many Egyptians, and not necessarily those affiliated with the movement, the Muslim Brothers were more than just an alternative. Since the mid-1980s and early 1990s, the movement had gained increasing popularity as a result of its impressive social services, which surpassed those of the regime, and despite its lack of formal state recognition the group enjoyed a popular base of social legitimacy. Although the Brothers' performance in power was not as impressive as when they were in the opposition (after just a year in power there were already public demands for Morsi to step down as President), it remains important to study and analyse this period, which enabled the Brothers following the 25 January revolution to emerge as the most organised force in Egypt.

On the extraordinary morning of 11 September 2001, I happened to be in the London office of the Muslim Brothers conducting interviews for this study. The faces of everyone in the office reflected the shocking scene of aeroplanes crashing into the towers of the World Trade Center in New York. Although the identity of the perpetrators was initially unclear, there were early fears that radical Islamists from Al-Qa'eda might be involved. The Brothers in the office were clearly uncomfortable about the potential implications. If Islamists were indeed involved, such an event would certainly heighten the fears of the Americans, and of the West at large, against Islam and Muslims, and would give more credibility to Huntington's notion of the "clash of civilisations". In the midst of these legitimate Western fears, the significantly visible line of differentiation between moderate and radical Islamists would become blurred or irrelevant. Not only would this register as a seriously mistaken attitude on the part of the United States and the West towards the sophisticated Islamist phenomenon, but it would encourage authoritarian Arab regimes to quell all Islamists indiscriminately, on the basis of would-be conventional wisdom that "all Islamists are potentially dangerous".

Egypt's President Mohammad Hosni Mubarak was among the Arab leaders who had already launched coercive campaigns against Islamists, both moderates and radicals, since the early and mid-1990s. His campaign reached its peak in 1995, when 95 civilian Islamists who were members of the Muslim Brotherhood, were put on trial in military courts, charged with belonging to an illegal organisation and conspiring to overthrow the government. But 11 September 2001, and the international anti-terror climate it created, certainly encouraged the regime to arrest and imprison civilian Islamist figures far more frequently. Atef Ebeid, the Egyptian prime minister, proudly invited Western countries to learn from Egypt's experience of dealing with Islamists instead of criticising its record on human rights, as they had done for the last 20 years. Ebeid's over-confident tone reflected the new realities of the post-September international and American mood. Whereas staff from the American Embassy would have been sent to observe the trials of opposition figures in the days prior to 11 September, more recent arrests of Islamic opposition figures drew no complaints or comments from the Embassy in Cairo.[1] Similar anti-terror measures taken in Britain and America eventually led Mubarak to boost that his military trials and other emergency measures against Islamists were always the "right policy".[2]

It is of course misleading to assume that Mubarak's relationship with the Islamists was characterised by coercion and repression alone. The policy of the state might indeed have been to use repression against such radical Islamists as *Al-Jihad* and *Al-Jama'at Al-Islamiyya*, but it was not used against the Muslim Brothers, who constituted the moderate wing of Islamism in Egypt. For much of the 1980s the movement was tacitly tolerated. (Not only were *Al-Ikhwan Al-Muslimin* allowed to function from their publicly-known headquarters in Ramsis Street in the crowded centre of Cairo, but they were also permitted to contest formal parliamentary elections in 1984 and 1987 under the banner of "Islam is the Solution"). Repression against the movement did not occur until the 1990s, when the movement's impact on Egypt's politics and society became an undeniable reality.

My intention is to examine the reasons behind the change in Mubarak's relationship with the Muslim Brothers, and to assess the extent to which it was linked to Islamic terrorism and conspiracies to overthrow the government. My argument concerning this change of attitude is not based on the fact that it simply characterised the nature of most authoritarian Arab regimes, which refused to tolerate Islamic opposition. Nor is it based on perceptions related to the impressive performance of Islamists in providing welfare services, albeit merged with religious rhetoric, and the threatening impact this has had on the regime. Both accounts are indeed accurate, but have been dealt with elsewhere and will not be duplicated here.

Instead, I seek to understand the change in the relationship between Mubarak and the Muslim Brothers by focusing on the state's persistent denial, in legal terms, of the Muslim Brothers and the impact of this on the movement and on its religious, social and political development during the 1980s and 1990s. Studies on the authoritarian nature of the Egyptian regime and the impressive social performance of the Brothers in syndicates, student unions and so on, are not sufficient on their own to explain Mubarak's change in attitude towards the reformist Islamists without the important dimension of the absence of state recognition and its implications. Moreover, the concept of legitimacy is significant not only for the Muslim Brothers but is equally important to Mubarak. Thus, while the Brother's impact on politics and society can be explained as one that is significantly governed by a desire for formal recognition by the state and its legal and political institutions, Mubarak's attitude towards reformist Islamists can equally be explained in the context of his desire to be recognised by society as a 'legitimate' ruler. The relationship between Mubarak and the

Muslim Brothers has therefore been shaped largely by their simultaneous pursuit of legitimacy, each on different terms.

Furthermore, while Mubarak tolerated the Brothers during the 1980s because he assumed, as a new leader, that such a policy would bolster his political legitimacy, he repressed them in the 1990s because he had by then redefined his pursuit of legitimacy. This pursuit was not compatible with a policy based on tolerating Islamists, especially when the Brothers were seen as a source of threat to his legitimacy. The Islamists' threat was not simply based on their effective social performance, but on *how* this performance was conducted and the impact it had on Mubarak's regime. Mubarak was threatened by the fact that, despite their denial by the state, the Brothers were able to pursue an alternative "resource of legitimacy" based on recognition of society rather than on recognition of the state, and that this legitimacy was used in mass mobilisation. Such mobilisation was intended not to 'overthrow the government', as the regime often claimed, but ultimately to impel the state to grant formal recognition to the Islamists. I will return to this theme later in the chapter, but at this point it is important to discuss what I mean by the concept of legitimacy and its 'resources'.

Approaches to Legitimacy

The debate over legitimacy, its definition, scope, relevance and various modes, is an ongoing one, which is why it becomes difficult, and perhaps unrealistic, to explain the attitude of particular political regimes in such controversial terms, especially when looking at authoritarian regimes or explaining state-society relations in the Arab world. Legitimacy or *shar'iyya* is a complex term and difficult to define, partly because the definition varies according to the ideological orientations and professional biases from which the definition has developed. For instance, the legal approach to legitimacy sees legitimacy as an extension of legality, which means that a legitimate regime is that which upholds and respects the rule of law.[3] The political approach to legitimacy tends to perceive legitimacy in connection with concepts such as power and authority. Although power, or *quwa*, is sometimes used interchangeably with authority, or *sulta*, the latter usually connotes a more formal legalistic meaning, which is why authority and its subsequent institutions are used to 'legitimise' power.[4] Furthermore, for a political authority to be legitimate (i.e. for its exercise of power to be acceptable) there must be a shared belief, on the part of both ruler and ruled, that a given political arrangement is valid.[5]

The connection between power and legitimacy was discussed in the work of Arthur Stinchcombe, who viewed legitimacy as a form of 'power reserve' located in 'strategic power centres', which in turn were located in notions such as public opinion, national myths, religion, etc.[6] According to Stinchcombe a good indicator of the legitimacy of any regime was to see how often this regime had to draw upon the 'power reserve' when carrying out particular decisions. A second indicator would be how frequently the regime felt compelled to resort to physical force or other obtrusive means of compulsion when implementing its decisions. Legitimacy was therefore connected to a process of consent without the need to resort to coercion, unless the stability of the regime was threatened – the case with most authoritarian regimes.

Max Weber has remained an influential contributor to the theme of political legitimacy and its forms. He famously spoke of the three forms of legitimacy, namely charismatic, traditional and rationally-based legitimacy. Charismatic leadership stemmed from 'extra-ordinary qualities' that evoked an immediate personal consent from the masses; traditional leadership comprised the rule of traditional forces and institutions, such as elders, tribes, customs and religions; while rational leadership referred to a type of authority, dependent on the acceptance of certain formal rules and procedures that were rationally valid and legally binding.[7] Further, a political regime generally established its rule using one or more of these kinds of legitimacy, but in time, and as challenges developed, a regime might adapt itself and rearrange its basis of legitimacy. For example, a ruler who might have based his legitimacy on charisma when he assumed power would often attempt to shift to impersonal or rational norms and procedures. Thus, a charismatic ruler 'routinised' his leadership in a constitution or particular codes of law and practice in an attempt to sustain his regime. The ultimate shift to rational norms was one reason why Weber viewed the rational–legal mode as the most grounded, in comparison with charisma and tradition.

Another important approach to legitimacy was that of David Easton.[8] Like Weber, Easton provided a useful classification of legitimacy modes, which he called personal, ideological and structural legitimacy. Personal legitimacy, "where the behaviour and personalities of the occupants of authority rule are of dominating importance" could become an important component in the overall legitimacy formula, to the extent that a leader "may violate the norms and prescribed procedures of the regime".[9] Easton's categories of legitimacy might appear essentially similar to Weber's, but are considered slightly broader. While Easton's 'personal' legitimacy included Weber's 'charismatic' legitimacy, it covered a wider range of leadership phenomena. As for ideologies, these were: "Articulated sets of ideals, ends, and purposes, which help the members of the system to interpret the past, explain the present and offer a vision for the future."[10] Easton's third category of legitimacy was the structure of the political system, as seen in the institutions and offices that made the political system functional. These institutions were the 'frameworks', where, to use Weber's expression, 'accepted norms and procedures' were preformed in a manner that bestowed legal legitimacy upon the system.

Structuring, or institutionalising, the system links with Samuel Huntington's concept of institutionalisation,[11] which he defined as "the process by which organisations and procedures acquire value and stability".[12] This institutionalisation was very much connected to the process of bureaucratic development and expansion. In addition to the works of Weber and Easton, there have been various Western attempts to argue for other modes of legitimacy.[13]

However, a practical problem remains – how can one 'measure' the legitimacy of a particular regime? There are two main approaches to measuring legitimacy: one based on assessing the efficacy of the system itself, and the other focusing on measuring public opinion. At the system level, legitimacy is viewed from above, where the focus is very much on the ability of the regime to establish opportunities for wide public participation. The emphasis is not so much on what people believe, but on the presence of attributes in the regime itself, such as accountability, efficiency and procedural fairness (e.g. majority rule, frequent elections, minority rights, etc.).[14] Of course the weakness of this approach is its tendency to concentrate on formal structures and aggregate processes, as well as its inadequate recognition of the complementary need to observe the "subjective" aspects of the political system.[15]

The second perspective, which views legitimacy from the grass roots level, focuses on the individual's beliefs and sentiments. This approach was made possible by the development of survey research methodology after World War II. It measures legitimacy based on questionnaires and surveys that ask citizens about their political interests and involvement, and probe their beliefs about social relations relevant to collective action, and their level of optimism about the responsiveness of the political system.[16]

The Legitimacy of Arab Regimes

How useful or relevant is the concept of legitimacy in explaining Arab regimes and the manner in which they control power? The answer to this important question is essential to the argument that sees Mubarak's relationship with Islamists in terms of a mutual struggle for legitimacy. Some scholars and students of the Middle East tend to neglect or underestimate the significance of legitimacy in the minds of many Arab rulers. John Waterbury, for example, in his discussion of corruption in Morocco suggested that the stability of the regime depended on its pervasive illegitimacy.[17] The undermining of legitimacy is usually coupled with an emphasis on concepts like 'power', 'authority', and 'coercion', which imply a form of rule that relies primarily on the use of physical force in maintaining authority. However, the relevance of legitimacy is an issue deeply rooted in the history of state formation in the Middle East, and is related to the manner in which Arab rulers assume leadership.

Michael Hudson has been a major contributor to the study of legitimacy in Arab politics. In reply to Waterbury's earlier assumption, which tended to downplay the importance of legitimacy to Arab regimes, Hudson noted that:

> Only the most cynical observers would contend that Arab political systems are totally devoid of legitimacy and thus completely dependent upon raw coercion for such stability as they may possess. Some systems enjoy greater legitimacy than others, and the legitimacy of particular ones fluctuates over time.[18]

In his study *Arab Politics: the Search for Legitimacy*, Hudson even applied Weber's and Easton's modes of legitimacy to explain how Arab regimes functioned. For example, he applied Weber's definition of charismatic leadership to rulers like Nasser and Bourguiba, and discussed the relevance of Easton's definition of personal legitimacy to other Arab regimes, especially those that were monarchies.[19] He also referred to Easton's notion of ideology and its functional role in legitimising Arab regimes. For Hudson, ideologies were, in varying degrees, important to almost all Arab regimes, whether "conservative" or "progressive".[20] Further, he employed what David Apter calls 'political religion' to illustrate how some revolutionary Arab regimes, such as Iraq, Syria, Libya and Algeria, used religion to mobilise the masses.[21] Other regimes such as Egypt, Tunisia and Yemen, would primarily invoke values of secular nationalism and modernity. Hudson's examinations of legitimacy and how it is used by Arab regimes is useful but not complete.

In the case of Egypt, the question of political legitimacy is particularly relevant, and the classifications proposed by Weber are useful in explaining how Egyptian rulers employed charisma, tradition and rational basis to legitimise their leadership. For instance, the earlier basis of the leadership of Gamal Abdel Nasser has been widely identified in terms of personal charisma, although his charisma was supplemented by the legitimacy of the revolution of 1952.[22] Mohammad Anwar Al-Sadat, on the other hand, was identified as a ruler who based his rule on more traditional and patrimonial forms of legitimacy, in addition to some form of rational legitimacy.[23] The concept of legitimacy in relation to Egyptian regimes is even more relevant because of the presence of a degree of public awareness or expectation that whatever the regime, it must be based on some kind of legitimacy. According to Sa'd Eddin Ibrahim, this political awareness or expectation had been deeply imbued in Egyptian society and in its political elite since Egypt's short-lived liberal era from 1920s until 1952:

> Legitimacy has always been, and continues to be, an essential concern for any ruling regime in Egypt. Any regime must claim some form of legitimacy, be it constitutional or political legitimacy. Whether rulers truly believe their own claim to legitimacy is something else. But when you look at their speeches and their policies, all this shows how attentive they are to legitimacy.[24]

The rise of a military regime after 1952 and its continuing survival did not erode this legacy of political expectation, however invisible it might have been. Its dormant presence is one reason why Mubarak appears cautiously reluctant to name his son, Jamal, as his potential heir. The issue of legitimacy also explains much of the tension undergone by the regime every time there is a presidential election. In short, the Egyptian public may not be able to create any sudden change in the current regime – and this is related to all sorts of reasons other than the fact that they are 'weak' or apathetic – but this should not imply that the political legitimacy of the ruler is outside the equation.

If legitimacy is therefore important to Arab regimes, including that of Egypt, can it be explained in the terms developed by Weber or Easton, or should one also develop new forms of legitimacy that are of relevance to their rule. This is a controversial theme and one that has raised many debates, especially in the Arab world where some Arab elites with nationalist or religious sentiments reject the categorisations of Weber and Easton, which they see as alien to the Arab political experience and incompatible with how Arab regimes maintain authority. This is, of course, a different attitude from the one that views the notion of legitimacy itself as irrelevant to Arab authoritarian regimes. Wahid Abdul Majid, editor of *Al-Nida'* magazine and a prominent analyst at the Al-Ahram Centre for Political and Strategic Studies in Cairo, argues that Weber's modes of legitimacy are inappropriate to many Arab regimes:

> The problem with Western notions of legitimacy is that they define modes in a rigid and inflexible manner. When it comes to Arab regimes, they simply identify everything that they could not comprehend as charismatic or rational-legal, as being 'traditional'.[25]

Instead, he prefers to describe the internal legitimacy of Arab regimes, including that of Egypt, as based largely on promises to improve peoples' living standards and welfare matters related to health, education and employment, even though these promises are rhetorical and not actualised or translated into real achievements. He also brings the foreign element into the equation of Arab legitimacy. In their political discourse, these regimes rely on the United States and Israel to evoke nationalist sentiments and thereby gain what he calls populist legitimacy.[26]

Abdul Majid's notion of promises of improved performances as a mode of legitimacy is an important one, because it emphasises the centrality of achievement for Arab regimes, where achievement in the social, political or economic spheres may be perceived as real or imagined. The closest interpretation of this mode of legitimacy is developed by Gehlen through his notion of eudaemonic legitimacy, which I will consider in some detail.[27]

Eudaemonic legitimacy

To Gehlen, eudaemonic legitimacy stems from acts of rule that assist the economic system to produce an increasing flow of goods and services for the consumer.[28] The concept is clearly tied to the development of the modern welfare state in the West, where the performance of the government plays a role in determining its legitimacy. According to Poggi, the development of the welfare state makes social eudaemonic legitimacy an important source of legitimacy, one that is independent of Weber's charismatic, traditional and rational dimensions.[29]

Weber recognised the significance of performance, but only in the context of an enduring charismatic legitimacy, arguing that when the supporters of a charismatic leader begin to perceive his performance as inconsistent with his promises, they usually start to withdraw their support, and alternative leaders will then tend to emerge. In this context, performance becomes much like a safety net, used only when the influence of legitimacy resources dries up. Moreover, in his assertion that traditional and rational types of legitimacy are more stable, Weber implies that the ruler's performance is not of great importance. This proposition contradicts historical evidence.

The concept of eudaemonic legitimacy is useful because it underlines social and economic achievements as an essential source of legitimacy. It credits the 'populace' with some weight in the legitimacy formula, in line with Ibrahim's "popular expectations" and Sadowski's strong societies.[30] Sadowki, (see bibliography for reference). This is in contrast to a primary focus on the leader's personal charisma, the norms of law, the powers of ideology, or the structure of the system. The people, along with their basic expectations, begin to assume a greater role in assessing the stability of regimes. Although eudaemonic legitimacy should not be viewed as a substitute or an alternative to other modes of legitimacy, some scholars, such as John Shaar, have argued that eudaemonic legitimacy has grown increasingly important in the last decades, in contrast to the Weberian types of legitimacy. Charismatic, traditional and rational legitimacy, according to Shaar, have been weakened by various political, social, and economic developments.[31]

Thus, with adaptation, eudaemonic legitimacy could be a useful notion in understanding how legitimacy functions in the Arab world, especially with regimes that view themselves as ruling welfarist states. This leads us first to define a welfarist state and secondly to establish the extent to which a country like Egypt identifies itself as one. One definition of a welfare state is that it is one that aims to reduce the negative impact of social divisions and mitigate social inequalities.[32]

Another emphasises the state's responsibilities for securing a basic level of welfare for its citizens.[33] Studies by Wilensky and Korpi focus on spending as the main criterion for defining a welfare state.[34] They assume that the level of social expenditure reflects a state's commitment to welfare. Expenditure alone as a criterion of a welfare state can be misleading, since not all spending carries the same weight or counts equally.[35] A third definition identifies a welfare state with that state's expansion of democracy. However, this definition overlooks the fact that the first welfare state initiatives occurred not only in countries which were not democracies but in autocracies such as France under Napoleon III and Germany under Bismarck.[36] One may then conclude that a welfare state is a state which is committed, or at least presents itself as being committed, to improving the socioeconomic welfare of its people.

To Egyptian elites and activists, whether socialist, Nasserist or *laisser-faire*, Egypt has largely been viewed as a welfare state.[37] Its welfarist system and culture was developed in the late 1950s and 1960s, at a time when, under Nasser, the state was indeed committed to improving the living conditions of the Egyptian people.[38] The state provided free education, free health services and employment to all high school and university graduates. It also guaranteed the poorer sector, if only rhetorically, an increase in income and progress in their living standards, providing these benefits in the form of subsidised basic goods and social services. This kind of commitment comprised what Waterbury calls the 'social contract' between the state and the people, whereby the state would provide goods and services in exchange for political docility and quiescence.[39] The social contract constituted an essential component of Nasser's legitimacy after 1954, and subsequently continued under successive military-based regimes. Even under Sadat's policy of *infitah* (open economy) or Mubarak's structural adjustment, according to Khalid Munir, a well known Egyptian journalist, "The post-1952 Egyptian state cannot simply abandon its social role, and if any regime did, it would automatically become illegitimate, because it would have terminated the base of its support."[40]

The Legitimacy of Mubarak

It is perhaps easier to talk about the modes of legitimacy that are claimed by the Mubarak regime to identify his rule, than to speak about how legitimate his regime might actually be. So far I have examined the charismatic, traditional, rational and eudaemonic modes of legitimacy, and have argued that legitimacy is an essential concept to the Egyptian regime. In analysing the discourse of Mubarak since he assumed power in 1981, one would have to make the following observations. Mubarak certainly lacked charismatic legitimacy, at least in contrast to Nasser; he did not bargain on traditional legitimacy (e.g. religion), as Sadat once did, although religious legitimacy is important to Mubarak; he depended on legal legitimacy, in so far as he was Sadat's vice-president and therefore, constitutionally, his expected heir; and counted on eudaemonic legitimacy since it constituted the state's contract with society.

I am aware that these observations may provoke some debate, especially since the definitions of the modes of legitimacy and how each is 'ideally' expected to materialise and function remain unsettled. The above observations, therefore, need to be situated within a particular theoretical context, which will become clearer in the following chapters. First, it is important to realise that the process by which a regime builds its legitimacy is far from rigid but is dynamic and ever shifting. In many cases, the process is inspired and conducted through the leader's unconscious instinct for survival, and thus cannot be ascribed to any particular mode. A ruler might not be consciously aware that, at a particular period, he is pursuing a particular mode of legitimacy. In theory, he would like to think that his authority encompasses different kinds of legitimacy; in other words, the broader his 'power reserve' the better. But in practice one must speak in terms of a "dominant" mode, which the ruler detects as being the most visible in the discourse. A rationally-oriented mode of legitimacy might, therefore, become the dominant discourse during parliamentary or presidential elections.

Secondly, what makes things seem even more complex is when modes of legitimacy appear so fluid that they become somewhat interchangeable. This means, for example, that if legal legitimacy entailed some kind of legal reform with social implications, it could be considered simultaneously as a variation of eudaemonic legitimacy. This then would suggest that at one particular moment there could be more than one dominant mode of legitimacy.

Thirdly, the process of building legitimacy does not emerge in a vacuum but is obviously a response to the surrounding social, political and economic orders. This of course entails a continuous change and reworking of modes of legitimacy in terms of priority or relevance, and again connects with what has already been mentioned about the dynamism and fluidity of modes of legitimacy. While a regime may not rely very much on religious legitimacy, it might well need to do so when a religious rival happens to exist.

Fourth, the process of building legitimacy is also complex because it often targets different audiences or constituencies. The achievements that the regime provides to gain the support of the military or the upper middle-class are obviously different from those that are proposed for the purpose of gaining the support of the lower-middle and poor classes. Moreover, the regime might at some point seek to legitimise itself differently for different constituencies. It might initiate particular policies in order to gain some form of legal legitimacy among the political elites, while initiating other policies to secure religious legitimacy among disenchanted youth.

Fifth, the legitimacy of the regime might be protected in urgent situations by the use of physical force, although frequent and consistent resort to coercion could at the same time easily lead to the erosion of that legitimacy. This implies that legitimacy is not an essentialist reality that at one extreme is either lacking or present, but is in fact viewed as a spectrum that includes variations like surplus legitimacy, crisis of legitimacy, legitimacy deficit, and illegitimacy.

The Legitimacy of Islamists

If legitimacy was an important concept in my attempt to explain the relationship between Mubarak and the Muslim Brothers, then it is equally important to examine how Islamists view the concept in relation to Arab regimes and then in relation to themselves. In theory, a legitimate rule is one which applies the Islamic *Shari'a*, and this is the classical understanding among scholars concerning the notion of *Al-Sulta Al-Shar'iyya* or legitimate authority.[41] Kamal Abu Al-Majd states that although legitimacy is essentially religious in Islamic political authority, the government and its bureaucracies are civil, not theocratic and its legitimacy therefore emanates from its commitment to Islamic teachings as well as from the consent of the people.[42] This definition on its own fails to provide an explanation of the emergence of political authorities that claimed to rule in the name of Islam but not necessarily through people's consent.

Further, Islamists are confused and ambiguous when it comes to examining the legitimacy of Arab nation-states or regimes. The views of Saif Abdul Fatah, an Islamist and lecturer in the Faculty of Politics at Cairo University, provide an interesting example of how the Islamists have struggled, since the demise of the Ottoman Empire in 1923, to develop the concept of *Al-Sulta Al-Shar'iyya*. Instead of relying on Weber's 'ideal' classifications of legitimacy, Abdul Fatah suggests a classification which he considers to be more useful to most Arab regimes. He argues that the legitimacy of Arab regimes should be looked at from three perspectives: the first is the ideological framework which gives the regime its identity; the second is the manner in which power is assumed and the subsequent nature of the contract binding the state to society; while the third is the legitimacy of practice, which focuses on the various policies pursued whilst a regime is in power.[43]

Abdul Fattah's differentiation between levels of authority in Arab regimes provides an incomplete yet useful framework for the way in which the Muslim Brothers view the Egyptian regime. Since Hassan Al-Banna, the movement has been careful not to engage itself publicly in issues related to the question of the regime's political legitimacy (*Al-shar'iyya al-siasiyya li-nizam*), perhaps because it was not of practical importance as long as the movement was officially recognised by the state, and while some form of co-operation existed between the movement and the King. Accordingly, Al-Banna saw no problem in contesting parliamentary elections, and did not prevent his followers from assuming high posts in state institutions. The confrontation between the movement and the state in the late 1930s and early 1940s, and the sudden murder of Al-Banna did not provide the movement with a focus to develop a proper attitude to the regime and to its legitimacy.

In the 1950s and 1960s, particularly after the clash with Nasser and the writings of Sayyid Qutb, the views of the Brothers towards legitimacy were rather ambiguous. To understand this ambiguity it is useful to divide the question of political legitimacy into three categories: that concerning the legitimacy of the president (*ra'is al-dawla*); the legitimacy of regime policies (*siyasat al-nizam*); and the legitimacy of the state's official institutions (*mu'sasat al-dawla*). The divisions are quite arbitrary because of the dominance of the person of the president over policy makers as well as over legislative and judicial institutions. The Muslim Brothers did not seem to express a consistent attitude with regard to the legitimacy of the person of Nasser. Initially they recognised the legitimacy of the revolution in 1952, and provided assistance to the military coup d'état by the Free Officers, but from 1954 they denied recognition for

Nasser. They also denied the legitimacy of the institutions of the state, whether in the government (by dismissing members who agreed to become ministers in Nasser's government), or in the parliamentary assembly. In the late 1950s and 1960s, the Brothers' view of Nasser's policies was unclear, largely because most members, including the leadership, had been put in prison. No particular public stance was therefore expressed.

The imprisonment of the Brothers continued until the early 1970s, which meant that the movement was still unable to express a definitive position on the legitimacy of Sadat when he assumed power in 1970. Even after their release from prison, and their subsequent co-operation with Sadat in his campaign against the leftists, the Brothers failed to articulate a response to his personal legitimacy. The movement's attitude to the state's institutions under Sadat also seemed to be contradictory. On the one hand, they refused to accept Sadat's offer to participate in his newly-formed political platforms (*manabir*), or to register as a charity organisation under the supervision of the Ministry of Social Affairs, or be appointed (in the person of their *murshid* 'Umar Al-Tilmesani) to the Consultative Council (or *majlis al-shura*). On the other hand, the movement did recognise the legitimacy of the state's legal institutions, possibly in order to use such institutions to appeal against their official ban, which had been in place since 1954.

Developments during the period of Mubarak are complicated. Again, the Brothers did not express a clear view on Mubarak's legitimacy because their leadership was again in prison when he assumed power in 1981. However, the legitimacy of Mubarak as president was categorically recognised by the Brothers when they voted in the 1987 Assembly for his second term presidency. The movement then voted against Mubarak's third term presidency, but argued that its vote was not against his legitimacy as president but against his policies. Though arbitrary, the distinction is crucial for a movement that knows it is functioning under authoritarian conditions and is therefore not prepared to enter into open confrontation with the regime on matters that appear already to have been decided. The Brothers avoided discussing the issue of Mubarak's legitimacy because, according to 'Esam Al-'Aryan, a prominent Ikhwan figure, the legitimacy of Mubarak's presidency, whether one liked it or not:

> The legitimacy of Mubarak is a reality, and despite the fact that we are against the way the referendum [for the President]

is conducted, and the way the President comes to power, we [the Ikhwan] are faced by a de facto President and a reality that we cannot ignore.[44]

Al-'Aryan's understanding of legitimacy is not unique but reflects the understanding of classical Sunni scholars, who recognise the legitimacy of a ruler, even if he is a tyrant, provided he maintains the minimum prerequisites of Islamic principles, or otherwise if his expulsion was a risky and bloody adventure. The reluctant acceptance of a ruler's leadership, in the interest (*maslaha*) of society, is confirmed by the late *murshid* of the movement, Ma'mun Al-Hudaybi, when he was asked about Mubarak's legitimacy:

> In principle, true legitimacy emanates from the people's choice. To the Muslims, they choose someone who rules them according to the teachings of the Qura'an and the Sunna (words and actions of Prophet Mohammad). This is the only *khalifa* (Islamic ruler) [considered legitimate] in Islam. Other than this, there is the *khalifa* of the status quo, and the imam of necessity or *imam al-darura*. When the latter becomes a reality and one which you cannot change, you then must obey this imam, otherwise the outcome of armed resistance would be social turmoil. This is the case of our President. He controls 90 per cent of state powers, including the army and the police forces.[45]

The 'politics of necessity' or *darura* was not confined to how the Brothers viewed the legitimacy of Mubarak but also concerned the legitimacy of his institutions. Although the movement had refused to engage in Sadat's Legislative or Consultative Councils, it constituted a strong presence in Mubarak's Assembly in the 1980s and in his Consultative Council in the 1990s. The 1980s saw the politics of alliance between the Brothers and other parties, whereas the movement had refused to be part of any political alliance in Sadat's *manabir* in the 1970s. The 1980s and 1990s also saw various attempts to establish a formal political party for the Ikhwan, an option which the movement had not entertained in the 1970s.[46] However, change in the attitude of the Brothers towards the Egyptian regime should not be sought in the extent to which they view the regime or institutions as legitimate, but in how the movement has come to view its own legitimacy, and the impact that this has had on its social and political developments.

The Legitimacy of the Muslim Brothers

The Muslim Brotherhood, founded in 1927, is regarded as one of the largest and most influential Islamic movements in Egypt. The Brotherhood is widely seen as the 'parent' of Islamic groups world-wide, and the emergence of extremist factions of Islamism like *Al-Jihad* is thought to be rooted in the movement. Their influence is confirmed by their transnational connections, which have helped to establish autonomous branches of the movement in most Arab, Islamic and even European states.[47] In Kuwait, for example, the movement is widely known as *Al-Haraka Al-Dusturiyya* (Constitutional Movement), in Jordan as *Jabhat Al-'Amal Al-Islamiyya* (Islamic Action Front), in Palestine as *Hamas*, in Yemen as *Harakat Al-Islah* (Reformation Movement), and in Algeria as *Harakat Al-Silm* (Peace Movement).[48]

However, whereas these groups are officially recognised by their individual states and are somehow incorporated into the social and political system, the 'parent' movement in Egypt is denied legal status. This has had a tremendous effect on how the movement has developed, and how this development has shaped its relations with state and society. Part of the movement's ability to survive in conditions of state denial has been its skill in expanding the organisation, or *tanzim*, creating new alliances and adapting ideas and attitudes concerning such issues as democracy, multi-party systems and women's rights. The ability to adapt to change and to address the social and religious concerns of its followers, makes it a powerful force, particularly among the young. However, these changes are frequently explained in terms of the socio-economic and political particularities of the 1980s and 1990s, even though they should be seen mainly in the context of the movement's desire to be recognised by the state and society.[49]

This study is intended to focus on the concept of legitimacy as a starting point in explaining the development of the Muslim Brothers, and how this development has affected their relations with the regime. I have already mentioned the significance to the Brothers of legal legitimacy (or the lack of it), but would like to expand my discussion to include other modes of legitimacy that will prove to be of equal importance.

Discussions on legitimacy by Weber, Easton, and (in the case of Egypt), Sa'd Eddin Ibrahim have all been preoccupied with the legitimacy of the political regime, and are therefore state-centric. With adaptations, charismatic, traditional, rational, and social eudaemonic modes of legitimacy become suited to discussions on the legitimacy of social movements, including Islamic movements that pose as 'legitimate' alternatives to political authorities. One problem with this approach is that one might then end up applying similar modes of legitimacy to the analysing of two different levels of power, one pertaining to the state, and the other to society. A ruling authority with control and distribution resources cannot be compared with a social power that is either dependent on state resources or has no access to them. Furthermore, social powers are influenced, restrained and obstructed by the state's bureaucracies, apparatuses and defined boundaries. However, this differentiation could prove useful when the relationship between Mubarak and the Muslim Brothers is seen as a mutual struggle for recognition. A comparison between the two levels of legitimacy or levels of power is then plausible, if legitimacy is seen in terms of public recognition and not just in terms of resources and capabilities.

Frequent comparisons have been made between the legitimacy of Arab regimes and the Islamists in response to social and economic changes, some of which are introduced by international actors. According to Lubeck and Britts, global pressure to restructure the economy has undermined the legitimacy of the nationalist state. This is partly because secular nationalism never originated from below, but was almost always a top-down, authoritarian project articulated from national military elites who assumed control over the authoritarian colonial apparatus.[50] The combined effect of disasters like the 1967 Arab–Israeli war, the stagnation of development, and the state's implementation of these structural adjustment programmes "destroyed the social contract between state elites and urban dwellers". Furthermore, the foreign elements and pressures in these structural programmes "rapidly evaporated any residual fig of legitimacy possessed by secular political elites" – a legitimacy that was presumably based on the welfarist responsibilities of the state.[51] The outcome of this stagnation, along with widespread corruption and bureaucratic incompetence, frustrates the mobility and security aspirations of the lower-middle classes (especially secondary school and university students) and makes them vulnerable to anti-state conscription. According to Sullivan, these recruits gradually become absorbed into a network of urban Islamist movements and civil society groups, as an alternative route towards the fulfilment of some or all of their aspirations.[52] The Islamists begin, therefore, to be viewed as 'legitimate' competitors to the state.[53]

What Lubeck, Britts and Sullivan are referring to in their writings is this mode of social legitimacy that the Islamists, in competition with the state, have adopted in recent decades. Other writers have attempted to compare the legitimacy of Islamists with that of the state in different Arab countries, where the comparisons have focused on material achievements.[54] The core contention of such case studies is that Islamism has emerged as a social movement protesting against the total failure of the social, economic and cultural modernist project once espoused by post-colonial secular nationalist states. Notwithstanding rhetoric and ambitious promises, these states have become practically incapable of securing the minimum needs of their continuously growing population. Ultimately, they cease to be seen as providers and, as a consequence, lose their legitimacy and their *raison d'être* in the eyes of their disenchanted populations. Through their limited resources and organisations (e.g. mosques, neighbourhoods, charitable clinics and schools), the Islamists then begin to offer an existential refuge, not just in terms of moral or religious values, but also in terms of material needs, and gradually begin to assume some degree of social legitimacy.

Some of the cases mentioned in another collection of studies[55] are interesting and are worth mentioning briefly. In explaining the emergence of the Islamic Salvation Front (FIS) as a popular power in the 1992 elections, Yahia Zoubir argues that the economic reforms of the 1980s aggravated the socio-economic conditions of most classes in Algeria, which resulted in a situation of acute housing shortages, water problems, diminished food supplies, high inflation, high unemployment and so on. The receding role of the state that resulted from such reforms violated the social contract that had been established under the Boumedienne regime, and the outcome of this was the remarkable decrease in the popularity of the *Front de Liberation Nationale* (FLN) and the nationalist values for which it stood.[56] The vacuum thus created was gradually filled by the religious discourse of the FIS, in addition to its modest but significant services.[57]

Hilal Khashan discusses the social achievements of Islamists in Lebanon as a source of their legitimacy, where legitimacy is again treated as a function of ideological affinity and the provision of services.[58] His main argument is that the provision of public services plays a decisive role in the extending of political legitimacy by the beneficiaries of the services to the agency providing them (in this case Islamists, as opposed to the national government). Having studied the responses of a random sample of 500 Muslim respondents, divided equally between Sunnis and Shi'is, who were asked about sources of popular legitimation and their actors, Khashan conclude that:

> The legitimacy of the Lebanese government receives low marks by the respondents, most of who describe the scope of its public oriented services as less than satisfactory. The deficiency in government services is compensated by private organisations, the most active among them being Islamic groups. Alarmingly, most respondents do not feel that the performance of the reformed Lebanese political system of the second republic (since 1989) has improved in relation to performance during the first republic (1943–75). Thus it does not surprise us to discover that many respondents support the activities of Islamic groups.[59]

The significance and implication of the achievements of the Islamists in Algeria and Lebanon (the study also speaks of Islamists in Jordan and Palestine) differ from those of the Muslim Brothers in Egypt. This is because the groups referred to above are officially recognised by their respective states, and enjoy some form of legitimacy, while the Brothers in Egypt are legally denied by the state. The distinction is not technical but it is important since it imposes a different agenda on the Brothers. Informal legitimacy gained via society is ultimately employed to secure recognition by the state, which is of course important for enabling the movement to function more effectively under authoritarian conditions.

Nonetheless the distinction is missing or is not sufficiently emphasised in the literature. In the past decade there have been several significant studies that have examined the relations between Mubarak and the Muslim Brothers. In her important contribution, Wickham[60] examines how Islamists such as the Muslim Brothers are able to sign up and mobilise their recruits under Mubarak's authoritarian rule. She argues that the partial liberalisation of the Egyptian polity from above, combined with erosion in state capacities for surveillance and control, has expanded the "structures of political opportunity" for Islamist outreach on the periphery of the formal political order. This outreach was possible through the dissemination of Islamist ideology and through the establishment of communal networks that created new motivations and venues for the political involvement of graduates. The Islamic mobilisation on the periphery has also had an impact on the politics of the centre by creating a support base for Islamist candidates in professional syndicates and parliamentary elections. Focusing on the Ikhwan in syndicates, Wickham coined the expression "parallel Islamic sector" to highlight the various services and projects carried out by the Muslim Brothers rather than the state, as a means of accumulating support.

Wickham relied on interviews with young Ikhwan leaders and on the extensive research on the Ikhwan in syndicates undertaken by Amani Qandil.[61] Qandil takes a different view from that of the state, since she regards the Ikhwan, with their powerful welfarist impact, as a legitimate movement in Egyptian society. Her main argument is that over the past 20 years, Egypt has witnessed dramatic social and economic changes that have led to the emergence of a size-able group of disenchanted lower middle class youth.[62] The regime failed to comprehend the changes, let alone their implications. The Ikhwan on the other hand were astute enough to sense the changes and to foresee their potential. Because syndicates epitomised essential core spaces where change was manifested, the movement invested its "resources of mobilisation" in these spaces. While Qandil has focused largely on the Islamists in the medical syndi-cate,[63] others have concentrated on the social role of the Ikhwan in the engineers' syndicate.[64] For example, Ahmad Hassan main-tains that the organisation's main mechanism to build influence was its initiation of social services and the use of Islamic codes and symbols, while Sullivan and Abed-Kotob, who looked at the social welfarist role of the Muslim Brothers through their charitable and voluntary associations, concluded that the Brothers constituted an essential element in Egypt's civil society, and should be recognised as such by the regime.[65]

Another important study of the relations between the Muslim Brothers and Mubarak is that of Hassanain Ibrahim, who examined the reasons behind the change in regime policy, and argued that the movement had assumed a significant role in society and poli-tics, which the regime was not prepared to tolerate.[66]

Research Method

This study aims to explain the relations between Mubarak and the Muslim Brothers in terms of a struggle for legitimacy, and argues that the state changed its attitude to the movement largely because the social performance of the Brothers (which it had tolerated in the past) began to assume an activist meaning. The components of this activism were first, a legitimacy gained from the social services; second, an organised network enabling such services to be deliv-ered effectively, and third, the politicisation of this legitimacy.

By legitimacy, I refer specifically to social legitimacy gained from material achievements. By an organised network I refer to the presence of a sophisticated structure of organised networks and connections among members active in different spaces and avenues. By politicisation of legitimacy, I mean the mobilisation of the recipients of the Brothers' services in support of a political agenda that concerns the movement and not necessarily the recipients.

The third of these components is important, because, among other things, it implies that in their mobilisation process the Brothers were not incorporating their beneficiaries in an adventurous project against the regime or the state itself. In other words, they were not "planning to overthrow the government", as the regime claimed, but were acting against the persistent refusal of the regime to recognise them. As Hamid Abdul Majid noted,

> The Brothers are sometimes allowed a de facto presence, yet are not recognized by the state. This contradictory situation created the Brother's real ambiguity, which is significant when wanting to understand their discourse. They are making inroads into all avenues in society to make a declaration to the state that: 'we enjoy status quo legitimacy, and thus should not be ignored'.[67]

The task of this study is complex because of the difficulties associated with the concept of legitimacy: how it is defined, its various modes, its target audience, and the way it is measured or 'quantified'. It becomes even more difficult because one is trying to speak about two levels of legitimacy, one related to the state, or the regime of Mubarak, and the other related to the Muslim Brothers. The process of comparison between the two levels is complicated by the dynamism involved in each level and the fact that each is competing against the other, even if it is only for a different mode of legitimacy.

To make this process more accessible, I will attempt to compare Mubarak's exploits with those of the Muslim Brothers in the political, social and economic fields, and to establish how each field requires its particular modes of legitimacy. The success or failure of the endeavour of each will be measured through simple social indicators, such as the percentage of turnouts in elections; the number of supporters of the ruling party; the occurrence (or absence) of socio-religious and political upheavals (e.g. riots, demonstrations, violence, etc.); and, in the case of the regime, how often it resorts to coercion to execute a particular policy.[68] It will be seen how legal legitimacy becomes significant in the political field whereas social legitimacy becomes more relevant in the economic field. In addition, I will focus on specific cases or institutions in the three main fields.

In the political field I examine the politics of parliamentary elections. In the social field I look at the professional syndicates and teachers' faculty clubs that are to be found on university campuses. Since university campuses and teachers' faculty clubs represent another variation of the Brothers' impact in Egyptian society, this analysis, based on primary documents and personal interviews, will be helpful in complementing previous studies (some of which are noted above) on the Brothers' impact in professional syndicates. My study of syndicates, likewise based on internal and unpublished documents, also contributes to current literature in showing how organised networks and structures affect, and are used in, the process of mobilisation. Earlier studies have tended to focus on only Cairo University, but my data sources also included the universities at Alexandria and Asyut.

Finally, in the economic field, I focus on Egypt's shift from a centrally-based economy to privatisation, and the impact of this shift on the regime's legitimacy. I also examine how Islamist institutions, particularly Islamic banks, Islamic investment companies and private business enterprises, have affected the impact and legitimacy of the Muslim Brothers.

Fieldwork

During my visits to Egypt in 2000, 2001, 2003, 2009 and 2011 I talked at length with figures from the Muslim Brotherhood. My aim was to collect as much information as possible about a period that has not yet been looked at in much detail. My in-depth interviews were based on open-ended questions that dealt mainly with the question of legitimacy, with Mubarak, and with the main developments between the Ikhwan and the Egyptian regime during the 1980s and 1990s. Initially I interviewed senior figures, including the former *murshids* Mustafa Mashhur and Ma'mun Al-Hudaybi, to find out how their perceptions of the regime of Mubarak compared with those of Sadat and Nasser. Later, I started to meet the younger cadres of the organisation, who were engaged in and occasionally more informed about activities at the grassroots level. My open-ended questions to the younger cadres, such as Anwar Shihata and Khairat Al-Shatir, focused on the impact of the Brothers on student unions, syndicates, banks and parliament. All interviews were taped and all were conducted in Cairo.

During my second visit to Egypt (June 2002 to August 2002) I continued to interview Cairo-based Muslim Brothers. However, I also
began to interview others who were based in Alexandria and Asyut,
since I wished to ascertain from Brothers in these areas whether
the strength of the Ikhwan was restricted to the capital, or included
other regions. Most studies on radical Islamists tend to focus on
areas in Upper Egypt (the *Sa'id*), while those on moderate Islamists tend to focus on the larger cosmopolitan cities like Cairo and
Alexandria. My investigations in Asyut showed that the Muslim
Brothers were a significant force in urban as well as village quarters.
In Asyut I also managed to meet with a Brother who was engaged
in the business and industrial sector. His insights on the role of
the movement in the economic arena were invaluable, since many
Brothers in Cairo or Alexandria were reluctant to discuss what they
felt was a highly sensitive theme.

One of the many benefits of my close encounters with the Brothers
in Cairo, Alexandria and Asyut was the fact that I gained access to a
number of internal and unpublished documents written by the political department of the Ikhwan. These documents (originally in Arabic)
are important as they shed considerable light on how the Mubarak
regime and factors that led to changes in official attitude were understood inside the movement. Although they were written when the confrontation between the regime and the movement was at a peak, none
of the documents mentioned "armed struggle" or plans "to overthrow
the government" as a response. Instead, they focused on the need to
expand quietly until the movement had become an undeniable reality.
These documents are looked at more closely in Chapter Seven.

During my second visit to Egypt I also managed to meet important independent thinkers, party activists and current or former
officials in the Mubarak regime, although I encountered numerous problems, especially when I wanted to meet security officials or
controversial figures like Sa'd Eddin Ibrahim, who at that time was
under police surveillance. One major problem was dealing with the
security services in certain governmental institutions and ministries
but I would like to think that such difficulties were no more than
might to be expected by anyone researching quite a sensitive theme.

Overview of Chapters

Following this brief introductory outline, Chapter Two offers a
brief historical background to the relationship between the Muslim

Brothers and Presidents Nasser and Sadat. The background is contextualised in conjunction with the various fields and the institutions identified with them, with the aim of comparing and contrasting the ways in which each regime utilised these spheres and institutions to build its legitimacy.

Chapters Three, Four and Five look specifically at the 1980s. Chapter Three deals with the period from 1981 to 1984, Chapter Four with the years from 1984 to 1987, and Chapter Five with the late 1980s, i.e., 1987–1990. Each chapter examines the impact of developments and changes in political, social and economic conditions on the Brothers and on the Mubarak regime, and how the terms under which legitimacy was pursued were defined. Although the early and mid 1980s lacked a context of confrontation, Chapter Five does show that the regime was starting to become alarmed at the increasing impact of Brothers on society and politics.

Chapters Six and Seven deal with the 1990s. Chapter Six considers the years from 1990 to 1995 and discusses the extent to which the Ikhwan's social legitimacy turned into a disturbing development for the regime. This was not because of the magnitude of its effectiveness, but because of its mobilising potential when organised and politicised. What exacerbated the situation further was the regime's concern with its own social legitimacy. Chapter Seven looks at the years from 1995 to 2000 and discusses the peak of the confrontation between Mubarak and the Brothers in 1995. During this period the military trials of the Brothers undermined the movement's impact, but at the same time deepened the crisis of the regime's legitimacy.

This legitimacy was then exploited in a political form not only in reaction to major developments such as the Gulf War and the devastating earthquake (that struck Cairo in 1992) but also in reaction to the regime's persistent refusal to recognise the organisation. The movement made political use of its organised social legitimacy to mobilise its lower middle class beneficiaries against the state's official denial of the Brothers. The organised and political form of social legitimacy challenged the regime's own quest for legitimacy and caused Mubarak to revoke his tolerant policies towards the Ikhwan and to take back the spaces he had opened up during the 1980s. This move might have deterred the Ikhwan and weakened the movement's legitimacy, but at the same time it undermined the legal legitimacy of Mubarak and exacerbated his legitimacy crisis. This legitimacy crisis was more noticeable in the mid-1990s.

Chapter 8 charts the process by which the Mubarak regime moved from trying to impede the Brotherhood and other Islamists to attempting to exclude them from politics by legalising its conflict with them. The chapter also considers the Brothers' relationship with the professional Syndicates, as well as with Egypt's university students, another significant group of supporters. It also considers how the Mubarak regime battled the Brothers on the financial front: arresting a number of their business financiers on charges of money laundering in 2006 and submitting them to military tribunal.

The extraordinary story of the fall of the Mubarak regime in 2011 and the rise to power of the Brotherhood's newly founded Freedom and Justice Party in 2013 is told in the Postscript to this book. The movement's period in power under President Morsi was short-lived, however, as the party failed to meet the high expectations of the Egyptian people, unleashed so unexpectedly after 30 years under Mubarak's iron thumb.

Notes

1 *Middle East Times*, 21 December 2001.
2 *Ibid.*
3 Franco Ferrarotti, "Legitimation, Representation and Power", *Current Sociology*, vol. 35, no. 2, Summer 1987, p. 23.
4 Faisal Hasan Tebeileh, *The Political Economy of Legitimacy in Rentier States: a Comparative Study of Saudi Arabia and Libya*, unpublished PhD thesis, University of California, Los Angeles, USA 1991, p. 16.
5 Max Weber, *The Theory of Social and Economic Organisations*, trans. A. Henderson and T. Parsons, New York, Oxford University Press, 1947, p. 213.
6 A. L. Stinchcombe, *Constructing Social Theories*, New York, Brace and World, 1968, p. 162.
7 For an elaboration of these trilogies see Max Weber, *The Theory of Social and Economic Organisations*, *op.cit.*
8 David Easton, *A Systems Analysis of Political Life*, New York, Wiley, 1965.
9 *Ibid.*, pp. 302–03.
10 Easton, *op.cit.*, p. 290.
11 Samuel Huntington, *Political Order in Changing Societies*, New Haven CT, Yale University Press, 1968, pp. 12–24.
12 Huntington, *op.cit.* pp. 12–20.
13 In his study on legitimacy in former communist Eastern Europe, Gary Lynch distinguishes between internal and external modes of legitimation. The internal modes emanate from within the political system, whilst the external comes from outside the system. The internal modes could include traditional, charismatic, nationalistic, legal-rational and goal-oriented legitimacies. The external modes could come from international organisations such as the United Nations (in the form of 'formal

recognition') or in the form of 'informal support' from powerful states. See G. Lynch, "The Legitimacy of Communism in Eastern Europe", cited from *http://members.tripod.com/index.html*, accessed March 2003.

14 See Robert Dahl, *A Preface to Democratic Theory*, Chicago, Illinois, University of Chicago Press, 1956.

15 Stephen Weatherford, "Measuring Political Legitimacy", *American Political Science Review*, vol. 86, no. 1, March 1992, p. 150.

16 *Ibid.*, p. 151.

17 John Waterbury, "Endemic and Planned Corruption in a Monarchical Regime", *World Politics*, vol. 4, no. 25, July 1973, pp. 533–55.

18 Michael Hudson, *Arab Politics: the Search for Legitimacy*, New Haven CT., Yale University Press, 1977, p. 16.

19 *Ibid.*, p. 19.

20 *Ibid.*, pp. 21–22.

21 David Apter, *The Politics of Modernization*, Chicago, University of Chicago Press, 1965, p. 266 and Ch. 8.

22 On Nasser's leadership style, see Hrair Dekmejian, *Egypt Under Nasser: A Study of Political Dynamics*, University of London Press, 1972; and James Bill and Robert Springborg, *Politics in The Middle East*, New York, Harper Collins, 1994, pp. 207–218.

23 On Sadat's leadership legitimacy see Bill and Springborg, *ibid.*, pp. 218–226. On general patterns of leadership exhibited by Nasser, Sadat and Mubarak, see Raymond Hinnebusch, "The Formation of the Contemporary Egyptian State from Nasser and Sadat to Mubarak", in Ibrahim Oweiss (ed.), *The Political Economy of Egypt*, Washington DC, Georgetown University, Centre for Contemporary Arab studies, 1990, pp. 188–209.

24 Personal interview with Sa'd Eddin Ibrahim, Cairo, 8 July 2002.

25 Personal interview with Wahid Abdul Majeed, Cairo, 15 July 2002.

26 *Ibid.*

27 A. Gehlen, *Studien zur Anthropologie und Soziologie*, Neuwied, 1963, p. 255.

28 G. Poggi, *The Development of the Modern State: A Sociological Introduction*, Palo Alto CA., Stanford University Press, 1978. p. 134.

29 *Ibid.*

30 Yahya Sadowski, *Political Vegetables? Businessman and Bureaucrat in the Development of Egyptian Agriculture*, Washington DC, The Brookings Institution, 1991, p. 90.

31 John Shaar, *Legitimacy in the Modern State*, New Brunswick, Transaction Studies, 1981, Ch. 1.

32 N. Ginsburg, *Divisions of Welfare*, London, Sage Publications, 1992, p. 2.

33 Gosta Esping-Anderson, *The Three Worlds of Welfare Capitalism*, Cambridge, Polity Press, 1990, p. 18.

34 See H. Wilensky, *The Welfare State and Equality: Structural Ideological Roots of Public Expenditure*, Berkeley CA., University of California Press, 1975; and Walter Korpi, "Power Resources Approach vs. Action and Conflict: On Casual and International Explanation in the Study of Power", *Sociological Theory*, vol. 3, no. 2, 1985, pp. 31–45.

35 For example, some welfare states spend a large share on benefits to privileged civil servants while other states spend on means-tested programmes.

36 Gosta Esping-Anderson, *op.cit.* p. 15.

37 Iman Bibars, *Victims and Heroines: Women, Welfare and the Egyptian State*, London, Zed Press, 2001, p. 77.

38 Mervat Hatem, "Economic and Political State Liberalisation in Egypt and the Demise of State Feminism", *International Journal of Middle East Studies*, vol. 24, no.2, 1992, p. 233.

39 John Waterbury, "The 'Soft State' and the Open Door: Egypt's Experience with Economic Liberalization 1974–84", *Comparative Politics*, vol. 18, October 1985, p. 69.

40 Personal interview with Khalid Munir, Cairo, 4 July 2002.

41 See for example Ibn Taymiyya, *Al-Siyasa al-shar'iyya fi islah al-ra'i wa al-ra'iyya* (Legitimate Politics in the Reform of Ruler and Ruled), Beirut, Dar Al-Afaq Al-Jadida, 1983.

42 Personal interview with Kamal Abu Al-Majd, Cairo, 12 December 2001. There are numerous modern writings on the subject of the state and political authority according to Islam. See, for example, Abdul Hamid Mitwali, *Mabadi' nizam al-hukm fi al-islam* [Principles of Government System in Islam], Cairo, Dar Al-Ma'arif, 1966.

43 Personal interview with Saif Abdul Fatah, Cairo, 20 July, 2002.

44 Personal interview with 'Esam Al-'Aryan, Cairo, 19 December, 2001.

45 Personal interview with Ma'mun Al-Hudaybi, Cairo, 18 December 2001.

46 Personal interview with Hamid Abdul Majid, London, 13 September 2001.

47 On the different 'schools' of Ikhwan in the Arab world, see F. Yakan, *Manhajiyyat al-imam al-shahid hasan al-banna wa madaris al-ikhwan al-muslimin* (The Methodology of the Martyred Imam Hasan Al-Banna and the Schools of the Muslim Brotherhood), Beirut, Al-Risalah Publishers, 1998; also A. Abu Azza, *Ma'a al-haraka al-islamiyya fi al-duwal al-'arabiyya* (With the Islamic Movement in the Arab Countries), Kuwait, Dar Al-Qalam, 1986.

48 For a perceptive comparative study of Islamists and Arab regimes, focusing particularly on the Egyptian case, see H. Abdul Majid, "Al-Haraka al-islamiyya wa al-nuzum al-siyasiyya al-'arabiyya ma'a ishira khassa lil al hala al-misriyya" (The Islamic Movement and the Arab Political Regimes, with Special Reference to the Egyptian Case), in M. Kharbousch, (ed.) *Al-Tatawwur al-siyasi fi misr 1982–1992* (Political development in Egypt 1982–1992), Cairo, Centre for Political Research and Studies, Cairo University, 1994, pp. 471–510.

49 See A. Qandil, *Al-Jam'iyyat al-ahliyya fi misr* (Informal Associations in Egypt), Cairo, Al-Ahram Centre for Political and Strategic Studies, 1994. For a well presented account on Islamic associations and agencies throughout Egypt, see also D. Sullivan and S. Abed-Kotob, *Islam In Contemporary Egypt: Civil Society vs. the State*, Boulder CO, Lynne Rienner Publishers Inc., 1999, esp. pp. 26–37 and Abdul Ghafar Shukr (ed.), *Al-Jam'iyyat al-islamiyya al-ahliya fi misr* (Islamic Informal Associations in Egypt), Markaz Al-Buhuth Al-Arabiyya, Dar Al-Amin, Cairo, 2001.

50 P. Lubeck and B. Britts, "Muslim Civil Society in Urban Spaces: Globalisation, Discursive Shifts and Social Movements", Working Papers Series, Centre for Global, International and Regional Studies (CGIRS), University of California, Santa Cruz., 2001, p. 7.

51 *Ibid.* p. 8.

52 D. Sullivan, *Private Voluntary Organisations in Egypt: Islamic Development, Private Initiative and State Control*, Gainesville FL, University Press of Florida, 1994.

53 These of course are not recent findings; see for instance Philip Khoury,

"Islamic Revivalism and the Crisis of the Secular State in the Arab World", in I. Ibrahim (ed.), *Arab Resources*, Centre for Contemporary Arab Studies, Georgetown University, 1983, pp. 215. This crisis, however, deepened in the 1990s, at least in so far as Egypt was concerned.

54 See for example, A. Moussalli (ed.), *Moderate and Radical Islamic Fundamentalism: the Quest for Modernity, Legitimacy and the Islamic State*, Gainesville FL, University Press of Florida, 1999.

55 A. Moussalli (ed.), *Islamic Fundamentalism: Myths and Realities*, Reading, Ithaca Press, 1998.

56 Yahia Zoubir, "State, Civil Society and the Question of Radical Fundamentalism in Algeria", in *ibid.*, pp. 123–167.

57 My focus on the social contribution of Islamists in Algeria is intentional, because many observers, including the Ikhwan, view the victory of the FIS in the 1992 elections as an important development that scared Mubarak about the Ikhwan in Egypt and prompted him to reverse his policies.

58 Hilal Kashan, "The Development Programme of Islamic Fundamentalist Groups in Lebanon as a Source of Popular Legitimation", in A. Moussalli (ed.), *op.cit.*, pp. 221–247.

59 *Ibid.* pp. 244–45.

60 Carri Rosefsky Wickham, *Mobilizing Islam*, New York, Columbia University Pres, 2002; see also Carrie Wickham, "Islamic Mobilisation and Political Change: The Islamist Trend in Egypt's Professional Associations", in Joel Beinin and Joe Stork, *Political Islam: Essays from Middle East Report*, 1997, pp. 120–135.

61 See, for example, Amani Qandil, "Taqyeem ada' al-islamiyin fi al-niqabat al-mihaniya" (An Evaluation of the Performance of the Islamists in Professional Syndicate), paper presented at the Fifth Franco-Egyptian Symposium on *The Phenomenon of Political Violence*, Research Centre for Political Studies, Cairo University, 1993, pp. 1–36; and "Al-Jama'at al-mihaniyya wa al-musharka al-siyasiyya" (Professional Groups and Political Participation), paper presented at the Symposium for Political Participation in Egypt, the Arab Centre for Research, Cairo, 1992, pp. 1–32.

62 Personal interview with Amani Qandil, Cairo, 2 July 2002.

63 A. Qandil, *Al-Dawr al-siyasi li jama'at al-masalih fi misr: dirasat halat li niqabat al-atiba' 1984–1995* (The Political Role of Interest Groups in Egypt: a Case Study of the Medical Syndicate 1984–95), Cairo, Al-Ahram Centre for Political and Strategic Studies, 1996.

64 Ahmad Hassan, *Al-Su'ud al-siyasi al-islami dakhil al-niqabat al-mihaniyya* (the Islamic Political Ascent to Professional Syndicates), Cairo, Al-Dar Al-Thaqafiyya li Al-Nashr, 2000.

65 D. Sullivan and S. Abed-Kotob (eds.) *Islam in Contemporary Egypt, Civil Society Vs. the State*, Lynne Rienner, Boulder, 1999. See also Amin Abdul Khaliq et al, *Al-Jam'iyyat al-ahliyya fi misr* (The Informal Associations in Egypt), Cairo, Dar Al-Amin, 2001.

66 Hassanain Ibrahim, *Al-Nizam al-siyasi wa al-ikhwan al-muslimun fi misr: min al-tasamuh ela al-muwajha 1981–1996* (The Political System and The Muslim Bothers in Egypt: From Tolerance to Confrontation 1981–1996), Beirut, Dar Al-Tali'ah, 1998, pp. 5–6.

67 Personal Interview with Hamid Abdul Majid, London, 13 September, 2001.

68 A. L. Stinchcombe, *Constructing Social Theories*, New York, Brace and World, 1968, p. 162.

2

THE REGIME AND
THE SOCIAL CONTRACT

From the founding of the movement in 1927, the relationship between the Muslim Brothers and the Egyptian regimes followed a sort of a cyclical pattern that usually began with an accommodation or an alliance, and ended with confrontation.[1] Hamid Abdul Majid, a Brother and a lecturer in Political Science at Cairo University, confirms this pattern, explaining how King Faruq accommodated the Ikhwan from 1942 to 1947 and repressed them until 1952, how Nasser accommodated them from 1952 to 1954 and repressed them until 1970, and how Sadat accommodated them in the early 1970s, and repressed them from 1978 until his assassination in 1981.[2] The reasons for the change in the relationship between the movement and each regime have been different in each case, but have never defied the logic of the pattern: accommodation followed by confrontation. In this chapter I examine the elements that shaped this pattern during the tenures of Nasser and Sadat; in subsequent chapters, I will try to establish the extent to which these elements have continued to affect Mubarak in his relations with the movement. My analysis will be based on the premise that much of the relationship between the Ikhwan and Nasser, as well as Sadat, was shaped by the struggle of each party for legitimacy, and that based on this struggle and the requirements of a pursued 'mode of legitimacy', the movement was either accommodated or repressed.

Nasser in Search of Legitimacy

When Nasser came to power in 1954, he already enjoyed certain degree of legitimacy that had been conferred on him by the

Revolution of 1952. During that period, the new President did not have a defined vision as to how Egypt was to be ruled, nor of the path it would pursue to confirm its political and ideological identity. In this confusion the Brothers were accommodated, as this would confrere religious legitimacy of the regime. But apart from revolutionary and religious legitimacy, Nasser had personal charisma which also gave legitimacy to his leadership.

In addition to his personal qualities, Nasser's charisma was augmented by the social and political context of Egypt in the 1950s and 1960s. As Tucker notes in his study on charisma in revolutionary situations, a charismatic leader often arises out of a movement for change or reform. Moreover, there has to be a widely-felt longing for salvation or else a crisis that demands immediate resolution, throughout the society in question.[3] Nasser was a young and enthusiastic political leader and a native Egyptian, in contrast to the previous foreign-born, corrupt ruling successors of Muhammad Ali. Egyptians longed to get rid of two major powers, the corrupt King and the British, and Nasser utilised his personal gifts to address these demands. His powerful speeches, charged with the appropriate rhetorical symbols, made the dreams that most Egyptians had cherished for many years into reality. To the ordinary citizen, much influenced by the state's powerful media propaganda, Nasser was regarded as Egypt's 'saviour' of the moment, a view that was confirmed by his decision to nationalise the Suez Canal in 1956. This was not portrayed as an angry response to America's refusal to provide funds for the building of the High Dam, but rather as a nationalist attempt to free Egypt from foreign dominance.

Populist Legitimacy

In addition to his charisma, an aura also began to develop around Nasser's personal leadership based on the line that he pursued through his policies. These aimed at giving his regime a populist legitimacy, based on his foreign policy approach towards Israel and the United States. Nasser played on the feelings of the Egyptian people, who although mostly hostile to Israel, believed in the possibility of political coexistence with the Hebrew state provided the rights of the Palestinians were restored.[4]

This attitude did not change, even following the aggressive action by Britain, France and Israel in 1956 since, according to Usama Al-Ghazali Harb, Nasser never took the issue of confronting Israel seriously.[5] The Palestine issue continued to be used by Nasser to mobilise and attract wider support for his leadership, as remains the case with most Arab regimes. He continued to portray his struggle for Palestine as part of the Arab nationalist struggle to confront Western imperialism and occupation,[6] and in the process used this rhetoric to modernise the army and consolidate control over the opposition.

Eudaemonic Legitimacy

On their own, charisma and political rhetoric concerning attitudes to Israel and the West were not sufficient to maintain a stable regime in the following years, and Nasser was expected to broaden his public appeal by matching slogans on 'national dignity and social justice' with achievements on the ground. That is to say, he was expected to supplant charisma and populism with a basis of eudaemonic legitimacy, through which he had also to project his period of tenure as one that would institute a solid welfare system for Egyptian people and confirm the state's responsibility for providing subsidised food, free education, and health services, as well as employment for new graduates. This was the price paid by Nasser in return for the consent of the rising middle-classes, and the social contract that he instituted in exchange for their political acquiescence.[7] The expanding bureaucratic structures required by the social contract were soon controlling political and social attitudes and organisations, and syndicates, trade unions, voluntary associations, university campuses, and social movements were forced to identify with the state and assimilate within its apparatuses. If they refused, as was the case with the Muslim Brothers, they were brutally repressed.

Two years after the success of the revolution, the popularity of Nasser was on the rise, and he felt that the support of the Brothers had become redundant. Having expected to assume a greater role in the new regime, and finding that this did not happen, the Brothers began to criticise Nasser's policies with regard to the British and to the role of religion in Egyptian society and politics. In the same year that Nasser assumed power, he moved to eliminate the movement as a political rival, disbanding it and confiscated its economic assets in 1954, despite its large membership.

Coercion of the Brothers

Following the elimination of his rivals, Nasser embarked on

creating an authoritarian state in which all power was concentrated in his hands. Institutions that included *majlis al-sha'b* (the People's Assembly), the university campuses, and professional syndicates were not permitted to function autonomously and independently of state patronage.

As far as the legislature was concerned, Nasser's period of tenure saw four assemblies in 1957, 1960, 1964 and 1969, none of which had any real power to legislate beyond the will of the regime. The National Union Executive Committee (headed by Nasser himself), approved the names of 1,748 candidates out of the 2,508 who were running for the 1957 elections, to make sure that no member of the Brotherhood or any sympathiser with their cause succeeded to the Assembly. In 1957 the Assembly had 342 seats, all of which were beneficiaries of state patronage: 94 seats were for police officers, 103 seats for professionals, and 124 seats for rural and urban capitalists.[8]

The freedom of the university campuses to hold elections was also suppressed by Nasser. Until the late 1940s and early 1950s the universities had returned representatives of the Brothers, who took charge of the student unions. In 1953, Nasser issued a law that gave the Minister of Education the right to transfer university lecturers suspected of loyalty to the Muslim Brotherhood movement or to the communists, to other posts outside the university. In February 1954 many Brothers were arrested and punished, following the eruption of large student demonstrations and strikes calling for a greater measure of democracy.[9]

Nasser had been aware of the strength of the Ikhwan on campuses even before he came to power in 1954. As Minister of the Interior in 1952, he had visited some of the Ikhwan's private training camps for students in Alexandria, Dumiat (Damietta) and Hilwan, and, according to Mahdi 'Akif, the former *murshid* of the Ikhwan, was "amazed by their size".[10] Nasser was also aware that the Brothers utilised university campuses as military training sites and sometimes used live ammunition; subsequently restrictions were imposed on students through security checks when entering campuses.[11]

Nasser also controlled professional syndicates, and membership was forbidden to the Brothers who were also prevented from running in the elections for membership on the boards of the syndicate councils.[12] Professional members who wished to contest these elections had to obtain membership of the National Union (later the Arab Socialist Union), which represented one of the state's largest mass organisations. Nasser considered abolishing the syndicates on many occasions, and in 1954, according to Bianchi, disbanded the syndicate councils of both the journalists and the lawyers when they called for the return of democratic rule.[13] When a syndicate's elections got out of hand, he suspended them and appointed a more loyal board's council.[14]

The Legitimacy Crisis of 1967

What has been discussed so far is the manner in which Nasser depended on certain modes of legitimacy to stabilise his leadership, and the way in which he employed coercion to eliminate his rivals, the Muslim Brothers and other political dissidents. Although the defeat against Israel in 1967 undermined Nasser's legitimacy, he survived by virtue of his charisma and coercion,[15] and by virtue of the social contract. Wahid Abdul Majid points to the significance of the latter as the element of support for Nasser's regime post-1967:

> Most of those who took to the streets urging Nasser not to go, following his resignation speech belonged to the middle class, who benefited from his achievements. They were mostly professionals, small merchants and public sector employees from Cairo. This was one reason why the demonstrators lacked support among the poorer classes, who came from Egypt's more rural provinces.[16]

However, as far as post-1967 was concerned Nasser had to pursue other modes of legitimacy to counter the effect of the crisis in his leadership and to accommodate the anger of most Egyptians about the failure of Arab nationalism.

In contrast to his repressive attitude during the 1950s and early 1960s, Nasser became increasingly responsive to public demands for democratic reform and the rule of law. At Cairo University, students, Islamists and communists chanted slogans calling for a free press, fair elections and removal of the security apparatus from campuses.[17] Nasser promised to undertake some of the reforms mentioned in his famous programme in March 1968, which was considered an attempt to displace charismatic and revolutionary legitimacy with a more rational form.[18] Nasser thereafter relaxed his authoritarian corporatism in syndicates that had enjoyed restricted freedoms and expressed different views. Economic policies also began to swing more than ever between centralised socialism and modest liberalisation, where the latter was motivated by widespread feelings that Egyptians had suffered enough from previous wars and foreign adventures, and that relaxed restrictions on private capital were essential to create alternative sources of income.

In addition to legal reform, Nasser also courted religious sentiments to maintain the stability of his regime after 1967. It would be misleading to assume that even during the heyday of his popularity, Nasser had neglected the religious legitimacy of his regime, but his attitude to religion varied according to prevailing social and political conditions. In her study of the political role of Al-Azhar, Majda Rabi' argues that Islam was a powerful tool for Nasser, especially during the peak of his confrontation with the Brothers in 1954 and 1965, and more so following his defeat in 1967.[19] Harb adds that for Nasser, religious legitimacy was also employed as a counter rhetoric to Israel's use of a religious discourse to mobilise Jews in support of the Hebrew state.[20] In doing so, Nasser sought the support of Al-Azhar.[21]

Nasser also appeared to court the Brothers by releasing many of their members from prison, to the extent that in 1971 no more than 140 Brothers remained in detention.[22] Mahdi 'Akif acknowledges that towards his final years, Nasser had released members of the Ikhwan, but that the number was far lower than his aides had claimed it to be.[23] In fact, most of the releases were the result of international pressure from Arab and Muslim countries following the execution of Sayyid Qutb in 1966.

Restrictions on the Brothers became comparatively relaxed, and the movement was able to assume some freedom. According to Zohurul Bari, and based on his interviews with 'Esam Al-'Aryan, the Brothers began to regroup in 1969, forming circles in mosques and on campuses.[24] However, a more robust existence did not begin until the years following Nasser's death, and after Anwar Sadat had assumed power in 1970.

Sadat in Search of a New Legitimacy

Because Sadat lacked the charisma of Nasser, he had therefore to build his rule on a more institutionalised base, which was the rule of the law. He was also known for his religiosity, at least in comparison with Nasser, which he also employed to counter the impact of the leftists, and what remained of the hardcore Nasserists. In this process of legitimation he accommodated the Brothers, but did not officially recognise their existence.

Instituting the 'State of Law'

Egyptian studies point out that Sadat's major contribution to the development of the Egyptian state was his shift from revolutionary to a legal legitimacy.[25] This did not mean that Egypt ceased to be ruled by a military and authoritarian regime, but that the authoritarian element was somehow institutionalised. A year after he came to power, Sadat reformed the Constitution, stressed the supremacy of law, and declared Egypt the "State of Law".[26] He promised a new period of judicial autonomy,[27] and declared an end to the imprisoning of people because of their political and religious persuasions.

In 1976 he moved from the one-party system based on the Arab Socialist Union, and introduced a restricted pluralism which accommodated three political platforms: the Progressive Unionist Party, representing the left; the Socialist Labour Party, representing the centre; and the Liberal Party, representing the centre-right. The regime also recognised the New Wafd as a fourth party in 1977, although a year later the New Wafd Party decided to dissolve itself in protest at Sadat's accusation that it had 'corrupted' political life.

The 'Believing President'

In addition to his personal religiosity, Sadat witnessed the rise of Islamism following Nasser's defeat in 1967 and utilised this to eliminate his leftists rivals, headed by his Vice-President, Ali Sabri, and his Interior Minister, Sha'rawi Gum'a. His permanent Constitution stipulated that "Islam is the religion of the state; Arabic is the official language; and the principles of Islamic *Shari'a* are a principal source of legislation". In the same way that Sadat declared Egypt the "State of Law", he also declared it "the State of Science and Faith" (*dawlat al-'ilm wa al –'ilman*).

He released Muslim Brothers from Nasser's prisons, restored their confiscated properties and resources, and permitted the Brothers who had lived in exile since the 1960s to return to Egypt.[28] He allowed the movement to reclaim its headquarters, reconvene its public meetings, and resume its press publication.[29] He encouraged the building of religious centres outside the sphere of Al-

Azhar, and the construction of mosques outside the supervision of the state. Following the victory over Israel in the 1973 war, under the banner of "God is Great" (*Allah-u-Akbar*), Sadat projected himself as the "Believer [in God] President" or *Al-Ra'is Al-Mu'min*. He used religious legitimacy when Islam seemed to support his policies, and where Nasser had employed Islam to justify his socialist predilection, Sadat did the same with *infitah* and capitalism. He initiated a debate in his semi-official press over what was described as the "Islamic economy", suggesting that Islam respected individual ownership and a person's endeavour to earn.[30] This led to the emergence of 'Islamic investment companies' and 'Islamic banks', which will be discussed in Chapter Three.[31]

Sadat's 1971 Constitution, which stipulated the prime role of Islam in legislation, brought to the forefront a wide public debate in Egypt on the place of religion in the Egyptian polity. When the Constitution was amended in 1980, making *Shari'a* the source of legislation, this debate gained even greater momentum. The religious legitimacy that the Ikhwan had accrued over the past decades enhanced their mass appeal, and through the movement's ideologues and printed literature, provided them with a convenient opportunity to enter the public arena. Since the beginning of the debate, the movement had become intensely preoccupied with the issue of applying the *Shari'a* in Sadat's state. Most of its editorials in *Al-Da'wa* and in other spaces it had occupied, were dedicated to this issue by the group (major contributors to the debate were 'Umar Tilmesani, via editorials and press interviews, and shaikhs Al-Ghazali and Kishk, via their populist mosques and Friday sermons).

The Social Contract

Sadat did not entirely abandon the state's Nasserist commitment to the middle classes. But from the mid-1970s to the 1980s, the regime gradually exhausted its capacities towards incorporation and welfare. According to Wickham, Sadat drained Egypt's revenues because although he wanted to affirm his commitments to Nasser's social contract, in practice he was unable to do so as the beneficiaries of the social contract grew wider.[32] Added to this was the gradual fragmentation of the middle class, which Nasser had harnessed to advance the expansion of his state bureaucracy, as a result of the opening up of the Egyptian economy to private investment. Sadat's *infitah* created new opportunities that did not necessarily match the skills and education this middle class had gained from the universities. In practice this meant the weakening of the capacity of the state to guarantee access to middle-class incomes for Egyptian degree-holders, and thereby to retain Nasser's 'social contract'.

In adiditon, it was obvious that Sadat was more biased towards the private bourgeoisie, who comprised the social base of his regime and who were the targets of *infitah*[33] and political liberalisation.[34] Hinnebusch maintains that this bias constituted the new social contract that Sadat had signed with a narrower social class. According to this tacit contract, Sadat would relax the state's interventionist role over society and the political arena, in exchange for a free hand in foreign policy and an unchallenged authoritarian presidency.[35]

In Pursuit of Recognition

When the Brothers were released from prison by Sadat they began to pursue two concurrent objectives: one was to secure the official recognition of the state, which they had lost since 1954, and the other was to rebuild the organisation or *tanzim*.[36] As far legal status was concerned, Sadat was prepared to tolerate the movement but without giving back its previous status, a situation which the Brothers did not accept. In light of their experience with Nasser, which had led to the elimination of their entire political, social and even economic existence, the Brothers decided not rely on the tacit tolerance of the regime or the president, unless this tolerance was established by a formal recognition.

In October 1977 'Umar Tilmesani filed a court case against Nasser's decision to disband the *tanzim*, arguing that since the Revolutionary Council had lacked legislative or constitutional rights, and its decision to disband the movement in 1954 was therefore illegal. Secondly, even if the decision was legally valid, it had been invalidated by Nasser's apologies for what he had done in 1954, and his release of the Brothers from prison, thereby permitting them to function freely. Thirdly, Sadat's political reforms, as manifested in the Parties Law of 1976, had automatically cancelled Nasser's decisions to disband political parties and political organisations, including the *tanzim*. Tilmesani's case was never settled by the court and at the time of writing continued to be in dispute. According to *Liwa' Al-Islam*, a magazine sympathetic to the cause of the Brothers, the movement's case was delayed by the court more than 40 times between 1977 and 1990.[37] The Brothers realised that even Sadat's courts, however 'independent' they appeared to be, were in reality subservient to the policies of the state.

The other approach was for the movement to make use of Sadat's pluralism and redefine itself in political terms. The shift imposed by the multi-party system in 1976 did not mark a transformation in the ideas of the Ikhwan towards party politics, but did provide an alternative route to securing recognition by the state. The ideal situation would, of course, have been for the regime, or for the courts, to grant the Brothers legal status to exist as a mass movement (*haraka islamiyya*) rather than as a political party (*hizb siyasi*); this was one reason why the shift from the *haraka* to the *hizb* was not an easy one, an why it was not accepted on absolute terms. During the 1970s, the majority of the Brothers were unable to envisage their mission in Egyptian society without the existence of the *haraka* as an idea and a *tanzim*. Rather than becoming a means to an end, according to Abdul Mun'em Abu Al-Futuh, a senior member in the Muslim Brotherhood, the *haraka* became an end in itself.[38] When Tilmesani spoke about the possibility of engaging in Sadat's parliament, Mahdi 'Akif, the Muslim Brothers' former *murshid*, objected strongly: "I told Tilmesani that my understanding of the Brotherhood was that it was a comprehensive organisation [and]. . . therefore would not accept or agree to its abolition or replacement by a political party regulated by the Parties' Law", 'Akif told me.[39] Tilmesani did not object to 'Akif's protest, but merely stressed the need to secure a legal umbrella beneath which to function publicly.

This did not mean that Tilmesani was prepared to abandon the *tanzim* for the sake of a political party. The *tanzim* was seen in totally different terms from a political party, which is generally far narrower in scope and appeal. Further, Tilmesani continued to uphold negative views on the idea of political pluralism based on partisanship (*hizbiyya*). In 1978 he criticised *hizbiyya* saying that the manifestos and policies of parties changed with the change in leaders and personalities, and were not related to the interests either of the nation or the *umma*.[40] In an article written in 1979 he repeated Al-Banna's sceptical remarks on *hizbiyya* to the effect that they were always related to quarrels and disputes, which divide society and tear it apart.[41] Tilmesani hoped that Sadat would agree to admit the Brothers into parliament as representing a sociopolitical trend and not as a political party in the strict technical sense, where the idea of political parties was firmly grounded and Sadat spoke of political pluralism in terms of platforms (*manabir*). The Brothers refused Sadat's offer to become affiliated with any of the three main platforms, since they saw themselves as representing an independent trend in society that should have separate representation in parliament. Thus the idea of *hizbiyya* was not yet an institutionalised reality in the politics of the 1970s, nor was it a political preference in the minds of the Brothers, as became the case in the 1980s and 1990s.

The Brothers applied for political recognition but as anticipated were refused. The Parties' Law had banned the formation of parties based on religious allegiances,[42] since, as the regime argued, the formation of parties based on religion would cause social and political rifts between Muslims and Copts. The Brothers, in turn, developed arguments which aimed to refute those of the regime. One argument, according to an unpublished study by a veteran Ikhwan lawyer in Cairo, was that the Muslim Brothers did not actually represent a religious movement in the traditional sense, but rather were concerned "with the political dimension of Islam". The author went on to say that the Brothers were engaged in the religious dimension of Islam only as part of their way of improving the spiritual status, education and behaviour of their individual members:

> . . . Otherwise, the movement is mainly concerned with the political dimension of Islam. The movement's engagement in politics is shaped by the principles of *Shari'a* and is confined to democratic and constitutional means to realise its goals, and it is this political engagement which distinguishes the Muslim Brothers from other Islamic groups which are concerned only with the pure religious aspect of Islam, such as Al-Jam'iyya Al-Shar'iyya, Ansar Al-Sunna and the Tabligh. [43]

The focus on the political element was not intended simply to distinguish the movement from other Islamic groups, but to redefine the movement's religious orientations in terms that would make it compatible with the new political arrangements. This approach to politics and religion was strikingly different from the movement's approach during the 1940s. According to Hamid Abdul Majid, a political science lecturer at Cairo University, who had once been involved in the political section of the Ikhwan, Hassan Al-Banna had presented the movement as one that was concerned more with religious reform, even if this led at one point to compromising a political gain. Al-Banna had, for example, agreed to withdraw his candidacy for the 1943 elections in return for a set of religious reforms.[44]

The second argument put forward by the Brothers against regime denial was that Egypt's 1971 Constitution stipulated that "Islam is the religion of the state" and that *Shari'a* comprised "a source of legislation" (the Constitution was amended in 1980 and the *Shari'a* became "the principal source of legislation"). The Muslim Brothers, who respect the Constitution and claim to reflect the aspirations and beliefs of Muslims in Egyptian society, therefore have the right to exist as a legally-recognised political party. Their third argument was that recognition of the Ikhwan would act as a bulwark against Islamist extremism and terrorism. This line of argument was well timed and placed before a regime that had witnessed a rise in Islamist violence since 1973, epitomised in 1974 by an attempt to assassinate Sadat.[45]

The Brothers saw themselves as an independent power, which deserved to be recognised as a *haraka* and if that was not possible then as a *hizb*. At that stage, and unlike in the eighties, it did not consider the possibility of establishing an alliance with political parties or platforms. The movement refused to a presidential offer to participate in parliament as affiliates with one of the three *manabir*. Tilmesani, nonetheless, permitted individual members like Hassan Al-Jamal to contest the elections, under the banner of the Socialist Arab Party.[46] Viorst states that such members secured six seats in the 1976 elections,[47] while Abdul Majid claims they secured five seats in the elections in 1979.[48] For the same reasons related to the issue of maintaining the independence of the movement, Tilmesani had refused Sadat's offer of a seat in the Consultative Council.[49] Tilmesani also refused Sadat's third offer to register the movement as a charitable organisation, so that the *haraka* would not be reduced to a charitable organisation dependent for its financial survival on the Ministry of Social Justice.

Building the Tanzim

In the early 1970s, the *tanzim* of the Ikhwan was weak and fragmented as a result of the long period of imprisonment and repression by Nasser. Tilmesani was in no hurry to embark on recruitment activities following the release of the Ikhwan from prison in the early 1970s, not wishing to aggravate the regime's fears and force it to revoke its tolerant policies. According to Mohammad Fu'ad, a veteran Ikhwan leader who lives in London, the movement did not begin serious recruitment until 1976, most visibly on university campuses and among students who were disenchanted with the failure of Arab nationalism and looked for an alternative ideology.[50]

The Islamist trend on campuses was called *Al-Jama'at Al-Islamiyya*, and was different and separate from the militant *Al-Jama'at Al-Islamiyya*. Its members were not affiliated with particular groups outside the university, although a large number of them were already influenced by the ideas of the Muslim Brothers from their readings of Sayyid Qutb and Shaikhs Mohammad al-Ghazali and Yusuf Al-Qaradawi. This had made campuses even more fertile places for recruitment. Two years after *Al-Jama'at* had won in the student elections at Cairo, Minya, and Alexandria Universities in 1976, the leaders of the Muslim Brothers held a meeting at the Presidents of these student unions. Tal'at Fu'ad Qasim, who eventually became a member of the militant *Al-Jama'at Al-Islamiyya* group, was present at this meeting:

[In the meeting]. . . the *Jama'at* was represented by three of its leaders, Muhyi Al-Din, Abu Al-'Ila Madi and myself from Al-Minya University, and by Najih Ibrahim and Usama Hafiz from Asyut. The Muslim Brothers' leaders who attended the meeting included Mustafa Mashhur and Salah Abu Ismail. They asked us frankly if we would join the Brothers. We refused because of the difference in our agenda. But they succeeded in influencing some *Jama'at* leaders, the most prominent being Muhyi Al-Din and Abu Al-'Ila Madi from the Sa'id [Upper Egypt]; 'Esam Al-'Aryan, Hilmi Al-Jazzar and Abdul Al-Mun'em Abu Al-Futuh from Cairo; and Ahmad 'Umar and Ibrahim Al-Za'farani from Alexandria University.[51]

Once they became members of the *tanzim*, students like Abu Al-'Ila Madi, 'Esam Al-'Aryan and Abdul Al-Mun'em Abu Al-Futuh, who became well-known activists in parliament and in professional syndicates during the 1980s, began to co-ordinate their efforts and resources to provide their fellow students with important services.[52]

As well as feeling an affinity for their ideology, students were attracted to the Islamists because of the services made available to them (e.g. cheap books, affordable accommodation, financial aid, suitable transport for female students), which contrasted noticeably with what the leftists had offered when they were in charge of the student union. According to a journalist from *Al-Da'wa* magazine who sought the views of students on the amenities provided by the Islamists, most answered favourably, remarking on the efficiency and effectiveness of the services.[53] It was obvious that the magazine's coverage of the students' comments served as a form of propaganda supported by practical action, or "propaganda by deed" that was intended to attract more students to the Islamists' cause.[54]

Initially Sadat and his close officials, such as Muhammad Othman Isma'il, viewed the rise of Islamist activism on university campuses as an asset to the state in its struggle to quell the effect of the leftists, even though the security services saw the Islamists as a threat. The confusion in state policies towards the Brothers' activism on campuses was confirmed by Fu'ad 'Alam, a senior security official in the 1970s and 1980s:

Sadat lent his support to the Ikhwan and other Islamic groups without even informing the security services of his decision to do so. He wanted relations with the Ikhwan to be based on political calculations, and did not want the security people to get involved in this. The file on Islamism, that is, during the 1970s, was in the hands of the politicians and not in the hands of security, and security did not start to comprehend this until later, because there was no real co-ordination between us and the politicians on this issue.[55]

Sadat's Dilemma of Legitimacy

This disparity between Sadat and the security services did not, however, continue for very long, since the Brothers began to grow increasingly powerful on campuses and in the society at large, and were becoming increasingly critical of the regime's policies. Sadat's *infitah* policies, and the announcement of his plans to reduce state subsidies on bread prompted the famous riots of 1977. These uprisings, which began in Cairo and Alexandria, spread to many other parts of the country and caused the deaths of more than 80 people, as well as extensive damage to public buildings and to the homes of government officials. The police required the backing of the armed forces as well as the imposition of a curfew to quell the rioters. The Ikhwan took the opportunity to criticise the regime and its failure to deal effectively with the wider problems of education, transportation and inflation.[56]

Abdul Mun'em Abu Al-Futuh, who was recruited to the *tanzim* wrote an article in *Al-Da'wa* on what he thought had led to these massive riots.[57] He attacked the regime's performance which, he claimed, had further increased the gap between expectations and achievements and had left the public more frustrated. He also referred to the growth of unjust practices and policies that had deepened the suffering of ordinary people, and increased their daily problems with transportation, food, clothing and housing. He complained that prices were on the rise and that the income of the majority remained fixed or had declined, while the regime and its close cronies continued to build luxurious houses and to live extravagantly.

Abu Al-Futuh also began to attack the religious slogans which the 'Believing President' had launched to legitimate his regime, pointing out that the regime's declared watchword of "Science and Faith" had remained an empty slogan: "People went on waiting for its implementation by the rulers but to no avail. Instead poisonous corruption was enveloping new generations which did not know anything about Islam except its name."[58]

Al-Da'wa magazine, which was after all sanctioned by the state, was also employed by the Brothers as a platform to undermine the modes of legitimacy used by Sadat to stabilise his regime, while simultaneously being utilised to promote the services of the *tanzim* to students as being "effective" and "efficient". According to Gilles Kepel, the Brothers were careful to cultivate their image as astute and honest administrators "at a time when Sadat's 'economic opening' had made corruption and misappropriation of public funds the two udders of the Egyptian milk-cow."[59]

The pressure from the Brothers and from other Islamists was felt still more strongly when Sadat signed a peace accord with Israel in 1979, and when the forces which he had encouraged and supported to bolster his legitimacy started to threaten this legitimacy. By the late 1970s, Sadat was beginning to encounter what I call 'the dilemma of legitimacy'; this is encountered by most authoritarian regimes when they open up to society, and then realise that the consequences of this 'opening' threatens their legitimacy. In September 1981 Sadat revoked his policies towards the Brothers, arrested many hundreds of them, and banned *Al-Da'wa* magazine. A month later he was assassinated by *Al-Jihad* and was immediately succeeded by Husni Mubarak, who had been his Vice-President.

Conclusion

I have illustrated here how the pursuit of legitimacy was an important factor in explaining the change in the relationship between the Muslim Brothers and the regimes of Nasser and Sadat, where both parties consolidated their power and recognition through the use of whatever modes of legitimacy they found feasible. Under Nasser, the Brothers did not benefit from any particular mode of legitimacy since they were in prison and absent from the public sphere during most of the period. Nasser, however, relied on various modes of legitimacy to consolidate his leadership, including charismatic and populist legitimacy. His more 'routinised' form of legitimacy was based on the arbitrary social contract that he signed with the rising middle class, and which promised subsidised services, free education and employment in the public sector in return for loyalty and political acquiescence.

Nasser's social contract was undermined by Sadat, who preferred to confirm his leadership with more rational and traditional modes of legitimacy. The Brothers exploited the regime's spirit of tolerance to rebuild the *tanzim* and to campaign for their own legitimacy, and although they failed to secure official recognition, they were nevertheless able to make a strong impact on campuses, revive their religious reputation and, most importantly, rehabilitate and expand the structure of the *tanzim*. The movement utilised this power to undermine the legitimacy of Sadat following his peace with Israel, and this contributed to a change in the relationship between the two protagonists towards the late 1970s.

Notes

1 P. Lubeck and B. Britts, "Muslim Civil Society in Urban Public Spaces: Globalisation, Discursive Shifts, and Social Movements", in J. Eade and C. Mele (eds.), *Urban Studies: Contemporary and Future Perspectives*, Oxford, Blackwell, 2000, p. 25.
2 Personal interview with Hamid Abdul Majid, Cairo, 13 September 2001.
3 Robert Tucker, "The Theory of Charismatic Leadership", *Daedalus*, summer 97, 3, 1968, pp. 731–56; esp. pp. 737–39, 743–46; cited from

Hudson, Michael. *Arab Politics: the Search for Legitimacy*, Yale University Press, New Haven, 1977, pp. 242–43.

4 Muhammad Al-Sayyid Salim, *Al-Tahlil al-siyasi al-nasiri* (Nasserite Political Analysis), Beirut, Markaz Dirasat Al-Wihda Al-Arabiyya, 1983, p. 361.

5 Usama Al-Ghazali Harb is a political analyst at Al-Ahram Centre of Strategic Studies. See his "Al-Mutaghiyyr al-khariji ka muhadid li al-shar'iyya" (The External Variable as a Determinant for Legitimacy) in Mustafa Kamil Al-Sayyid (ed.), *Al-Tahwulat al-siyasiyya al-haditha fi al-watan al-'arabi* (Modern Political Change in the Arab Homeland), Centre for Political Research and Studies, Cairo University, Egypt, 1989, pp. 698–999.

6 Hudson, *op.ci.t*, p. 240.

7 This social contract, according to Waterbury, was "centred on the commitment of the state to provide goods and services to the public in exchange for political docility and quiescence". John Waterbury, "The 'Soft State' and the Open Door: Egypt's Experience with Economic Liberalization 1974–84", *Comparative Politics* Vol. 18, October 1985, p. 69.

8 Hilal, A. *op.cit.* pp. 182–183.

9 Kirk Beattie, *Egypt During the Nasser Years: Ideology, Politics and Civil Society*, Boulder CO, Westview Press, 1994, p. 139.

10 *Ibid.* 'Akif was in charge of *maktab al-tulab* (the Student Section) during the 1940s and 1950s and used to organise and train participants (including students, and also merchants, farmers and professionals) in these camps. When parts of the training programme comprised talks, prominent speakers such as Rahman Azzam (Egypt), Amin Al-Husseini (Palestine), and Mujadidi (Afghanistan) were invited.

11 Personal interview with Mahdi 'Akif, Cairo, 2 August 2002.

12 For instance, according to Beattie, no candidate suspected of belonging to the movement was allowed to run for the elections of the journalists' syndicate council between 1954 and 1969. Beattie, *op.cit.*, p. 139.

13 Bianchi, R. *Unruly Corporatism: Associational Life in Twentieth Century Egypt*, Oxford, Oxford University Press, 1989, p. 91.

14 This occurred from 1954 to 1959. See Mustafa K. Al-Sayyid, "A Civil Society in Egypt?", *Middle East Journal*, vol. 47, no. 2, 1993, p. 228–242.

15 Hudson, *op.cit.* p. 245.

16 Personal interview with Wahid Abdul Majid, Cairo, 15 July 2002. Abdul Majid's argument on the role of the social contract after the defeat of 1967 is also supported by Hasan Naf'a in "Al-Nizam al-siyyasi al-'arabi: halat misr", (The Political Arab Regime: the Case of Egypt), *Al-Mustaqbal Al-'Arabi*, no. 112, June 1988, p. 75.

17 See Al-Miligi, *Tarikh al-haraka al-islamiyya fi sahat al-ta'lim* (The History of the Islamic Movement in the Education Field), , Cairo, Maktbat Wahba, 1994, pp. 24–25.

18 'Usama Harb, "Al-Mutghair al-khariji. . .", *op.cit.*, p. 708.

19 Majda Rabi', *Al-Dawr al-siyyasi li al-azhar: 1952–1981* (The Political Role of Al-Azhar: 1952–1981), Centre for Research and Political Studies, Cairo University, Cairo, 1992, pp. 109–110.

20 Usama Harb, "Al-Mutghair al-khariji..", *op.cit.* p. 709.

21 Jamil Muhammad, *Al-'Ilaqa bain al-nizam al-siyyasi wa al-harakat al-islamiyya fi misr, 1970–1977*, (The Relation Between the Political Regime and the Islamic Movements in Egypt), unpublished MA Dissertation, Cairo University, Cairo, 1996, p. 32.

22 See S. Sharaf, *Abdul Nasser: kaifa hakam misr?* (Nasser: How Did He Rule Egypt?), Cairo, Madbuli Al-Sagir, 1996.

23 Personal interview with Mahdi 'Akif, Cairo, 2 August, 2001.

24 Zohurul Bari. *The Re-emergence of the Muslim Brothers in Egypt*, New Delhi, Lancer Studies, 1995, pp. 82–83.

25 Bakr Taneera. *Tatwur al-nizam al-siyyasi fi misr 1952–1976* (The Development of the Political Regime in Egypt 1952–1976), unpublished PhD thesis, Cairo University, Egypt, 1979, pp. 530–567.

26 For an analysis of the 1971Constitution, see: Ali Hilal (ed.), *Democracy in Egypt: Quarter of a Century After the July Revolution*, Cairo Papers in Social Sciences, vol. 1, no.2, Cairo, American University in Cairo, 1978.

27 R. Hinnebusch, *Egyptian Politics Under Sadat: The Post-Populist Development of an Authoritarian- Modernizing State*, Cambridge, Cambridge University Press, 1985, p. 183.

28 These included Ikhwan veterans like Yusuf Al-Qaradawi, Ahmad Al-'Asal and Salim Nijm. See Mahmud Jami', *'Araft al-sadat* (I Knew Sadat), Cairo, Al-Maktab Al-Misri Al-Hadith, 1999, p. 189.

29 R. Hinnebusch, *Egyptian Politics, op.cit.*, p. 205.

30 See for example *Al-Akhbar*, 15 July 1976.

31 According to Haddad, the Ikhwan benefited from Sadat's economic policies and from overseas employment to accumulate wealth. See Yvonne Haddad, "Islamic 'Awakening' in Egypt", *Arab Studies Quarterly*, Vol. 9, No. 3, p. 255.

32 Carrie Wickham, *Political Mobilisation Under Authoritarian Rule: Explaining Islamic Activism in Mubarak's Egypt*, unpublished PhD thesis, Princeton University, New Jersey, 1996, pp. 113–116.

33 Personal interview with Hussein Abdul Raziq, Cairo, 18 July 2002.

34 Ali Hilal, *Tatawwur al-nizam . . .*, *ibid.* p. 202.

35 R. Hinnebusch, "The Formation of the Contemporary Egyptian State From Nasser and Sadat to Mubarak", in Ibrahim Oweiss, *The Political Economy of Contemporary Egypt*, Washington DC, Georgetown University, Centre for Contemporary Arab Studies, 1990, p. 195.

36 B. Rubin, *Islamic Fundamentalism in Egyptian Politics*, London, Macmillan, 1990, p. 31.

37 *Liwa' Al-Islam*, 23 June 1990, p. 47.

38 Personal interview with Abdul Mun'em Abu Al-Futuh, Cairo, 23 July 2002.

39 Personal interview with 'Akif Mahdi, Cairo, 2 August 2001.

40 *Al-Da'wa*, Issue 31, December 1978.

41 *Al-Da'wa*, Issue 40, September 1979.

42 Jakob Skovgaard-Peterson, *Defining Islam for the Egyptian State*, Brill, Leiden, 1997, pp. 208–9.

43 *Al Mashru'iyya al-dusturiyya wa al-qanuniyya lil jama'a*, (The Legal and Constitutional Legitimacy of the Group), unpublished, undated internal document, p. 5.

44 Personal interviews with Hamid Abdul Majid, London, 13 September 2001.

45 Sa'd Eddin Ibrahim, "The Islamic Alternative in Egypt: The Muslim Brotherhood and Sadat" in S. Ibrahim (ed.), *Egypt, Islam and Democracy: Twelve Critical Essays*, American University in Cairo, Cairo, 1996, p. 33. The assassination attempt was led by Salih Sariyya, who headed a radical group in the Military Academy.

46 I am indebted to Muhammad Al-Jamal, son of Hasan Al-Jamal, who supplied me with documents and papers relating to his father's involvement in Egyptian politics since 1976.

47 Milton Viorst, *In the Shadow of the Prophet: The struggle for the Soul of Islam*, New York, Anchor Studies, 1998, p. 72.

48 Personal interview with Hamid Abdul Majid, London, 13 September 2001.

49 The Consultative Council, *majlis al-shura*, was founded by Sadat on 22 May 1980. According to the amended Constitution of 1980, the Assembly is concerned with the study and proposal of what it deems necessary to preserve the principles of the Revolution of 23 July 1952 and the Revolution of 15 May 1971. Unlike the parliament, the Assembly does not enjoy an independent legislative role. 'Umar Tilmesani, *Ayyam ma'a al-sadat* (Days With Sadat), Cairo, Dar Al-I'tisam, 1984, p. 17.

50 Personal interview with Mohammad Fu'ad, London, 9 November 2001.

51 Hisham Mubarak, "What Does the Gama'a Islamiyya Want?", in J. Beinin, and J. Stork, *Political Islam: Essays from Middle East Report*, London, I. B. Tauris, 1997, p. 316.

52 Maha Azzam, *Islamic Oriented Protest Groups in Egypt 1971–1981: Theory, Politics and Dogma*, unpublished PhD thesis, Oxford University Faculty of Social Studies, 1989, esp. pp. 132–157; and Muhammad Badr, *Al-Jama'a al-islamiyya fi jami'at misr* (The Jama'a Al-Islamiyya in Egyptian Universities), no publisher, 1989.

53 Gilles Kepel, *Muslim Extremism in Egypt: The Prophet and the Pharaoh*, Berkley CA, University of California Press, 1985, p. 144.

54 The expression "propaganda by deed" was coined by Charles Tripp in "Islam and the Secular Logic of the State", in Abdul Salam Sidahmed and Anoushiravan. Ehteshami (eds.), *Islamic Fundamentalism*, Boulder, Westview Press, 1996, p. 62.

55 Personal interview with Fu'ad 'Alam, Cairo, 8 July 2002.

56 Sa'd Eddin Ibrahim, "An Islamic Alternative in Egypt: The Muslim Brotherhood and Sadat", in Ibrahim, Sa'd Eddin. *Egypt, Islam and Democracy: Twelve Critical Essays*, Cairo, American University in Cairo, 1996, pp. 39–40.

57 *Al-Da'wa*, February 1977, pp. 16–17.

58 *Ibid.* p. 17.

59 Gilles Kepel, *Muslim Extremism in Egypt, op.cit.*, p. 144.

3

MUBARAK IN PURSUIT
OF LEGITIMACY

When Mubarak assumed power in October 1981 he lacked any legitimacy of his own, apart from the fact that as Sadat's Vice-President, he was therefore, constitutionally speaking, his expected successor. This was a major reason why Mubarak attempted, during the early 1980s, to develop a stronger and more lasting basis for legitimacy beyond that of the constitutional element. His regime launched a series of policies and reforms that aimed to bolster the populist and legal basis of his legitimacy. While many of the policies were based largely on rhetoric and symbolic gestures rather than on real reform, the general spirit during this period was one of tolerance and conciliation. The Muslim Brothers tapped into that spirit and tried to achieve two main objectives. One was to resume their activities and expand the structure of the *tanzim*; the second to secure the recognition of the state.

The first aim of this chapter is to examine the ways in which Mubarak led Egypt into the early 1980s, with a particular focus on the years from 1981 to 1984, and the efforts he made to establish his political authority. The second is to examine how the Brothers made use of Mubarak's efforts to expand their organisation and to secure legal status. The second of these objectives was obviously not realised, since Mubarak was not prepared, at least officially, openly to unleash the Islamists and thereby repeat Sadat's mistake. However, the first objective was partly achieved, since it was taking place gradually and in secret. To understand this latter development it is important to say something on the personal characteristics of Mubarak when he first came to power, and also to look at conditions during the transition period from Sadat to Mubarak.

This is because these two elements acted as essential factors in Mubarak's tolerant attitude and created an opportunity for the movement to resume its activism.

Certain aspects of Mubarak's personality were conducive to a spirit of tolerance in the early 1980s. The first relates simply to his background. Until appointed by Sadat as his Vice-President in 1975, Mubarak had never had any political responsibilities,[1] since his education and his successive postings had been purely military.[2] Such an a-political background meant that he had no previous disagreements with, or antagonism towards any particular political force, based on a specific political tendency. The second aspect relates to Mubarak's own generation. Although he came from a military background, he did not belong to the generation of the Free Officers who had gained power in 1952.[3] This meant that he had not inherited Nasser's antagonistic views, whether against the Brothers or even the communists. On the contrary, his past record with the Brothers had been one of co-operation.

It must be remembered that the first time Mubarak assumed any political responsibility was in 1975, when he took up his public position as Vice-President. At this time Sadat's accommodation of the Islamists was at its peak. Personal interviews with veterans of the movement reveal that Mubarak did not entertain any particular suspicions about the Ikhwan; indeed on occasions he was on quite friendly terms with figures like 'Umar Tilmesani, who was himself close to Sadat. In addition to his a-political background Mubarak, perhaps unlike Sadat, was known to be quite cautious. His decisions were usually based on careful calculation and wide consultation. This suggested, among many other things, that at least his impartial attitude towards the Brothers would not suddenly change once he came to power. This was especially the case in the early 1980s, when conditions in Egypt were not favourable to such change.

Up to and following the assassination of Sadat in 1981, Egypt was in a state of turmoil. This was because Sadat's authoritarian policies had increased public dissent and alienated people from the regime. It was therefore to be expected that if Mubarak wanted to stabilise his new regime, he would have to become more tolerant towards the opposition. This was particularly the case when the immediate enemies were religious extremists. The regime would need to create a broader nationalist front and to mobilise the moderate Islamists, such as the Muslim Brothers, against such force.

In addition to local/domestic considerations, the 1980s also saw a global wave of democratisation, to which most regimes in the Third World became vulnerable. Any Arab regime that needed to secure some form of economic and political support from the West had first to show its willingness to democratise and to introduce political reforms, even if only superficially. To a certain extent the Brothers benefited from this wave.

This spirit of tolerance offered Mubarak and the Brothers the respite needed for each to consolidate a form of authority. This was achieved by the potential opportunities embedded in the political, social and economic fields. The following section will discuss Egypt's political situation in the early 1980s, and will examine the ways in which Mubarak utilised political turmoil to gain a degree of legitimacy.

The Build-up of Legitimacy

One could argue that potentially Egypt's political situation in the early 1980s offered Mubarak an opportunity to boost both his populist and his legal modes of legitimacy. Here I confine 'populist legitimacy' to the sort of rhetoric and foreign policies that were proposed in answer to pressure from the United States, Israel and the Arab countries, with the aim of winning nationalist sentiments and local credibility. And by legal legitimacy, I refer to the sort of legal reforms that Mubarak undertook to emphasise his regime's respect for the rule of law. These modes of legitimacy, certainly as far as the political dimension was concerned, were the most convenient alternatives to charisma, which Mubarak obviously lacked, or to traditional modes, which he was not prepared to consider.[4]

Populist Legitimacy

If populist legitimacy is understood in relation to foreign and regional policies then it is correct to argue that Sadat's legitimacy was undermined by three factors: his visible economic and political dependence on the United States, his peace with Israel and the consequent break up of Egypt's relations with the rest of the Arab World. It was only logical therefore for the new regime to redefine, if partly or rhetorically, its relations with the United States, Israel and the Arab countries.

In his first speech to the Egyptians, Mubarak declared his plan to continue with Sadat's policies but in a "dynamic and wise" manner.[5] Although this meant that he was indeed committed to retaining Egypt's special relations with the United States, he wished to avoid whatever negative implications this had on the legitimacy of the regime, and would thus hope to come across as a more independent leader than Sadat. One manifestation of this desire was his refusal to accept American aid amounting to about US$500 million in 1983 to develop Egypt's Ra's Banas naval military base. Mubarak also refused to give in to American pressures in 1985 and 1986 to join a military operation against Libya.

With regard to Israel, Mubarak emphasised his commitment to the Camp David peace plan,[6] but at the same time made sure that this peace did not translate into a complete normalisation of social or economic relations. Mubarak, who had also gained an element of legitimacy for his role in the October War of 1973, wanted to assure Egyptians that the regime would not rush towards real peace until Egypt had regained its lands, occupied since 1967, and until the Palestinians had regained their homeland.[7] The sentiment was confirmed in 1982 when Mubarak immediately withdrew his ambassador in Tel Aviv in protest against Israel's invasion of Lebanon.

In contrast, Mubarak was eager to warm up relations with the Arab world. He had instructed the Egyptian press to end its hostile campaigns against Arab states, especially Libya and Syria, that were strong critics of Egypt's peace with Israel. Mubarak's move was in sharp contrast to Sadat's hostile discourse defending his unilateral decision to recognise the state of Israel in 1979.[8] The Mubarak gesture was undoubtedly welcomed just as much by Arab regimes as it was by Egyptian nationalists and Islamists.

Further, Mubarak's position on the Iran-Iraq War (1980–1988) and his support for Iraq as "an Arab country"[9] boosted the image of the new regime, not just in Iraq but also among the Gulf States, who saw themselves as equally vulnerable to the Iranian threat. Egypt's position with regard to the War was among the factors that improved its relations with the Gulf, and this in turn created new opportunities for Egyptians to work abroad. Remittances from Egyptians working in Iraq and in the Gulf constituted an important source of income for the Egyptian economy. In the fiscal years between 1980/81 and 1984/85 they accounted for 10 per cent of Egypt's Gross Domestic Product (GDP), a level that increased to 18 per cent in 1989/90.[10] In addition to the amount of aid (US$2 billion) received annually from the United States, remittances contributed to improving the living standards of working and middle class Egyptians. On a state level, the regime used remittances, along with aid and loans from Iraq and the Gulf, for infrastructure-related reconstruction projects, such as communications, transport and drainage, etc.

Legal Legitimacy

Mubarak's discourse in the early 1980s was intended to emphasise his regime's commitment to the rule of law. This was seen in the way he accentuated his respect for equal rights, for the independence of the judiciary, and for the sovereignty of law. In one of his speeches, Mubarak emphasised that the sovereignty of law "was the basis of state governance and . . . no authority should interfere in court cases and justice . . . Since the first day [in power] I have abided by the rule of justice."[11] He consolidated the power of the judiciary by introducing a new law which provided full immunity and protection to members of the prosecuting tribunal and the State Court. He also reformed the Council of the Supreme Court by placing an independent judge at its head, rather than the Minster of Justice who was counted as belonging more to the executive rather than as being an independent figure.[12] Tariq Al-Bishri, an independent thinker and former judge in the Supreme Constitutional Court, stressed the importance to Mubarak of legal legitimacy:

> It was an important issue for Mubarak not to appear as against the rulings of the court or against the legislations of the Assembly. He also tended to project himself as an executer of the legislation, and certainly in contrast to Nasser, he cared more about the legal legitimacy of his leadership.[13]

In her research on the position of legal authority in the Egyptian political regime, Ahlam Farhud concluded that court rulings, particularly in the first seven years of Mubarak's rule, were generally respected by the regime and were used as a guide in taking political decisions.[14] In the past, the courts had been subordinated by the person of Nasser and, to a lesser extent, Sadat, and were exploited to issue rulings that would give legitimacy to authoritarian policies. With Mubarak, at least far as the early 1980s were concerned, the case was different. According to Farhud's study, Mubarak did not use his presidential powers to pressurise the courts to issue new rulings that would restrict social and political freedoms, but on the contrary, left the courts to initiate a series of limited but significant legal reforms in social and political areas.

Connected to the spirit of reform was Mubarak's famous campaign against institutionalized corruption or *fasad*. The campaign targeted important figures, most noticeably Sadat's brother, 'Ismat, who was tried in 1983 for extensive illicit dealings.[15] The campaign won wide media coverage which was obviously aimed at showing the public that the new regime was committed to rooting out corruption; that the regime knew no favouritism; and that all were equal before the law. Although Mubarak's campaign was "short-lived", to use Nazih Ayubi's expression, it was sufficient to deliver the message.[16] The campaign was coupled with Mubarak's emphasis on freedom of the press.[17] He continued to remind Egyptians that freedom of political expression under his leadership was 'unprecedented' in Egypt's history.

Nonetheless, one should not conclude that Mubarak's reforms were absolute, since most of the restrictive laws that had been issued during Sadat's later tenure (most notoriously the Emergency Law launched in 1981) were retained by the new regime. Mubarak continued to be in command of most powers, and his respect for the law was in those areas that did not threaten the survival of the regime. One area of restraint remained that of politics and political freedoms.

While Mubarak stressed his support for political pluralism, in practice he did nothing to further it, and in fact retained the essential constraints on the formation of new parties, which would otherwise have threatened his *Al-Hizb Al-Watani Al-Dimuqrati* or the National Democratic Party (NDP). The regime's authoritarian tendencies were confirmed by the creation of the Parties' Committee (*lagnat al-ahzab*), which was responsible for granting licences and legal status to newly-formed parties. The setting up of the Committee was rejected by the opposition, who viewed it not as an independent organisation but as one that was essentially controlled by the government. As a way of affirming the independent powers of the judiciary, the regime did permit rejected political parties to appeal to the courts against the Committee's decisions.[18] However, this alone did not guarantee the transformation to pluralism, since the courts remained subordinated to the will of the head of state. From the many parties that did appeal to the courts during this period, only the New Wafd and the Umma were granted recognition in 1983. As much as the latter development strengthened the legal legitimacy of the regime, it also revealed the extent of its limitations.

The Brothers and Formal Politics

The Muslim Brothers aimed to utilise Mubarak's tolerant spirit to achieve two main objectives: to continue to rebuild the *tanzim* and to reintegrate fully in society and politics. The latter objective would not be wholly achieved if the movement lacked a form of legal recognition from the state, its courts, or its Parties Committee.

Initially, Mubarak's emphasis on the rule of law kindled the Brothers' hopes that the state might recognise them as a mass movement, especially when Mubarak agreed to allow the return from exile of leading Muslim Brothers figures, such as the former *murshid* Mustafa Mashhur, and complied with the court's decision to allow the resumption of publications, such as *Al-I'tisam* and *Al-Mukhtar al-Islami*, that were close to the ideas of the movement. The Brothers were, however, disappointed with a regime that was not prepared to tolerate the legal existence of Islamist organisations or to propose alternatives similar to those that had been proposed by the previous regime (e.g. a charity organisation). The Ikhwan's court case, that had been filed in 1977, continued to be delayed by the Constitutional Court.

Mubarak's 1983 electoral law institutionalised the political culture of *hizbiyya* and this compelled the Brothers to think in terms of *hizbiyya* if they wanted to enjoy the protection of a 'legal umbrella'. In the 1970s, the Brothers had been negotiating alternatives to their existence as a mass movement (the ideal option). Sadat's *hizbiyya* was still in its formatives stages, and the Brothers thought, reluctantly, that they could perhaps negotiate a place in the political process on their own terms. Sadat's political tolerance extended beyond parliament, and that gave them a variety of options. Mubarak's political tolerance, on the other hand, was confined to political parties, and that limited their options. What was also limiting was the restrictive implication of the Parties' Law itself. The Parties' Committee had been governed since 1976 by the multi-party laws which prohibited the formation of parties on religious grounds. At that stage, the leadership of the movement was less concerned with assuming an institutionally-based political role than with rebuilding the organisation and re-establishing its presence on a wider mass level. Even so, the restrictive conditions in the law had deterred the Brothers from thinking with any enthusiasm in terms of establishing a proper political party. However, the thinking of the 1970s changed, and during the 1980s the movement began to consider the idea of engaging in formal politics by establishing an alliance with a legal party.

Thus the early 1980s saw two main developments in the political thinking of the Muslim Brothers. The first was the decision to participate in parliamentary politics, this time as an organised bloc and not as individuals (as had been the case in the 1970s), and the second was the resolve to take part in the parliamentary elections in alliance with a political party that was promoting another political trend in society. Both developments were quite separate from the enthusiasm for establishing a proper political party, with a proper manifesto – a development that crystallised in the mid-1980s. I will briefly discuss the first development (that of entering parliament): the second development will be looked at in the next chapter when I examine the Brothers' alliance with the New Wafd Party in 1984.

There is no clear date as to when the Brothers decided to join Mubarak's parliament, although Abdul Mun'em Abu Al-Futuh claims that the idea began to crystallise in Tilmesani's mind as early as 1983.[19] But the decision to participate in parliament in the name of the outlawed movement was a brave one, and not everybody was prepared to take its consequences. Badr Mohammad Badr, who had been a student activist in the 1970s, and had worked closely with Tilmesani in the 1980s, told me that the issue had been hotly debated, not just among both the younger and older generations of the movement but even among the senior members of the Guidance Bureau or *maktab al-irshad*.[20] I referred in Chapter Two to the discussion that took place between 'Akif, the *murshid* of the Ikhwan, and Tilmesani, the former *murshid*. In the 1980s, however, the discussions took on wider dimensions. According to Badr, in 1983 quite a large meeting was held in Cairo, presided over by Tilmesani whose intention was to persuade the participating representatives and officials of the movement, from the capital and from regional cities, to his way of thinking.

At the time, the Ikhwan had recently come out of prison, and were reluctant to engage so rapidly in public arenas. Some were still haunted by the period of Nasser and what he had done to them, while others thought that more time and energy needed to be devoted to building the *tanzim*. Tilmesani argued that building the *tanzim* and engaging in the political process could take place simultaneously, and that it was not necessary publicly to reveal all aspects of the *tanzim* and its members. Secondly, the Brothers should ultimately stop functioning as a secret movement and instead try to explore all possible means of propagating their ideas. Thirdly, they needed to become more experienced in the political process, and that sort of experience could only come from participating in parliament. Fourthly, their presence in parliament would give the movement a valuable opportunity to reform the laws based on *Shari'a*. Finally, this would also provide the Brothers with access to ministers and officials, who could be persuaded of the movement's non-violent approach to state and society.

The Spirit of Tolerance

Mubarak's tolerant attitude was aimed at defusing the tensions in state-society relations created by Sadat. In 1982 he released political activists who had been arrested and imprisoned by Sadat; among more than a thousand prisoners were individuals from various sections of society, such as religious leaders, journalists, students, members of professional syndicates, and trade unionists. Mubarak also wanted to unite social forces and institutions against the religious extremists who were regarded by the regime as an immediate threat. This was one of the reasons why he tolerated moderate Islamists as well as Al-Azhar. Mubarak also opened up some social spaces, maintained their semi-autonomous structures, and allowed the opposition to operate inside them within limits. The professional syndicates (*al-niqabat al-mihaniyya*) constituted one of the obvious spaces that benefited from Mubarak's reforms.

Professional Syndicates

It was expected that if Mubarak aspired to win the support of the lower middle classes, once alienated by Sadat, he would introduce some reforms within the professional syndicates. As a way of controlling the growing activism of the professional syndicates that had followed his unpopular policies during the late 1970s, Sadat had introduced a number of restrictive bylaws against them. In 1981, Sadat had disbanded the elected council of the lawyers' syndicate because of its increasing rejection of peace with Israel.

When Mubarak came to power he wanted to show that things had changed for the better. In 1983 he revoked Sadat's decision and issued a new law that reinstated the disbanded council of the lawyers' syndicate.[21] Syndicate members welcomed Mubarak's action, although they objected to the fact that parts of the reformed law remained essentially restrictive.[22] As a way of giving lawyers working in the public sector greater powers in the decision-making process, the new version now transferred considerable powers to the board of the council's syndicate, rather than to the elected board.[23] Following active lobbying, Mubarak conceded to the objectors and agreed to introduce further reforms. The president of the syndicate (the *naqib*), was invited to attend the National Assembly discussions that dealt with the new draft, and the reformed law received further approval in 1984.[24]

The case of the lawyers' syndicate was a clear example of how Mubarak gave way to the demands of professionals in exchange for their support. According to Bianchi, Egypt's relations with Israel and the United States "had deteriorated" in the early 1980s, and this was another reason why Mubarak did not take action as Sadat had done against the lawyers' syndicate when it resumed its criticisms of the Camp David Treaty.[25] Mubarak effectively employed syndicates to bolster his legal as well as his populist legitimacy.

Apart from legitimising his regime, Mubarak tolerated syndicates, partly because he did not expect them to turn into sources of mobilisation in the way they were to become in the 1990s. He assumed that his attitude to political reform and pluralism, as seen in the new Parties' Law of 1983, provided the opposition with a sufficient democratic margin. He seems also to have assumed that the 'corporatist' links between the state and these syndicates offered sufficient guarantees against forces that aimed to undermine the regime's authoritarian controls. These controls had been manifested in a series of restrictive measures embedded in the bureaucratic structure of syndicates since the days of Nasser. Even then, Mubarak was still prepared to tolerate a marginal political role played by syndicates provided this role was strictly retained within the syndicates' boundaries and was supervised by the state.

Al-Azhar

As noted above, in order to combat the threat of *Al-Jihad* and *Al-Jama'at Al-Islamiyya*, both of which had been responsible for the outbursts of violence in Asyut, Mansura and Cairo, Mubarak tolerated Islamists and Al-Azhar. In the process, he wanted also to appeal to religious legitimacy. In 1983, at an event celebrating the religious institution's millennium[26] he awarded medals to some of Al-Azhar's *'ulama* (religious scholars; pl. *'alim*). Mubarak frequently met the Shaikh of Al-Azhar, Gad Al-Haqq (who had been appointed to the position in 1982). In these meetings with the former *mufti* and Minister of *waqfs*, Mubarak stressed the importance of Al-Azhar's role in ridding Egypt of its growing wave of Islamic radicalism.[27] Several shaikhs appeared on television to contradict the ideas of the *Jama'at* and to promote thinking along lines that were formally recognised by the state. New specialised committees were set up in Al-Azhar to recommend ways in which religious values could be propagated in the media.

The appeal to religious legitimacy was coupled with the use of security forces, which began a massive crackdown on people suspected of violence. During the weeks following Sadat's assassination, it was estimated that more than four thousand people were arrested.[28] Human rights reports claimed that the arrests continued during 1982, "where detainees were held for a renewable period of six months, with no recourse to a court of law to challenge their detention".[29] Al-Azhar co-operated with the security apparatuses to support the regime in its fight against Islamist radicals, and organised various 'convoys' (*qwafil*) to visit different towns and debate with young Islamists.[30] The alliance certainly undermined the credibility of the religious institution of Al-Azhar among the youth, many of whom constituted potential recruits for the extremists.

University Campuses

University campuses represented both the exception to Mubarak's tolerant spirit and reforms, and a continuation of the regime's campaign to crack down on extremism. This is easily enough understood since student campuses constituted a major breeding ground for the Islamists' radical ideas and for the Islamist groups that (as interrogations subsequently showed) had been responsible for the assassination of Sadat. Badr Mohammad Badr, who had been an active Ikhwan student at Cairo University, confirms that following the murder of Sadat the University had been subjected to visible tight controls and checks, because of fears that its faculties were becoming "strong recruiting points for militants".[31]

Mubarak maintained Sadat's 1979 amendment of the Student Charter, which essentially was intended to undermine the power and activism of students on campus by dissolving the representative student bodies, including the elected General Union of Egyptian Students. It also placed student activities under the complete supervision of the teaching body, which was not independent but reflected the mood of the government and obeyed its orders, and at the same time legalised the presence of security guards inside campuses. Students continued to persist with efforts to change the Charter, as was evident in the relentless visits of student representatives to government officials and members of parliament. However, and differently from the case of the lawyers' syndicate, the new regime rebuffed their demands.[32]

Against this tight security presence, the Muslim Brothers were unable to resume their activities on campuses until 1984, when Mubarak introduced trivial but significant reforms to the Student Charter. During the first couple of years after the assassination of Sadat, most campuses were politically inactive and in a state of inertia. Although student union elections resumed a year later after Sadat's death, most students who ran the elections in 1982 and in 1983 were unaffiliated to a group or did not identify with a particular ideology. Most students who were released from prison after the assassination of Sadat became more concerned with their personal affairs and the progress of their delayed studies rather than with group activism. Many were also frightened away from engaging directly in campus activities because of increased security interventions and surveillance.

The interviews I conducted with the students' representatives in Cairo, Alexandria and Asyut showed that this stagnation was not confined to a particular university or a particular region, but reflected a general phenomenon throughout Egypt. The situation in Asyut University was understandably tenser than in Cairo because of the existence of extremist groups like *Al-Jama'at Al-Islamiyya*.[33]

During this period, and although the Muslim Brothers could not engage in student activism, partly because some of its young members were still in prison, the objectives of most Ikhwan students was

to focus on their academic progress while at the same time maintaining organisational links inside and outside campuses. In a way,
such links implied that even during the early 1980s, and under tight
security conditions, campuses were not totally devoid of activism in
its quietest form. According to Ahmad Abdullah, an Ikhwan student
activist and later President of Cairo's Student Union, informal
meetings between student members of the university used to take
place quite regularly inside the university mosque.[34] He and other
students I met in Alexandria and Asyut confirmed that such meetings
were also used for recruiting new members into the movement.

The *Tanzim* in the 1980s

Abdullah's revelations showed that during this difficult period, the
Brothers placed more emphasis on maintaining and expanding the
organisation or the *tanzim* than on resuming public activism. The
entire process had been initiated in the 1970s by 'Umar Tilmesani,
but was soon obstructed by Sadat's arrests among the movement's
members in September 1981. However, shortly after the Brothers
had been released from prison in 1982 and 1983, the group
resumed its uncompleted mission. As in the case of the university
campuses, the process was achieved quietly and gradually.

The process was accompanied by a growing conviction among
most Brothers that the movement needed to coexist publicly and
peacefully alongside the state and within its institutions. This
conclusion was prompted by several developments. First, there was
the movement's serious repudiation of the use of violence to realise
its goals. The commitment to peaceful methods to achieve reform
had been endorsed in the 1970s as a result of the positive outcome
of interaction with the society at large. Second, was the central role
played by 'Umar Tilmesani in accelerating the process of change.
Tilmesani, the *murshid* of the movement, was a courteous man. A
lawyer by profession, he enjoyed the respect of many Egyptian
officials including Sadat. In addition, the fact that Tilmesani was
never a member of the Special Apparatus, *al-nizam al-khass* (later
the main source of violent operations), meant that he was a more
acceptable face for the group.

Third was the growing influence of the group's younger cadres.
These cadres did not share the grievances against the regime held
by the veterans, most of whom had been tortured by Nasser. Even
so, moderate tendencies would not have crystallised without some

sort of positive overtures from the state. Mubarak's spirit of tolerance, his populist foreign policies and appeal to justice and equal rights undoubtedly encouraged the movement towards this more conciliatory attitude.

Soon after Mubarak's accession to the leadership, the Muslim Brothers began their organised plan to expand in Egyptian society. In mosques, local towns, urban and rural neighbourhoods and villages, the movement relied on traditional and religious forms of influence to regain its popularity. Religious discourse and symbols continue until today to be a powerful means of recruiting new members into the organisation. It was through these means that the Muslim Brothers were able to rebuild the *tanzim* and reconstruct its internal structures.

But what in fact was the *tanzim* and what did rebuilding it mean? How does the *tanzim* help us in understanding the reasons behind the movement's strength and effectiveness as far as social institutions, such as syndicates or student unions, are concerned? And finally, how does the *tanzim* link to the movement's objective of gaining recognition by the state? The *tanzim* is the inner structure, dynamics and hierarchies of the movement's organisation. During the days of its founder, Hassan Al-Banna, most of its hierarchies and dynamics, perhaps with the exception of the Special Apparatus, were openly known and defined by the movement's special constitution. However, after the movement was disbanded in 1954, issues concerning the *tanzim* became highly secretive.

My questions on the *tanzim* and the changes it has undergone since the 1970s were frequently answered with equivocation by the late *murshids*, Mustafa Mashhur and Ma'mun Al-Hudaybi, the current *murshid*. My interviews with the Ikhwan leadership were taking place during the period when confrontations with the regime were at their peak, and I soon realised that questions on this subject were highly sensitive. Later I discovered that the younger cadres were more disposed to speak on the issue. 'Esam Al-'Aryan, an influential member in *maktab al-irshad*, was one useful informer. He admitted that the *tanzim* was a central concept to the Muslim Brotherhood and that it is still considered the main source of their power. The Brotherhood had always been a mass movement that included members from various social backgrounds, specialised departments, and local branches. During the early 1980s, the movement continued to rebuild its specialised departments and branches, to which it added new ones that had been developed to cater for its new role in society and politics.[35]

According to Al-'Aryan, there are about eleven departments or sections inside the organisation for Social Services, *Da'wa* (Islamic call), Students, Workers, Teachers Faculty Clubs, Sisters (like the Girl Guides movement in the UK), Education, Families, Physical Training, Muslim World, and Professional Syndicates. Some sections can include specialised committees such as the Financial Committee, the History Committee, and the Scholars' Committee. The Scholars Committee is responsible for ensuring that the movement's views and positions are in accordance with the *Shari'a*, while the History Committee, whose office I visited and some of whose members I interviewed, is entrusted with writing a 'formal' version of the history of the Muslim Brotherhood. Other sections have recently been developed to cater for the new political role of the Brothers in parliament. The Political Section, which includes the Media Committee, is rather like a think tank and specialises in co-ordinating studies on various political issues and developments. Some of the studies relating to the movement and to the Egyptian regime are discussed in Chapter Seven. The Political Section also includes the Parliamentary Committee, whose members include the Brothers' deputies in parliament.

A second development during the 1980s concerned the way the *tanzim* was run, and involved the institutionalising of a decentralised system of management and administration. Decentralisation was introduced in the 1980s as a way of improving the movement's effectiveness and because it seemed a convenient operational arrangement, given the prevailing authoritarian conditions and state denial. In the decentralised structure, the central leadership was based in the capital, and was in charge of formulating the movement's major policies, especially those related directly to the state. Such policies were frequently articulated in political statements, press releases, general sermons etc. The regional leadership decided on regional policies. The eleven internal departments referred to above existed twice, i.e., at two main levels: a central level administered from the Cairo headquarters, and a provincial level. The provincial level was spread through Egypt's 28 governorates. The larger departments, especially those with similar concerns, were linked together and co-ordinated on a regular basis, either through personal meetings or use of modern technologies such as the Internet. Regular meetings and contacts also took place between members of the central and regional departments in order to share experiences and unify approaches.

The third major development was that the leadership in the movement and within its departments was formally elected, rather than appointed on the traditional basis of seniority as might have been the case in the past. This development, even if it was not ideal in practice, was a significant one, partly because it was at odds with the prevailing political culture practised by most Arab regimes. Members of each section within the *tanzim* were also elected by their central or regional constituencies, and when this was not possible for reasons related to availability, were appointed. Members of one section, especially the more senior and experienced, might shift from one department to another, or simply be members of more than one section. This ensured that experience was rarely wasted but could be shared and accumulated. The connection between the role of the *tanzim* and the impact of the Brothers on society and politics is discussed in more details in Chapter Four.

Maintaining the Social Contract

Egypt's economy has presented a formidable challenge to almost all Egyptian regimes since 1952. Unlike the social or the political field, where the president could improve his public image by symbolic gestures such as releasing political prisoners or introducing minor social reforms, reforms in the economic field are difficult, time consuming and more constrained. Most of Egypt's economic problems were shaped by the revenues from four sources of income: dues from the Suez Canal, income from oil and from tourism, and workers' remittances, all of which are uncontrollable and unpredictable.[36] Mubarak's unique predicament in this regard is that he inherited a series of institutionalised policies that were inherently in contradiction with each other, reflecting the conflicting tenures of Nasser and Sadat.[37] Mubarak's challenge was that at the outset he could not simply abolish the policies of Nasser and, even more so, of Sadat, since these were not just the product of presidential initiatives and vision. Rather they reflected the socio-economic changes that had been taking place within and outside Egypt, and whose effects were still being felt until Mubarak's era.

I will not provide a critical account of Egypt's economy under Mubarak, since this has been undertaken elsewhere, but instead will examine how Mubarak responded to Egypt's economic realities

with the intention of enhancing his legitimacy. It would be somewhat of an exaggeration to assume that in the earlier stages of his
leadership Mubarak, who was essentially a military pilot, had any
clear vision or ready-made plan as to how Egypt might be freed
from its economic problems. But for the purpose of our analysis it
is sufficient to assume that his generally cautious attitude to society
and his reluctance to introduce radical changes, particularly if
these were unpopular, meant that he continued to emphasise the
role of the state in Nasser's established 'social contract', without
forsaking Sadat's *infitah*, albeit in a more regulated fashion. In his
speeches and interviews in the early 1980s, Mubarak never spoke
directly of dismantling the public sector or even privatising parts of
it, but merely talked about the need to reform it and make it more
productive. In one interview, he affirmed his commitment to the
public sector, and proudly boosted that in 1983 his regime had
allocated £E700 million from its budget specifically to support
manufacturing in the public sector.[38] Mubarak stressed that he
wanted to rehabilitate the public sector, maximise its productivity
levels and promote investment,[39] since this, he reiterated, was the
only solution to Egypt's economic problems.[40]

At the same time, Mubarak resisted pressure from donor
agencies and the International Monetary Fund (IMF) to introduce
structural reforms, so as not to provoke riots similar to those that
had erupted in 1977 when Sadat reduced food subsidies.[41] Instead,
he preferred to solve Egypt's pressing problems with increased
external borrowing, which was facilitated by all sorts of external
credits and loans from the United States.[42] If reductions in subsidies
were in fact taking place as a continuation of Sadat's *infitah* policies,
which Mubarak had said he would reform rather than repeal, such
reductions were either applied to non-essential commodities or
were happening only quietly.

However, most Egyptians expected to see more than just maintenance of the public sector from the new regime. They expected
to sense real improvements in their living conditions and in welfare
services. Although Sadat's *infitah* had benefited a narrow sector of
society, it had alienated most lower classes who continued to lack
access to services and to a well built infrastructure. Sadat had
initiated important industrial projects, factories and areas for urban
activities and accommodation (e.g. Al-'Ashir min Ramadan City).
According to Ayubi, his government had allocated 45 per cent of
all public investment to infrastructure facilities and services (about

9 per cent for power, 27 per cent for transport and telecommunications and the rest for housing and construction) in its 1978–1982 Five Year Plan.[43] Most of these projects were not finished under Sadat but were completed during Mubarak's era. From 1982, a large share of Egypt's investment went into the infrastructure.[44] The results of these investments were celebrated by the state-owned magazine *Al-Ahram Al-Iqtisadi*, which claimed that from 1981 to 1986:

> The road network increased from 26,000 to 42,000 kilometres; the number of trucks more than doubled; the number of telephone lines increased more than two-and-a-half times; and electricity generation increased from 18 billion kilowatt/hours to 45 billion. As a result electricity, which had been connected to 5.2 million homes in 1981, was connected to 8.2 million in 1986; and townships supplied with fresh water increased from 4200 to 4500 towns.[45]

Ibrahim Oweiss is right in suggesting that the figures above were not real indicators of the performance of the new regime when measured against a substantial growth in population.[46] But however modest the performance of the regime, it certainly provided the state-owned media and press and, most importantly, the presidential speeches, with the substance needed in the campaign for eudaemonic legitimacy. In conferences, speeches and interviews to the foreign and domestic press, Mubarak referred proudly to his achievements since he had come to power. It is worth noting the fact that Mubarak had spoken of his achievements to the foreign press, since this was an indication that he was also intending to attract foreign investors, as much as to satisfy the Egyptians.[47] The two strands are not, of course, mutually exclusive, since foreign investment and the revenues it yields will eventually strengthen the local economy and, in the words of Mubarak himself, create job opportunities for graduates.[48]

The Emergence of Islamist Finance

The Muslim Brothers were able to develop their own financial ventures, partly because of the regime's prevailing spirit of tolerance, and partly because they did not appear to pose any particular threat. Indeed it could be argued that at one stage the regime and its cronies thought that they might benefit from such ventures, either as a source of aid to the state economy or in the form of increased personal wealth. Both possibilities were seen in the case of the Islamic investment companies that sprang up in the 1980s and the state's ambiguous response to them. In examining the financial activities of the Brothers during the early 1980s, I will also discuss the role of the Islamic banks and of individual private enterprises.

Investment Companies

I must make it clear from the outset that I am not offering an account of the emergence and/or the politics of the Islamic Investment companies. I am more concerned to study the Brothers' link to these companies, as one manifestation of their financial activities. Islamic investment companies, or *sharikat tawzif al-amwal*, are frequently and mistakenly confused with the Brotherhood organisation itself, perhaps because in practice, due to the confidentiality of the information, it is difficult to work out whether personal owners of investment companies were affiliated in any way to the movement. To an outsider, or even to local Egyptian analysts, the easiest option seems to be to lump all bearded Islamists together, particularly if this phenomenon is scrutinised on the basis of its Islamic credentials, whereby organisational differentiation becomes irrelevant. For the purpose of this study, organisational difference is obviously essential if one is to present an accurate view of the Ikhwan's financial performance, and the impact this has had on the *tanzim* as well as on the regime.

When I went to Egypt to investigate the role of the Muslim Brothers in the emergence and development of Islamic investment companies, the name of Ahmad 'Ubayd became familiar. In public circles, 'Ubayd might not have been as well-known an activist as 'Esam Al-'Aryan, for instance, but he certainly represented one of the financial arms of the movement. An Ikhwan veteran, and owner of the small but powerful *Al-Hijaz* Investment Company, 'Ubayd played a tremendous role in the emergence and expansion of the larger conglomerate investment companies owned by the more famous Al-Sharif, Al-Sa'd and Al-Raiyyan families. Although the Brothers deny that 'Ubayd represented anyone other than himself and his own initiatives, in practical terms his affiliation to the movement meant that his financial achievements were utilised in funding the organisation and employing its cadres.

In Cairo, I met 'Asim Shalabi and his older brother Mohammad Shalabi, both of whom are Islamist entrepreneurs who once owned an Islamic investment company (before it was dissolved by the regime in 1989) and worked closely with 'Ubayd. 'Asim currently owns Dar al-Wafa', an Islamic publishing house, while Mohammad owns a large construction factory, and both retained documents and accounts that recorded the story of 'Ubayd and his connections to *sharikat tawzif al-amwal.*

In the early 1970s 'Ubayd was released from Nasser's prison by Sadat and subsequently started to work for Abdul Latif Al-Sharif, an independent Islamist and entrepreneur who owned a small plastics manufacturing firm. Al-Sharif benefited from Sadat's *infitah* and his business expanded rapidly throughout the 1970s. Even with increasing profits more funds were still needed to expand into a larger enterprise that would be equipped with more modern (and expensive) machines. 'Ubayd used his organisational network to persuade members of the Brotherhood who were working in the Gulf and looking for safe opportunities to invest back home, to deposit their savings with Al-Sharif. In return, Al-Sharif employed many of the recently-released Ikhwan who were unable to travel to the Gulf and who preferred to work in Egypt in the private sector.

By the late 1970s, Al-Sharif's total assets had reached no less than £E300 million, and his conglomerate was engaged in various businesses that ranged from the construction of apartments to the manufacture of plastics, lights, detergents and electronic equipment. 'Ubayd was rewarded for his efforts by being promoted to the Board of Directors of the various companies, for which he received a monthly salary of £E5000. This was a remarkable increase in a very short period, certainly when compared with the £E180 he had been paid when he started his job in 1974. But in 1979, 'Ubayd decided to leave his job as a result of a dispute with Al-Sharif over the way the latter managed the business.

Together with Mohammad 'Elaiwa, a Brother and an influential entrepreneur, 'Ubayd then launched *Al-Hijaz* Investment Company. Among various other developments, this led to the deposits of the Ikhwan members shifting from Al-Sharif to *Al-Hijaz* which, if nothing else, illustrates the value of organisational affiliations and loyalties. From the early 1980s, *Al-Hijaz* engaged in limited investment projects, but one of its significant actions was to provide loans to small entrepreneurs who wished to invest in property.

Chapter Four will discuss the crucial role played by such loans in the emergence of Al-Sa'd and Al-Raiyyan, other prominent Islamic tycoons. During the period, 'Ubayd's affiliations were quite well known to the security apparatuses, and the activities of *Al-Hijaz* were generally tolerated by the regime.

Islamic Banks

Islamic banks were another form of financial institution tolerated in the early 1980s, and the Brothers had played a conspicuous role in their establishment and development. During the late 1970s and early 1980s, Egypt had two main Islamic banks: the Islamic International Bank of Investment and Development (IIBID), and the Faisal Islamic Bank, both founded in 1979. Both were developed and supported by the Muslim Brothers. At one stage the Executive Director of the Faisal Bank was Ahmad 'Adel Kamal, a Brother with a specialist interest in Islamic economics. Other known Brothers included Hilmi Abdul Majid and Tawfiq Al-Shawi, who were both on the Bank's Board of Directors.[49] Similarly the Board of Directors of the Islamic International Bank of Investment and Development included Abdul Hamid Al-Ghazali, Said 'Umara, and Khairat Al-Shatir. Al-Ghazali and Al-Shatir are both influential members of *maktab al-irshad.*

According to Abdul Hamid Al-Ghazali, a known activist and a lecturer in economics at Cairo University whom I interviewed in 2002, the IIBID was established during Sadat's era with a capital of £E12 million.[50] However, the bank did not expand significantly until the early years of the Mubarak era. From 1981 to 1983 the bank paid profits to its depositors of up to 14.7 per cent (compared to the 10 to 11 per cent paid by the state's banks). The IIBID made sure that the majority of its depositors belonged to the lower-middle class of Egyptians, "in order to help improve their living standards".[51] According to Al-Ghazali, the banks assets were invested in major industrial and agriculture-related projects. Islamic banks were useful institutions that showed the Brothers' commitment to providing Egyptians with an Islamic alternative to Western-based and state-sponsored banks, but the movement did not achieve great success in this field, partly because these banks were experiencing many problems, mostly related to personal disputes and lack of organised management systems. Personal disagreements, along with increasing state pressures, had a considerable negative impact on the fate of Islamic banks, particularly during the late 1980s, as will be discussed in Chapter Five.

Private Enterprises

The Muslim Brothers warn against confusion between a member's private business property and ventures that represent the movement's property. Following the ban on the movement in 1954, the *tanzim* of the Brotherhood claimed to have terminated most, if not all of its formal enterprises, with the possible exception of Dar al-Tawzi' wa al-Nashr al-Islamiyya, a house that publishes and distributes general Islamic books and audio materials, in addition to the books of the *tanzim.* Even so, the connection between the individual and the movement remains, at least as far as donations are concerned. This is something that the leadership does not deny, since it lacks proper sources of funding and depends mainly on the subscriptions of its members to carry forward its activities. State denial has had a serious impact on the development of the Ikhwan in terms of the movement's need to rely on subscriptions, rather on more consistent revenue sources.

It was not easy to persuade certain Ikhwan entrepreneurs to speak about their private businesses and the progress they had made under Mubarak during the early 1980s. Some of the rather wealthy Brothers whom I managed to meet in Egypt were willing to speak about abstract ideas related to Islamic ethics in running a successful business, but were unwilling to say anything about their own experiences in business. My fieldwork took place during the period of Mubarak's confrontation with the movement. Understandably most Brothers were not prepared to sacrifice their commercial enterprises for the sake of published research on the subject, especially as the regime had accused some Ikhwan businessmen of financing the movement's political activities. As one Brother remarked, according to the well-known Egyptian saying: *ras al mal gaban* or "Capital is coward".

However, an exception to the Egyptian saying was Khalid 'Auda, an Ikhwan businessman from Asyut who was prepared to speak to me. I met 'Auda at his lavish apartment in Cairo, a day before he flew to the United States to attend a geology conference. 'Auda, the son of the famous Abdul Qadir 'Auda who was hanged by Nasser in the 1960s, lectured in geology at Asyut University and also owned a chain of companies and factories in his home town of Asyut. In

2000, he contested the parliamentary elections in Asyut but claimed that he had failed because the violent intervention of the security forces to prevent his victory.

'Auda started his business in 1980, with a small factory, *Al-Ribat*, for making clothes. The factory had only twelve sewing machines and no more than twenty workers. During the 1980s, the factory expanded and was not much affected by Sadat's brief arrests of the Brothers in 1981. 'Auda explained that "Sadat's arrests were not against the Brothers, but was a campaign against the entire opposition, including the Copts, and therefore not all Ikhwan suffered."[52] When Mubarak came to power, the factory flourished even more rapidly, and was soon selected by the Ministry of Supplies to make inexpensive clothing for the public sector:

> We were selected because we had cheap labour in Asyut. The Ministry of Supply sent us the fabrics and we made all kinds of clothes for men, women and children. The Ministry would give the clothes to the public sector to be sold at quite cheap prices. The people were happy with the project's products.[53]

This meant that by the late 1980s, 'Auda's factory had forty-five sewing machines and about 100 workers. In 1982 'Auda established another factory, *Al-Buniyyan Al-Marsos*, for making building bricks.[54] Again this factory flourished, and was not harmed by the troubles of *Al-Jama'at Al-Islamiyya* in Asyut. 'Auda stressed that the regime had differentiated between extremist and moderate Islamists.

Conclusion

Accounts of the political, social and economic fields show that the early 1980s in Egypt lacked the context for conflict between the Ikhwan and the state. The Brothers were not connected to the assassination of Sadat, nor were they prepared to use violence against the state. The regime was more occupied with broadening its legitimacy and was thus not prepared to engage in unjustified or unpopular confrontations. The concern for stability required Mubarak to develop a spirit of tolerance that had been lacking under his predecessor, Sadat. Mubarak therefore emphasised the rule of law, slowed down the normalisation with Israel, improved relations with the Arab countries, and set out to improve Egypt's infrastructure. To enhance his religious image in his struggle against Islamist radicals, he also sought to accommodate Al-Azhar. Although the regime did not settle the question of its own legitimacy, Mubarak did gain a degree of public acceptance, which was largely indicated by the low level of social and religious violence in the initial years of his leadership, and by the participation of major political powers in the 1984 elections.

The Muslim Brotherhood seized upon Mubarak's conciliatory mood to rebuild the *tanzim* and to gain legal status, succeeding in the former endeavour but failing in the latter. Religious legitimacy continued to be employed as a means to recruit new members and to appeal to particular sectors in the society, particularly through the traditional avenues of mosques and neighbourhoods. Religious discourses and practices were also used to initiate economic ventures that might have been modest, but were nevertheless sufficient to provide support and funding for the movement's expansion.

Notes

1 Hasan Naf'a "Mulahzat Hawl Intikhabat 1984" (Comments on the Elections of 1984), in A. Hilal, *Al-Tatwur al-dimuqrati fi misr: qadaya wa munaqashat*, (Democratic Development in Egypt: Issues and Discussions), Cairo, Nahdat Al-Sharq, 1986, p. 36.

2 Mubarak entered the Military Academy in 1947, graduating in February 1949. He then entered the Air Academy and graduated in 1950. In 1952, he became an instructor at the Air Academy and in 1967 was promoted to Director-General of the Air Academy. In 1969, he was appointed by Nasser as Chief-of-Staff of the air force and in 1972 was made Commander-in-Chief by Sadat him. See A. McDermott, *Egypt From Nasser to Mubarak: A Flawed Revolution*, London, Croom Helm, 1988, pp. 69–71.

3 On the major difference in character between Nasser and Mubarak, see Salwa Jum'a, "Al-Tagiur wa al-istimrariyya fi mu'sasat al-riyasa: halat misr" (Change and Continuity in the Presidential Institution: the Case of Egypt), in A. Hilal (ed.), *Al-Nizam al-siyasi al-misri: Al-tagiur wa al-istimrar* (The Egyptian Political Regime: Change and Continuity), Cairo University, Egypt, 1988, pp. 139–163.

4 In fact, when asked in his first interview as President about what he feared, Mubarak replied "Nothing". Springborg comments on such an uncalculated reply by asserting that "to a Muslim audience, a man not fearing God, especially when his predecessor had just been gunned down by Islamic extremists, was either a fool or a non-believer". See Robert Springborg, *Mubarak's Egypt: Fragmentation of Political Order*, Boulder CO, Westview Press, 1989, p. 25.

5 See Mubarak's speech in *Al-Ahram*, 15 October 1981, p. 6.

6 *Akhbar Al-Khalij*, 27 April 1982.

7 The Palestinian issue was a major card exploited by Mubarak and the
  other opposition groups to increase legitimacy, as shown by Mubarak's
  persistent refusal to visit Israel until the Palestinians secured their
  rights.

8 Ali Hilal, "Egyptian Foreign Policy Since Camp David" in William B.
  Quandt (ed.), *The Middle East: Ten Years After Camp David*, Washington
  DC, Brookings Institution, 1988, pp. 94–111.

9 *Akhbar Al-Khalij*, 27 April 1982.

10 Huda Al-Sayyid, "Ather tahwilat al-'amilin bi al-kharij 'ala al-fi'at
   al-ijtima'iyya wa al-iqtisadiyya fi misr 1980–1991" (The Effect of
   Remittances from Workers Abroad on the Social and Economic Sectors
   in Egypt 1980–1991", *Misr al-Mu'asira*, issue 429, July 1992, pp. 63–64.

11 Mubarak's speech on 25 April 1986, *Al-Ahram*, 26 April 1986.

12 Jamal Zahran, "Al-Dawr al-siyasi li al-qada' al-misri fi 'amaliyat sun'
   al-qarar" (The Political Role of the Judiciary in Decision-Making), in
   A. Hilal, (ed.) *Al-Nizam al-siyasi al-misri: al-tagiyur wa al-istimrar*, (The
   Political Egyptian Regime: Change and Continuity), Cairo, Cairo
   University, Egypt, 1988, p. 362.

13 Personal interview with Tariq al-Bishri, Cairo, 18 January2001.

14 Ahlam Farhud, *Mawqif al-sulta al-qada'iyya fi al-nizam al-siyasi al-misri*
   (The Position of the Legal Authority in the Egyptian Political Regime),
   unpublished PhD thesis, Cairo University, Egypt, 1998, p. 318.

15 Muhammad Abu al-Is'ad, *Zahirat al-fasad al-siyasi fi misr al-mu'asira* (The
   Phenomenon of Political Corruption in Contemporary Egypt), Cairo,
   no publisher, 1996, pp. 27–8.

16 Nazih Ayubi, *The State and Public Policies Since Sadat*, Reading, Ithaca
   Press, 1991, p. 227.

17 Egyptian official reports estimate that between 1981 and 1989, the
   Supreme Council of Journalism issued publishing licences to over 160
   Egyptian newspapers and magazines, 36 of which were the newspapers
   of political parties. *Al-Taqrir al istratiji al-'arabi*,1988, (The Arabic
   Strategic Report, 1988), Cairo, Al-Ahram Centre for Strategic and
   Political Studies, 1989, p. 472.

18 Amani Qandil, *"Amaliyyat al-tahawul al-dimuqrati fi misr 1981–1993* (The
   Process of Democratic Transformation in Egypt 1981–1993), Ibn
   Khaldun Centre, Cairo, 1995, p. 81.

19 Personal interview with Abdul Mun'em Abu al-Futuh, Cairo, 23 July 2002.

20 Personal interview with Badr Mohammad Badr, Cairo, 14 January
   2001.

21 For the text of the 1983 law, see Abdul Fattah Samruh, *Qanun al-
   muhamah al-mu'adal* [The Reformed Law of the Lawyers], Zaqaziq, n.p.,
   1993.

22 For reactions on this new law, see *Al-Ahrar*, 10 January 1983; also *Al-
   Sha'b*, 22 and 29 February 1983.

23 Robert Bianchi, *Unruly Corporatism: Associational Life in Twentieth-Century
   Egypt*, Oxford, Oxford University Press, 1989, p. 87.

24 Ahmad Abdul Mun'em, "Al-Sulta al-siyasiyya wa al-tanmiyya munzu
   1805 hata al-'an" (Political Authority and Development from 1805 to
   the Present), *Al-Ahram Al-Iqtisadi*, issue 64, June 1993, 1989.

25 Bianchi, *op.cit.*, p. 105.
26 Malika Zeghal, "Religion and Politics in Egypt: 'ulama' of al-Azhar, Radical Islam and the State (1952–94)", *International Journal of Middle East Studies*, vol. 31, no. 3, 1999, p. 385. This celebration should have taken place in 1979 but had been postponed by Sadat.
27 *Taqrir al-hala al-diniyya fi misr* 1995 (Report on the Religious Condition in Egypt, 1995) Cairo, Al-Ahram Centre for Political and Strategic Studies, 1996, p. 29.
28 *Al-Ahram*, 4 June 1982.
29 Amnesty International, Annual Report, 1983, pp. 301–2.
30 Personal interview with Fu'ad 'Alam, the formal deputy of the security forces in Cairo, Cairo, 8 July 2002.
31 Personal interview with Badr Mohammad Badr, Cairo, 14 January 2001.
32 For a full account of the student movement in Egyptian politics, see A. Abdullah, *The Student Movement and National Politics in Egypt, 1923–1973*, London, Al-Saqi, 1985.
33 Personal interview with Ahmad Abdullah, Cairo, 16 January 2001.
34 Personal interview with Ahmad Abdullah, Cairo, 16 January 2001.
35 *Taqrir al-hala al-diniyya fi misr* 1995, (Report on the Religious Condition in Egypt, 1995), Cairo, al-Ahram Centre for Political and Strategic Studies, 1996, p. 163.
36 Beshai, A., "Interpretations and Misinterpretations of the Egyptian Economy", in Tripp, C. (ed.) *Contemporary Egypt Through Egyptian Eyes*, London, Routledge, 1993, pp. 132–41.
37 Lillian Craig Harris, (ed.), *Egypt: Internal Challenges and Regional Stability*, London, Routledge and Kegan Paul for the Royal Institute of International Affairs, 1988, pp. 33–47.
38 Interview with Mubarak, *Al-Sharq Al-Awsat*, 23 January 1983, p. 6.
39 *Ibid.* p. 6.
40 *Ibid.* p. 6.
41 M. Zaki, *Civil Society and Democratisation*, Ibn Khaldoun Centre, Cairo, 1995, 164.
42 Alan Richards, *The Political Economy of Dilatory Reform: Egypt in the 1980s*, Amsterdam, Stichting, Middle East Research Associates, 1990, pp. 6–7.
43 Nazih Ayubi, *The State and Public Policies Since Sadat*, Reading, Ithaca Press, 1991, p. 58.
44 Alan Richards, *The Political Economy of Dilatory Reform: Egypt in the 1980s*, *op.cit.* pp. 6–7.
45 *Al-Ahram Al-Iqtisadi*, January 1988. Quoted from Oweiss, Ibrahim. "Egypt's Economy: the Pressing Issues" in Ibrahim Oweiss (ed.), *The Political Economy of Contemporary Egypt*, Centre for Contemporary Arab Studies, Georgetown University, 1990, p. 4.
46 *Ibid.* pp. 4–5.
47 Personal interview with Jalal Amin, an economist at the American University in Cairo, Cambridge, 27 August, 2002.
48 Asked about what he thought was the worst problem facing him, Mubarak responded: "The population. Their growth rate is below what used to be, it not about 2 per cent. But we need 900,000 jobs this year.

That is why I am trying to look for investment and job opportunities for these people". Interview with Mubarak, *Newsweek*, 10 April 2001, p. 14.

49 Personal interview with Hassanain Shihata, an Ikhwan veteran and leading Islamic accountant, Cairo, 12 January 2001.

50 Personal interview with Abdul Hamid al-Ghazali, Alexandria, 3 August 2002.

51 Personal interview with Abdul Hamid al-Ghazali, Alexandria, 3 August 2002.

52 Personal interview with Khalid 'Auda, 7 July 2002.

53 Personal interview with Khalid 'Auda, 7 July, 2002.

54 According to 'Auda, this was the first factory in Upper Egypt to make such bricks. The factory had 100 workers and was relatively successful.

4

THE ISLAMIST SOCIAL
CONTRACT

The early 1980s did not provide Mubarak with an independent source of legitimacy, apart from the fact that he was Sadat's expected successor. For this reason he adopted a spirit of tolerance which aimed to provide the regime with new foundations of credibility. As far as the political opposition and the Muslim Brothers were concerned, Mubarak's efforts paid off, and the 1984 elections provided an opportunity for such forces to make a strong reappearance on the political scene. The elections provided him with the first appropriate context in which to pursue the notion of legal legitimacy as the 'dominant mode' of the period, and this in turn strengthened the position of the Brothers, not just in parliamentary politics, but also in society generally and in its influential institutions. Although the Brothers were still in the process of rebuilding the *tanzim*, they were now in a stronger position to contest elections in student unions and professional syndicates. Their ultimate goal was to influence the spaces they occupied and gradually to create a broader public opinion that would put pressure on the regime to grant them legal status. At this stage, legal status did not necessarily mean that they would become an Islamic movement, or *haraka islamiyya*, but that they would perhaps achieve the status of a political party (*hizb siyasi*).

Apart from the Muslim Brothers and other political activists, the vast majority of Egyptians did not really benefit from the regime's political overtures since they were not particularly interested in political affairs and elections. What was more important for most Egyptians was whether or not the new regime would be able to improve their living standards and conditions. Chapter Three showed that Mubarak did initially emphasise his commitment to improving the public sector and the infrastructure, and that this position remained unchanged in the following years. However, because of the economic crisis and other economic problems in the mid-1980s the regime was unable to deliver its promises. In contrast to the earlier periods when public hopes had been quite high, the later years saw increasing frustration and dissension. Only five years after Mubarak had come to power Egypt again saw unexpected riots among the central security forces, reminiscent of the food riots in 1977, as well as the re-emergence of Islamist violence. The latter trend constituted a new element that complicated the relationship between the Muslim Brothers and the regime.

This chapter examines the new developments and assesses how each influenced Mubarak and the Brothers in their pursuit for legitimacy. In the political field, Mubarak used the elections to bolster his 'democratic image' inside Egypt and abroad, while the Brothers used them as another means of securing official recognition. The Brothers utilised the social field to make a strong comeback on campuses, but more importantly they emerged this time in professional syndicates as well. The economic field presented Mubarak with his most significant challenge. The economic crisis of the mid-1980s undermined the state's commitment to the 'social contract', and this soon unleashed social rebellion. The regime's performance on the economic side was in contrast to the growing role of the Brothers in Islamic investment companies and their success in the private enterprises that were used to fund the *tanzim*.

Mubarak and the 1984 Elections

The elections that took place in May 1984 were particularly significant for Mubarak, simply because, as the first to be held during his tenure, they provided an opportunity to endorse his commitment to political pluralism. The elections provided a strong context for Mubarak to develop new foundations of legitimacy, which this time would make legal legitimacy the 'dominant mode'. The elections also provided Mubarak with the democratic and legal prerequisites needed to establish his regime and to form a government with loyal political elite. In his discourse, he used the elections to re-emphasise his respect for the Constitution and the peoples' choices in electing their representatives in parliament.

Prior to the elections, Mubarak promised Egyptians that his version of democracy would "become obvious, contrary to the

conditions at the time of Abdul Nasser and Sadat."[1] According to
Hasan Naf'a, a political science lecturer at Cairo University, who
had been a candidate for the Tajammu' Party in 1984, the elections
were not directly related to Mubarak and the extent of his presidential legitimacy, but were in fact related to the legitimacy of his
regime and government. Nonetheless, Mubarak reused the elections in such a way that he made "the legitimacy of the regime and
the government become the new sources of the legitimacy of the
President."[2] Naf'a argues that the elections represented a more
important element for Mubarak's legitimacy than the fact that he
had been Sadat's Vice-President. According to Naf'a, "In Egypt
people do not really care how you have assumed power; rather they
care how you intend to continue to remain in power."

To enhance the credibility of the elections, and therefore the
credibility of the expected results, Mubarak accommodated the
political opposition and permitted the Muslim Brothers to
participate in the elections in alliance with the New Wafd Party. Even
though the Brothers were not a recognised political party, the regime
did not intervene to prevent their alliance, in spite of the fact that the
1983 election law did ban alliances between recognised political
parties. Mubarak might perhaps have allowed the alliance to take
place in order to broaden his coalition in confronting Islamist
militancy. By permitting the Brothers to enter the political process,
Mubarak could make the point that he was not anti-Islamic but was
only against extremism. According to one interpretation, Mubarak,
who did not yet perceive the Brothers as a short-term threat, wished
to assess the resources and influence of the secret movement.[3]

As expected the elections ended with the victory of the National
Democratic Party (NDP), which secured a majority of 390 out of
448 seats (87 per cent), leaving the rest of the 58 seats to the
opposition.[4] What might have been surprising, at least for the
regime, was that the opposition in parliament consisted only of the
New Wafd Party, in alliance with the Muslim Brothers. Well known
parties like the Tajammu' and the 'Amal failed to secure the
necessary eight per cent to be in parliament.[5]

The political opposition were obviously disappointed with the
results, and defeated candidates like Naf'a concluded that there was
no real difference between Mubarak's pluralism and that of Sadat,
and that true democratic elections were practically absent. Instead,
each of the rulers had sought to secure victory for his party in order
to control the legislature. There was a wide belief that the

government usually fiddled with the ballot boxes to ensure favourable results, and this lack of confidence in the government's intentions, in addition to wider political apathy, were largely responsible for the low turn-out of voters (only 43 per cent of those eligible). The discourse of Mubarak during the entire period of the elections revolved round the themes of political pluralism and respect for the law.

However, the law itself was in essence restrictive and not conducive to real political pluralism. As already mentioned, the electoral law confined political contest to recognised political parties, thereby denying independent candidates their political right to participation. The conditions for establishing a party were difficult and have not changed since Sadat introduced his electoral laws in 1976. What was even harder in 1984 was that parties wishing to be represented in the Assembly were required to secure eight per cent of the vote, and those who secured less were not represented. Further, whatever votes the defeated parties had secured were in the end added to the party with the majority of votes – in this case the NDP.[6]

Parties were also asked to provide a second reserve list of candidates whenever it was needed.[7] The main objective of the regime was to secure a fragile foundation of legitimacy rather than a real one. The law was harshly criticised by most political parties as being restrictive and tailored to guarantee an NDP majority. To stipulate eight per cent of the votes was not only a hurdle but 'practically speaking was unfeasible'.[8] And in practice, demanding that parties should present two lists of candidates meant that each party was expected to provide the names of twice as many candidates as there were actual parliamentary seats. The regime claimed that it wanted to make sure that only the genuinely popular parties entered the Assembly, and that securing the eight per cent minimum was one way of achieving this. If this was indeed the case, the results showed that, apart from the NDP, it was the New Wafd, in alliance with the Muslim Brothers that constituted the 'genuinely popular' forces in Egypt.

The Brothers in Parliament

Mubarak's 1983 Electoral Law restricted political activism to political parties, where the parties gained legal status by way of the state-dominated Parties' Committee (or *lagnat al-ahzab*). The Law led the Brothers to think in new and different terms from those prevailing in the 1970s, and they began to consider more seriously the option of establishing an alliance with political parties. In due course this developed into the idea of establishing an independent political party. The Brothers anticipated that in either case, access to parliament would provide them with an opportunity to initiate reform from within the political system, and that they would be able to show the officials and the public that the movement had adopted a non-violent approach to the state and to society. As Abdul Mun'em Abu Al-Futuh commented

> We were not much concerned with how large our number was in parliament in 1984. This was our first experience and we just wanted to make our presence felt. We wanted to prove our presence to those who despised us; we wanted to have a presence in the society and to function through legal and open channels. Otherwise we would not have engaged in the political process in the first place.[9]

Tilmesani's initiative to ally the movement with the secular New Wafd in 1984 was an interesting development. The movement had managed to redefine its stand with regard to the complexities of the political reality and of Muslim society, in contrast to the position of Sayyid Qutb, which continued to exert a powerful influence until the late 1970s. Unlike Qutb, who had drawn strict boundaries between 'genuine' and 'fake' Muslims, Tilmesani practiced a more flexible strategy and aimed to forge relations with his political and ideological opponents. From the 1980s, Tilmesani co-operated with former adversaries such as Nasserites and communists, and championed broader 'national' causes rather than 'religious' ones with the aim of 'normalising' ideas about, and images of, the Brothers within the society and among the various elites.

The Wafd had always identified itself as a secular nationalist party that rejected the mixing of religion and politics, and since 1924 this had created animosity between the Wafd and the Muslim Brothers. When Sadat introduced his controlled liberalisation measures in 1976, relations between the Brothers and the Wafd began to improve. Tilmesani, himself a former member of the Wafd, enjoyed a close relationship with the Wafd's leader Fu'ad Siraj al-Din. For the Brothers, an alliance with a popular party such as the Wafd was a cleverly calculated move to which Fu'ad Siraj Al-Din agreed. In 1983, the New Wafd had just reappeared on the political scene and the idea of an alliance with the popular

Brothers was not a bad idea, especially when an eight per cent hurdle needed to be overcome.[10]

This particular obstacle raised by the Electoral Law haunted the less well-known political parties even more, and they also approached the Brothers with the idea of forming an alliance. According to a private hand-written document, the Brothers claimed that parties as diverse as the 'Amal, the Umma, and the Tajammu' asked the movement to form an alliance with them, but the movement refused.[11] The document, written by someone called Abu Ayman (possibly Mustafa Mashhur, the former *murshid*) claimed that the Ikhwan had turned down the Umma because of disputes with its leader, Ahmad Al-Sabahi, and rejected the Tajammu' because of its anti-religious views. According to Abu Ayman, the reasons put for turning down the 'Amal were because:

> The Party had recently shown closer relations with the Nasserists, by commemorating the death of the greatest tyrant of the century: Abdul Nasser. Second, [the leader of the 'Amal Party] Ibrahim Shukri, in a delegation with the Tajammu', presented [President of Syria] Hafiz Al-Assad, trader of the Golan, with a Medal of Peace, after he had demolished the City of Hamah and killed 40 thousand Syrian people. Third, the 'Amal had approved the Camp David Treaty in the National Assembly [. . .]. Fourth, the 'Amal Party is a feeble party with no popular base and no clear principles.[12]

This quotation is interesting, because only few years after the alliance between the New Wafd and the Ikhwan failed, the movement did decide to form a new alliance with the 'Amal in the 1987 elections.

The alliance between the Brotherhood and the New Wafd was successful, securing a total of 58 seats of which eight belonged to the Muslim Brothers. The results had various implications for the regime, the Brothers and society. First, the presence of the out-lawed organisation in the legislature constituted an embarrassing pointer to the deficiencies of Mubarak's pluralism. Mubarak's persistence in denying a popular power that had secured eight seats in parliament undermined his claim that he wished to introduce genuine reform into the political system. Secondly, it revealed the Ikhwan's political weight, something that Tilmesani wanted to be sure of.[13] As far as political experience and performance were

concerned, the Brothers showed modest but significant profession-
alism in parliament. Contrary to what had been widely expected,
especially among secular political elites, the Ikhwan did not indulge
in religious rhetoric, but engaged efficiently in addressing the
socio-economic concerns of their constituencies. Finally, the presence of the Brothers in parliament generated a wider debate as to
whether Mubarak's political process reflected the genuine powers
in society, and why the state continued to deny a reformist and non-
violent movement like the Ikhwan.[14]

The Shift to Hizbiyya

The success of the Brothers in parliament crystallised the option of
establishing an independent political party. The Parties Law
stipulated that a political group would not be eligible to apply for a
party until it was able to secure at least 20 seats in the National
Assembly. According to Abu Al-Futuh, who was working closely with
Tilmesani at the time, it was this that led Tilmesani to think
seriously about establishing a political party, especially as the
number of Ikhwan in the parliament could well increase in the
following assemblies.[15] In the minds of many Brothers who despised
the political culture of partisanship (*hizbiyya*), this was not an easy
option. Hasan Al-Banna expressed what was at best an ambiguous
view of *hizbiyya*.

One argument maintains that Al-Banna rejected the principles
of *hizbiyya*, considering its foundations to be incompatible with
Islam.[16] While Islam aims to establish a peaceful and united society,
hizbiyya leads to a society's weakness and division. The other argument contends that Al-Banna rejected only the negative influences
of *hizbiyya* and not *hizbiyya* itself. Certainly he viewed the *hizbiyya* of
the 1930s and 1940s as a divisive element in Egyptian's struggle for
independence.[17] Abdul Al-Futuh is among those who think that Al-
Banna had negative views on *hizbiyya* and that there was nothing
wrong with admitting this, provided the movement was prepared to
change these views:

> Some Ikhwan are embarrassed about saying that Al-Banna
> had negative views of *hizbiyya* rather than admitting that we
> have developed and reconsidered our ideas towards parties,
> in the same way that we developed our position on the
> political rights of women, for example.[18]

Roel Meijer is correct in saying that the Brothers' adoption of
hizbiyya was not a smooth process.[19] After all, Tilmesani did not
become an enthusiastic supporter of *hizbiyya* even when he had
lobbied for one. Two years after the Brothers had drafted a party
manifesto in 1984, Tilmesani admitted that the movement was
compelled to adopt *hizbiyya* to make its voice heard in parliament
after other means had been blocked.[20] Hassanain Ibrahim argues
that the shift to a *hizb siyasi* was a part of the movement's pursuit of
legitimacy.[21] More importantly, the *hizb* was in no way an alternative
to the *tanzim*. Again, according to Tilmesani:

> The Ikhwan is an international organisation, and their con-
> cerns encompass the entire world and continents. This is
> different from political parties, which have domestic con-
> cerns. The [ruling] Democratic Party [for instance] does not
> have branches in England or America, while the Ikhwan has
> branches all over the world.[22]

In 1984, Tilmesani formed a special committee, headed by Salah
Shadi, a prominent figure in the *tanzim*, which had the task of
preparing drafts for a party manifesto. Mohammad Fuda, one of
those who worked closely with this committee, told me that during
this time the Brothers had used their local resources and transnational links to consult about the issue by approaching Islamists in
Jordan, Turkey and Yemen who had some practical experience of
hizbiyya.[23] Fuda also showed me two separate drafts of a party
manifesto which had been prepared by the Brothers; one draft was
for the Egyptian Reform Party or *Hizb Al-Islah Al-Misri* and the other
was for the Consultation Party or *Hizb Al-Shura*.[24] Neither draft was
ever formally submitted to *lagnat al-ahzab*, for fear that they would
be rejected.

It is interesting to compare and contrast the two drafts of the
manifesto, since they show how the Islamists were reorganising
their ideologies in response to modern realities such as the nation-
state, and how they had repositioned themselves in the process.
According to *Al-Shura* Party, the aim was:

> . . .to establish the *Islamic* Egyptian state that aimed to
> combine between being a state of guidance, guided by the
> light of Islam and committed to its rules, and being a welfare
> state that provides services to its citizens and works to ensure

freedom and security, and makes available to its citizens all necessary needs.[25]

On the other hand, the *Islah* Party, which seem less ideological and more pragmatic aimed to: "Reform the affairs of the Egyptian state so it becomes able to provide citizens with services and work to ensure freedom and security, and makes available to its citizens all necessary needs."[26]

It is worth noting that the text produced by the *Islah* became the more popular draft among the inner circles of the Brothers, especially the younger generations, who had begun to make inroads into Egypt's associational life since the mid-1980s. This was so much so that the draft was slightly reworked to produce the *Wasat* Party's manifesto, which was submitted to, and soon rejected by, the *lagnat al-ahzab* in 1996. Moreover, much of what was mentioned in the *Islah* document was repeated (almost word for word) in the election programmes of candidate Brothers like the former *murshid*, Ma'mun Al-Hudaybi, during his campaign for the 1995 elections.[27]

According to *Al-Islah* the state was expected to protect the general freedom and liberty of its citizens.[28] There should not be any form of restriction on "establishing parties, organisations or political gatherings that intend to express the views of a particular group as regards a particular issue",[29] and neither the state, nor any of its institutions, had the right to ban or prevent Egyptians from engaging in political or social action. This included the right to establish professional syndicates and public associations, regardless of affiliations, political views or ideological orientations. The *Islah* draft reflected the views of the Brothers towards the military forces (p.33), the economy, agriculture (p.49), industry (p.54), and energy (p.52). It discussed and put forward solutions and reforms to Egypt's rampant economic problems, including external debts (p.64), unemployment (p.73) and population growth. The manifesto also referred to social problems such as drugs (p.79), and emphasised the importance of sport (p.107) and health (p.101).

Criticisms levelled at the performance of the state in the areas of welfare and the economy were at the heart of the state's social contract. In this respect, *Al-Islah*'s draft stressed, for instance, the need to improve and increase medical health centres in cities as well as in remote villages and rural areas, where the costs of the health services should be made free of change or nominally priced (p.72).

It also emphasised that the state should facilitate the establishment of private hospitals that provided good but inexpensive treatment (p.102). For Islamists to put forward such solutions for repairing the social contract showed the extent of the contract's weakness under both the current and the previous regimes. Many of the solutions proposed were put into practice and implemented by the Brothers in and through the institutions they later controlled.[30]

Joining Parties

In addition to forming alliances and entertaining the idea of establishing a political party of their own, the Brothers, or at least some of them, allegedly became affiliates of the National Democratic Party (NDP) and other political parties, in the hope of being able to effect reform from within.[31] Because of the lack of data in literature concerning the Islamists and politics in Egypt, such claims are hard to verify, but if they are indeed true, they reveal important information as to how the Brothers were re-working their political attitudes in ways that had formerly been rejected. The NDP appeared to have no objection to these affiliations, particularly when it needed Islamic-oriented candidates to contest elections in certain constituencies. I was told by Hamid Abdul Majid that Abdul Sabur Shahin, a former member of the Brothers, headed the Religious Committee of the NDP, and that the Brothers had also affiliates in *Al-Ahrar* Party,[32] while a source from the State Security apparatus claims that the movement had affiliates in the Tajammu' Party.[33]

The Rise of Social Dissent

The mid-1980s saw the re-emergence of social and religious disturbance, in contrast to the relative calm that had prevailed in 1981when Mubarak came to power.[34] Such disturbances were scattered and were motivated by different circumstances, but most reflected widening dissension with regard to the regime's failure to address the needs and concerns of the population. The limited satisfaction derived by the political opposition from Mubarak's democratic reforms in 1984 was irrelevant to the rest of the Egyptian people, who felt betrayed and abandoned by the state. Part of the regime's failure to address public anger was related to the economic crisis, exacerbated in 1985 by the fall in international oil prices. Mounting debts and lack of new resources made it extremely difficult for the troubled regime to react swiftly and effectively to the problems of unemployment and poverty, and to the rapid increase in population. The result of all this was social turmoil, manifested in the dramatic riots among the central security forces and the reappearance of terrorism.

Central Security Riots

The central security rioting was the most shocking development to have confronted Mubarak since he came to power. Early on the morning of 25 February, Cairo experienced the worst disorder since the 1977 food riots. Hundreds of policemen assigned to guard embassies, bridges and other sites in and around the capital took to the streets and began to vandalise and burn hotels, nightclubs, cars and other state- owned installations.[35] The riots continued to the following day, and spread throughout Cairo, Giza, Isma'iliyya, Qaliubiyya, Asyut and Suhaj. No one is sure of the reasons behind the riots, although it was widely believed that they were sparked off by a rumour that the government intended to extend the period of service in the central security forces for a fourth year.

To this day it is not known who was behind such a rumour and why, but the fact that such a rumour provoked this degree of anger says something about the way certain sectors in Egyptian society felt about the state. Most recruits in the Central Security forces are from modest social backgrounds and from the poorer regions in Egypt. At work they are mistreated by their superiors and are underpaid for the long hours they spend in guarding. Targeting and demolishing state installations was their angry statement against a government which, they felt, had failed to address their needs. These angry rioters were also joined by a wider public, most of whom were young and unemployed. In response to the rioting, Mubarak immediately called out the army, led by Defence Minister Abdul Hamid Abu Gazala, and employed tanks, artillery and special commando units to confront the rebels. For the first time since Sadat's assassination a massive military presence was to be seen at all major locations and interchanges in the city. The government also imposed a complete curfew on Cairo, and cancelled classes in all universities and schools. According to some estimates, around 2,000 rebels from the central security and several hundred civilians had been arrested when the riots eventually ended.[36]

The Role of the Security Apparatuses

The riots, along with major incidents such as the vast 'Green March', which demanded the establishment of *Shari'a* and developed into certain violent acts, exacerbated the fears of the regime and led to an increase in the role of the security forces in the politics of Mubarak. This ultimately created a visible paradox, whereby some policies aimed to pursue authority through the manufacture of consent while others pursued authority through coercion. In one way this disparity and incoherence in policies reflects the competing forces and priorities inside the apparatuses of the state, and make it difficult to speak of the regime as a unified entity. An extreme manifestation of this incoherence and what amounted to a more or less total lack of co-operation, could be seen in the case of Sadat and the Islamists, where Sadat supported the Islamists against the wishes of the security officials.[37]

Over a period of time policies had tended to be incoherent, even within the security apparatuses, largely due to changing circumstances and to the personalities of those in charge. Ministers of the interior play a tremendous role in shaping the regime's security policies, and this will ultimately affect state-society relations. The Interior Minister appointed by Mubarak when he came to power was Hasan Abu Basha, a well-known figure in the political police in Nasser's time. Abu Basha preferred to deal with instigators of social and political troubles through dialogue and not coercion,[38] and his style of management accorded with Mubarak's spirit of tolerance and concern for establishing the rule of law. During his period in office from 1981 to 1984, Abu Basha initiated a series of extensive dialogues with leaders of extremist groups which were conducted by the *'ulama* of Al-Azhar and broadcast on Egyptian national television. Although he disliked the Muslim Brothers Abu Basha did not intervene to halt their alliance with the New Wafd since, legally speaking, the alliance was not against "Mubarak's constitutional legitimacy".[39]

Abu Basha's approach was carried on by his successor Ahmad Rushdi, who became the new Minister of Interior in July 1984 and whose appointment again reflected Mubarak's spirit of tolerance. Rushdi's attitude, in contrast to that of Abu Basha, had a more positive influence on the Muslim Brothers. Ibrahim Munir, an Ikhwan veteran who lives in London, maintains that the presence of Rushdi in the government was one of the factors that contributed to a neutral relationship between Mubarak and the movement. On becoming minister, Rushdi summoned Hasan Abdul Baqi, an Ikhwan

veteran who had been a candidate in the 1984 elections, and affably
rebuked him: "Since I became a minister, why have the Muslim
Brothers never sent me formal congratulations?" According to
Munir, the Brothers soon decided to send a delegation, headed by
Tilmesani, to visit Rushdi in his office:

> When Rushdi met the delegation he left his desk and sat with
> them in the living room. He asked Tilmesani not to hold him
> responsible for his past actions in the security services during
> the Nasser era, when he had taken part in the torture. He
> pointed out that at the time he was only doing his job. 'Now',
> he added, 'I am in charge of making policies'.[40]

It was during the period of Rushdi that the Brothers made inroads
into syndicates and campuses without any visible interventions from
the security services. However, Rushdi was dismissed soon after the
eruption of the central security riots and was replaced by Zaki Badr,
a brutal man whose time in office will be discussed in Chapter Five.

The disparities in agendas and priorities between the political
and security apparatuses make it difficult to generalise about the
way the regime reacted to the progress of the Brothers in various
spaces in Egyptian society. For example, in the case of syndicates,
which are discussed in more details below, the disparity was very
much related to the regime's lack of expectation that the syndicates
would later threaten its legitimacy. Amani Qandil, who examined
the question of Islamists in syndicates, argues that the regime "did
not have a clue" as to what was going on inside syndicates:

> Mubarak focused on political reform to consolidate his
> legitimacy, but ignored the social sphere. In the eighties,
> Egypt saw serious socio-economic changes, which led to the
> emergence of a new professional middle class. The regime
> was simply unaware of these changes and unaware of the new
> professional class and how it is mobilised in syndicates.[41]

Professional syndicates saw a dramatic expansion in the decade
between the mid-1970s and the mid-1980s, which reflected the
accelerated growth in university enrolments during the Sadat era.
By the early 1990s, membership in Egypt's professional syndicates
had grown to more than 2 million individuals, most of whom held
professional degrees in medicine, engineering and law. This

expansion in the new professional middle class was the result of Nasser's social contract, which had promised social mobilisation through free education and employment within the state bureaucracy. However, since Sadat's *infitah*, and due to Mubarak's subsequent inability to instigate radical reforms with regard to the future of Egypt's graduates, this new class became increasingly frustrated and disappointed with the state.

It is perhaps inaccurate to say that the regime was entirely unaware of the impact of socio-economic change on the alienation of the new professional middle-class. The regime continued to woo middle-class constituencies in the significant syndicates and in the syndicates that remained under its control. In the journalists' syndicate, the regime's candidates promised their supporters an increase in allowances if they were elected as presidents or *naqib*s. In 1985, the journalists voted for Makram Muhammad Ahmad, editor of *Al-Musawwar* magazine, and received £E20 a month extra allowance.[42] These allowances continued to increase regularly after Ibrahim Nafi', editor of *Al-Ahram* newspaper, became *naqib*, and had reached £E320 in 2002.[43] This indicates that the regime was aware of the frustrations of the middle class, but addressed them through what it thought were the most important syndicates.

An Islamist Social Contract

Until Mubarak made up his mind to exercise repression on syndicates and campuses in the 1990s, the Brothers were able to utilise the second half of the 1980s to accommodate the angry middle classes and address their concerns. This process provided the movement with a new avenue through which to pursue legitimacy, defined in eudaemonic terms and sought from society rather than from the state, its courts or the parliament. This process, which was undertaken by the younger generation of the Brothers, should not be viewed as an alternative but complementary to the efforts pursued by the older generation in seeking legitimacy via the courts. By exploiting available spaces in society to gain social legitimacy, this legitimacy could then be used to pressurise the state and translate it into official legitimacy. It was anticipated that while this pressure would not come directly from the Brothers, it would come from the beneficiaries and recipients of their services, as well as from political elites. These elites would perceive the movement to be a crucial element in Egypt's civil society and, hence one that had to be acknowledged and supported by the regime.

However, the reactivation of spaces like campuses and professional syndicates, at least in the earlier phases, should not be seen only as an orchestrated plan by the Brothers ultimately to achieve legal status, but also as a reflection of other dimensions. First, the Brothers constituted a social movement composed of students and professionals, and their presence in universities to earn degrees and to obtain decent jobs, or in syndicates as a prerequisite for employment in most fields, was therefore an expected reality. Second, whatever services the Brothers developed on campuses or in the syndicates (e.g. cheap books, pensions, health care, etc.) were also for the immediate benefit of the members of the movement as well as for the rest of the constituency. Third, the Ikhwan was also an activist movement that would engage the masses with its religious and political agenda, regardless of whether or not it enjoyed a legal status. The movement's expected and increasingly powerful presence and activism was soon to be organised and placed in the service of its relentless struggle for legitimacy.

Before discussing the Brothers' approach on campuses and in syndicates, it is important to touch on the major patterns of change that characterised the movement's younger generation during the 1980s, as opposed to the 1970s, since it was this generation that played a remarkable role in these institutions. In many ways the changes are a reflection, or an outcome, of the socio-economic developments referred to by Qandil (above), that influenced the new middle-class at large, and that were a product of the movement's efforts to normalise and integrate itself into society.

One of the immediate contrasts between the older members and the younger Brothers of the 1970s and 1980s was related to articulating their religious identity. In the 1980s religious expressions were pronounced quite indirectly, compared with the explicitness of the 1970s. Hilmi Al-Jazzar, an Ikhwan member who was active in the medical syndicate of Giza in Cairo, and a former President of Cairo University's Student Union, says that in the 1970s most of the Brothers grew beards and wore *galabiyya* or *julbab* (the long flowing garments traditionally worn by Egyptian men). This changed in the 1980s: "If you look at campuses in the eighties, you would not see an Ikhwan with a beard and all were now wearing Western clothes".[44] Al-Jazzar, Al-'Aryan and Abu Al-Futuh all had long beards and wore traditional clothes in the 1970s (which gave them more of a fundamentalist or *salafi* appearance), whereas they were now clean shaven, wore fashionable suits and spoke eloquent English to Western journalists and researchers.

In the 1970s, according to Al-Jazzar, the discourse was predominantly "religious in a direct manner, and focused on issues such as the importance of the Islamic dress (for females)". In the 1980s:

> . . .our discourse changed and began to emphasise freedom and democracy, and serving the needs of students and providing them with cheap references and revision manuals. This was the more logical discourse through which to attract students and win elections. I see this as a positive development, and not a negative one. For any social sector, the one who claims to represent it is the one who serves it.[45]

Students in the 1970s were still engaged in reformulating their long-lost Islamic identity, perceived in its most literal and traditional sense. A good Muslim was one who practised the customs of the Prophet, including his dress code. This understanding was encouraged by Sadat, who wanted to offset the influence of the left. There were still no proper organisational links between the majority of activist students and the Muslim Brothers, since most of the latter were still in prison during this period.

However, thanks to the writings of Qutb and Al-Banna and figures like Al-Tilmesani, Al-Qaradawi and Al-Ghazali who used to be invited to speak on campuses, the ideas of the Brothers were much admired. In addition, their books and lecturers were again sanctioned by the regime. Serious recruitment of students like Al-'Aryan, Abu Al-Futuh, Al-Jazzar and Madi, did not begin until in the late 1970s, by which time most of the Brothers were out of prison and Tilmesani had begun to rebuild the *tanzim*. Al-Jazzar notes that tensions between Sadat and the Islamists in the early 1980s made it difficult for students, who were forced to shave off their beards and wear Western clothes to disguise their true identity from increased surveillance by the security apparatus.

This situation continued under Mubarak, and for the younger Brothers freedom and democracy became paramount issues rather than the beard and the *galabiyya*. Salah Abdul Al-Maqsud, an Ikhwan journalist who worked for *Al-Da'wa* during the 1970s and

1980s, confirmed the shift in discourse and argues that it was also coloured by the way each regime chose to project itself:

> In the 1970s the Brothers focused more on the issue of implementing the *Shari'a*, following Sadat's 1971 Constitution and his referendum, which led to the Constitutional amendments in 1980. This changed in the 1980s and the demand for *Shari'a* receded and was overtaken by the demand for freedom to establish political parties and join the elections of 1984, and to have our own newspapers.[46]

The issue of freedoms became even more important when the students of the 1970s graduated and wished to take up jobs in the state's hospitals, universities and courts. They wanted to make sure that they were not discriminated against because of their religious affiliations, but at the same time they wanted to express their activism wherever they went. Graduates like Al-'Aryan, Abu Al-Futuh, Al-Jazzar and Madi continued to be active in syndicates while at the same time retaining organisational links and contacts with university campuses. Because of their long-term experience in student work most of them took charge of the students' section (*maktab al-tulab*) within the *tanzim*. This section formulated student policies and co-ordinated relations between campuses and the movement.

University Campuses

In the mid-1980s, the Brothers needed to interact closely with the more sophisticated and mature student movement to know exactly what they wanted. This close interaction with students was identified by 'Amr Abu Khalil, President of the Student Union of Alexandria University in 1984–85, as an important feature of the Islamic student movement in the 1980s:

> Our functions and services in the eighties depended very much on the interaction with students. This was something that we considered important for our election campaigns. We used to assess our performances regularly and think how to improve them, based on student feedback and comments. For example, distributing questionnaires, something that was uncommon in the seventies, became one of the techniques that we made use of to familiarise ourselves with what students

wanted. We also used to ask students to donate money towards various causes to get them engaged.[47]

The Brothers soon became the most powerful force on campuses. As early as 1984, and despite continued security surveillance, they were controlling student union elections, and continued to do so from the mid-1980s until the late 1990s. They were not only popular in the large universities of Cairo and Alexandria but were also to be found in universities in cities like Asyut, far away in Upper Egypt. Mubarak's policies were partly responsible for the success of the Brothers, especially the Student Charter reform in 1984 which, though limited, was still significant because it restored some of their lost powers to the student unions. According to the 1979 Charter, the student council for an entire university consisted of 12 members: five students and seven members of staff. The input of the staff members was binding on many of the student union's policies and procedures, including who was to become the union's president. As a result of Mubarak's 1984 reform, the student council now consisted of 18 members, 12 students and six members of staff, and students formally had a say on the selection of the new president of the student union.

Many student services continued to be basically similar to the services provided in the 1970s, since the basic needs of students (e.g. for cheap textbooks, revision manuals and revision classes) remained unchanged, while new ones were introduced in the 1980s. During my research in Egypt, I met students from Cairo, Alexandria and Asyut universities to compare how the Brothers' services in the 1970s differed from those in the 1980s. These were the oldest and largest universities in Egypt, and had been strongholds of the Brothers for many years. Asyut was particularly interesting because it defies the common perception that tends to identify Upper Egypt (the *Sa'id*) with radical Islamism only.[48]

Since the late 1970s, Alexandria University had been a stronghold of the Brothers and more so from 1984 when 'Amr Abu Khalil, at that time President of Alexandria's Student Union, was also elected to the presidency of all student unions in Egyptian universities. The Egyptian Universities' Student Union had been disbanded by the 1979 Charter, and the election of Abu Khalil was a symbolic protest against the Charter. It also reflected the popularity of the Brothers with regard to the kind of services offered to students. One such service was the Family Medical Project:

> We agreed with some doctors in the medical department of
> the university to provide students in the department with
> medical treatment free of charge. This service began in 1985
> and was so popular that it later developed into an inde-
> pendent club called The Family Medical Club, and later
> replicated by other departments in the University.[49]

At Asyut University students received medical treatment in the
private surgeries of the Ikhwan doctors or whoever was sympathetic
to their cause. According to the Brother in charge of the *tanzim*'s
student section in Asyut:

> We used to dispatch medical convoys made up of medical
> students and teachers to go to the villages and treat the cattle.
> We used to organise what was called the Cure Week, or the
> Cure Month, where we would go to the villages and provide
> medicine to people free of charge. On occasions, we would
> encourage students to donate blood for the villagers and for
> people who were sick.[50]

Asyut University was different from Alexandria and Cairo in that
while the Muslim Brothers elsewhere struggled against interference
from the security services, the additional challenge in Asyut came
from *Al-Jama'at Al-Islamiyya*.[51] This was the name given in the late
1970s to the Islamist trend among students in universities though
it was not yet connected to any particular group or organisation.
The first President or *amir* of *Al-Jama'at* in 1979 was affiliated with
the Muslim Brothers, but following protests about his election from
radical Islamists, he was displaced from his post by force and one
of their own team was appointed in his place.

According to the Brother in charge of the student section in Asyut,
hostility continued until the mid-1980s between the moderate and
radical Islamists.[52] Both groups contested for student representation
under the name of *Al-Jama'at Al-Islamiyya*. On many occasions, the
radical Islamists would resort to physical force to obstruct the
activities of the Brothers on campus as well as threatening their
supporters. The security personnel would witness these often violent
confrontations but would not intervene, appearing not to mind
Islamists fighting each other as long this did not impact in any way
on the regime's stability. Because the security services were passive,
the Brothers acted to defend themselves, and fought back.

Only when the radical Islamists began, in the name of *Al-Jama'at Al-Islamiyya*, to conduct violent operations outside the campus against the state and society did the security forces intervene. At this point, the Muslim Brothers decided to abandon the name of *Al-Jama'at* and renamed themselves the Islamic Trend (*Al-Taiyyar Al-Islami*).

Professional Syndicates

The presence of the Muslim Brothers in professional syndicates was a 'normal' phenomenon rather than a planned one. Most of the Brothers who had been students in the 1970s had now graduated and needed to look for jobs in the appropriate professional field. Membership in the relevant syndicate was a prerequisite for employment, and it also offered benefits such as pensions, subsidised health insurance and help in obtaining visa to work abroad. Whether or not they were employed, degree holders in most professions were eligible for membership in the specific syndicate. The Brothers soon assumed an activist role when they started, during the mid-1980s, to organise themselves and contest council board elections. Wherever they went, whether on campuses or in syndicates, they were functioning as activists and were serving their political mission. But unlike on campuses, activism in syndicates had a more serious implication.

Most members of syndicates consisted of middle-class professionals, who had more sophisticated demands and concerns than cheap books and revision classes. Many were already employed in the public or the private sector, and enjoyed a degree of financial independence as well as wider prospects for social mobility and social impact. Unlike most students, they were eligible to vote in parliament, and thus had a powerful political impact as well.

Prior to the mid-1980s, most syndicates were inert spaces, used (or abused) by the president or the *naqib* and his close circle to accumulate status as well as financial privileges. The syndicates had tight budgets and it was not possible to offer significant subsidised benefits to their large memberships. Right from the start, activists such Al-'Aryan, Abu Al-Futuh, Al-Jazzar and Madi, who aspired to contest the elections, would promise their voters not just to provide services, but also to fight administrative and financial corruption.[53]

Campaigns against corruption or *fasad* were always attractive and powerful elements in Arab political discourse. Mubarak himself began his era with an organised campaign against corruption as a way of winning public support. The Muslim Brothers did the same in syndicates, except that they carried out their policies more consistently and more seriously. Amani Qandil studied the performance of the Brothers in syndicates, and based on her access to large numbers of documents concerning the way syndicates were run before the mid-1980s, claims that the movement did well in fighting corruption:

> I have looked at many court cases filed by the Muslim Brothers against various corrupt practices that used to take place in syndicates. Mohammad Salim Al-'Awa, the Ikhwan's solicitor, showed me documents revealing how the seventeen companies owned by the engineers' syndicate, and run by cronies of 'Uthman Ahmad 'Uthman [the *naqib*], were making big losses.[54]

Qandil argues that Islamists in syndicates succeeded in stopping major abuses of resources, and for the first time were able to create large surpluses in the syndicates' budgets. According to Ahmad Al-Nahas, treasurer of the Alexandria branch of the engineers' syndicate, the 1994 budget reached £E15 million, compared to only £E230 in 1986.[55]

The Brothers in the syndicates had been previously active in student unions, and the experience they had gained on the campuses was not lost or dispersed. Thanks to the *tanzim* and its structured networks, such experience was developed and transmitted to syndicates. According to Abu Al-'Ila Madi, one figure who retained the campus-syndicate connection was Abdul Mun'em Abu Al-Futuh:

> Abu Al-Futuh was an important figure for our performance in syndicates, because he had been an important figure in the student movement in the 1970s. In the same way that he believed Islamists should participate in student unions, he believed that we should do the same in syndicates.[56]

The success of Abu Al-Futuh in the medical syndicates in 1984 led the Brothers to contest the elections in other syndicates, and they were soon on the council boards of the engineers' syndicate (in 1986) and the pharmacists' syndicate (in 1988).[57] Initially, and because they were fighting institutionalised corruption, the Brothers could only reintroduce some of the popular services that they had provided to the students in the 1970s. This happened most noticeably in the syndicate branches since they were less hampered by corruption. Ahmad Al-Nahas had been a leading Ikhwan student at Alexandria University in 1978, and had organised sales of durable goods (e.g. washing machines, refrigerators, house furniture etc.) on campus for students and their families. When he became treasurer of the Alexandria branch of the engineers' syndicate, he organised similar sales from 1985. The first two sales were virtually the same as the ones he had organised in the 1970s, but they soon developed significantly to accommodate the different needs of the professional members.[58] The sales were so popular that profits for the syndicate could reach £E20 million.

Al-Nahas was aware of the importance of services, rather than political rhetoric, in winning people's support:

> In the first couple of years after we established our presence in the syndicates we did nothing but provide services. We knew that people would listen to us if we first addressed their needs and concerns in a practical way, instead of just speaking to them about politics right from the beginning. This was the best way to mobilise people in support of our policies. Politics could then come later.[59]

Such an a-political approach to services, which addressed the needs of the young constituencies, was what made the Brothers popular and won them votes in the elections. According to Al-Nahas:

> Most of those who voted for us in the syndicate elections, whether they numbered three or four thousand, were essentially young professionals whom we had known since we were students. This made it easy for us to communicate with them in a language they could understand and relate to. The more senior constituencies who had not known us before, preferred to vote for their familiar cronies in exchange for personal privileges.[60]

In 1986 the Brothers in the medical syndicate in Cairo introduced their famous project for subsidised health insurance. Most graduate doctors could not afford the high costs of treatment in private hospitals, and many felt humiliated in government hospitals as they did not receive proper attention or proper services. According to Anwar Shihata, treasurer of the syndicate, the project was successful among the young doctors because it aimed to restore their "self-respect and prestige in society".[61] It offered them, and their families, decent health care at affordable prices.

A Worn-out Social Contract

In the mid-1980s it became clearer that Mubarak wanted Egypt to pursue a liberalised economy along the lines of Sadat's *infitah*, albeit in a more rationalised form. However, the on-going problem was how to market this line of policy to the poor and lower middle classes without seeming to abandon Nasser's social contract and without risking the de-legitimisation of his rule. Mubarak continued to defend Sadat's *infitah* and continued to confront its negatives impacts (manifested in the rampant consumption of luxuries and rapid accumulation of wealth via unproductive and corrupt means). He emphasised the importance of a productive rather than a consumerist *infitah*, but without spelling out precisely the fate of the public sector. And although he stressed that it needed reform, he continued to pledge the state's commitment to the public sector, as well as to improvement of the infrastructure.

With regard to the latter, Mubarak did achieve undeniable results by improving the outdated sewage system, building bridges and roads, and increasing houses and transport, including Cairo's underground metro network. Though modest, the improvements were significant in giving substance to the regime's claim that it 'did something' for the people. In speeches and interviews, Mubarak would almost always refer to his achievements since coming to power, and promise more achievements in the future. In one speech he reminded Egyptians that progress in development had been far quicker and more extensive during the first two of years of the Five Year Plan than it had been during the "entire twenty-year period preceding it." Such results, he insisted, "evoked confidence and optimism".[62]

Rhetoric notwithstanding, however, Mubarak's performance failed to please the majority of Egyptians, who did not benefit from *infitah*, or from improvements in basic services. The average Egyptian living in Embaba or Boulaq could not discern any improvement in his or her daily life. An article by an Egyptian in

1984 in *Ruz Al-Yusuf* magazine described how numerous Egyptians lacked the basics of life, including "the ability to move in the streets, whether in vehicles or on foot, without tripping and failing or becoming stranded", and how they inhabited quarters "contaminated by pools of sewage and piles of refuse".[63]

Mubarak's improvements focused on Egypt's more urbanised regions (particularly the large cosmopolitan cities of Cairo and Alexandria) and neglected the poorer and less urbanised provincial towns of Upper Egypt in the south. Figures show that between 1983 and 1984 the regime invested 29 per cent of its budget in improving Cairo and 15,8 per cent on improving Alexandria. Less than 4 per cent of the budget was invested in the southern governorates.[64] Eudaemonic legitimacy seemed to be sought from the more privileged classes, who included individuals in the military and the commercial bourgeoisie who attracted foreign revenues to the state. The public anger aggravated by this bias towards the wealthy was manifested in the re-emergence of socio-religious disturbances after 1985. I have already referred to the Central Security Forces riots that erupted in 1986. Kafr Al-Dawar saw similar violent disturbances by textile workers when the government announced cuts in subsidies. The reasons for each outbreak might have varied but all disturbances were related to a general feeling of frustration with the state's failure to secure basic needs.

In the mid-1980s Egypt suffered from high inflation and increased debts, and was a victim of the international oil crisis. The fall in oil prices affected the government budget because of the decline in revenues from public-sector oil production and the decline of tax payments received from oil companies operating in the country. It also had a negative impact on the economy of the United States and this reduced some of America's aid commitments to Egypt. The crisis ultimately led Egypt to become more vulnerable to pressures from the International Monetary Fund and the World Bank. Mubarak was aware of the criticisms indicated above, but mounting economic pressures and what Rodney Wilson calls "his lack of vision", prevented him from pursuing a coherent policy to allay these grievances.[65] Instead he pursued what Brumberg describes as "survival strategies", aimed at prolonging the existence of the regime.[66] On the one hand, he hoped to 'let out steam' by creating a margin of democracy, which for a time could compensate for failure to reform the economy.[67] This 'margin' was evident in the elections of 1984 and 1987, although I have argued that it was more relevant to the political elite than to the wider public. This was confirmed by Hassanain Ibrahim's study, which found that in developing countries the legitimacy of ruling regimes was determined by their ability to secure equal distribution of wealth and not just margins of political freedoms.[68] Ironically, the re-emergence of violence in Egypt was taking place at the midst of Mubarak's political and legal reforms.

Mubarak's second 'survival strategy' was to initiate a local campaign of 'national revival' aimed at those Egyptians who could contribute financially to reduce the dramatic effects of Egypt's economic problems. The recession of the mid-1980s had major effects on Egypt's revenues, including those from tourism (which was harmed by violent acts of Islamist extremism). Mubarak had no choice but to engage his people and confront them with the harsh realities:

> We do not underestimate the severity and difficulty of the problem we are facing. The problem has been made acute by two fundamental factors. The first was the amazing drop in oil prices [. . .]. The second factor was that the size of the repayments resulting from our external commitments, which must be met, reach their peak in the current year [1986] and the next two years. We will be under considerable pressure for these three years. We will be compelled to face them.[69]

He also referred to the problem of rapid population growth and the negative effect it had on the standard of living.[70] Turning to different sectors of society for help, he requested "everyone who has lawfully gained much. . .to contribute. . .from a national and spiritual conscience, to the solutions that will ensure the interests of the majority of Egyptians who are suffering because of limited income and high prices". He asked "parties, trade unions and [the] many organisations in Egypt" especially "those with abundant money. . .to set in motion a process to help alleviate the burdens of those with limited income". He reminded Egyptians working abroad that they all "benefited in every aspect" from the support of their families and their country, and asked them "to pay back this favour and to lead the ranks in participating in [the country's] great awakening". He also launched a 'debt campaign', in which "every citizen would contribute what he could without over-burdening himself" in order to reduce the heavy national debt.[71]

By the end of 1985, Egypt's external debt had reached US$33 billion and the servicing of this consumed 35 per cent of the annual current account receipts.[72] The failure of the 'national revival' and 'debt campaigns' was a serious indicator of the Egyptians' perception of the legitimacy of the regime.

The Expansion of Islamist Finance

The economic predicaments of the Egyptian state did not seem to show a negative impact on the financial activities and fortunes of the Islamists. On the contrary, from the mid-1980s the gradual liberalisation of the economy, the receding role of the state in economic planning and management and the spirit of Mubarak's tolerance towards society and moderate political forces, led to the growth of Islamic activity in the economic field. This could be seen in the expansion of investment companies, banks and personal enterprises.

Investment Companies

The mid-1980s saw the growing importance of the role of Ahmad 'Ubayd, a veteran member of the Brothers and owner of *Al-Hijaz* Investment Company, in the emergence of conglomerates besides those of Al-Sharif, most crucially that of Ashraf Al-Sa'd and Ahmad Al-Raiyyan (who were not members of the Brotherhood). Al-Sa'd and the three Al-Raiyyan brothers (Ahmad, Fathi and Mohammad) had been beneficiaries of Sadat's *infitah*, which, through its unregulated status, created easy ways to make money through foreign currency dealing. Though blessed by bankers, Western governments and Egyptian workers,[73] such dealings occurred illicitly in the black market, and/or lacked strict control by the state or the supervision of international financial bodies. By the mid-1980s there were state efforts to regulate the process of foreign exchange and to strengthen the role of state banks. Mustafa Sa'id, Minister of the Economy from 1983 to 1985, mounted a serious campaign against Ashraf Al-Sa'd and Ahmad Al-Raiyyan and more than 50 other unlawful dealers, in an attempt to abolish the black market and impose a new official exchange rate. Al-Sa'd and Al-Raiyyan were soon arrested but later released on bail. It was 'Ubayd who paid the bail after the government had confiscated the money the two men had accumulated. He compensated them both for some of the wealth they had lost, and agreed to enter into partnerships with them in small scale ventures at a later stage.[74]

Al-Sa'd re-launched his financial career in the mid-1980s by establishing the Ashraf Al-Sa'd and Partner Car Company, with the Partner (who was 'Ubayd) providing 80 per cent of the capital. The company traded in new cars, and customers consisted mainly of Egyptians working in the Gulf and Iraq. Mohammad Shalabi, a former owner of *Al-Sharika Al-'Aqariyya* Investment Company, saw the creation and development of the Al-Sa'd-'Ubayd alliance:

> I was there when Ashraf Al-Sa'd went to 'Ubayd and persuaded him to be his partner in the car company. 'Ubayd agreed and shortly after, Al-Sa'd founded the car company in *simbilawin* [in Daqahliyya Province], where 'Ubayd contributed 80 per cent of capital. The Company grew bigger and bigger and Al-Sa'd wanted to have it for himself. Eventually Al-Sa'd decided to end his partnership with 'Ubayd.[75]

Unlike Al-Sa'd, Ahmad Al-Raiyyan wanted to establish a company to trade in foreign currency again.[76] 'Ubayd preferred to invest his money in a less risky and more beneficial venture and therefore refused to form a partnership with Al-Raiyyan, but did agree to lend Al-Raiyyan the necessary capital to establish the company, which soon became known as Al-Raiyyan Investment Company.

These brief accounts of the emergence of the Al-Sa'd and Al-Raiyyan conglomerates are intended to illustrate the role played by the Brothers in the expansion of the Islamic investment companies in the 1980s, and to show how this period saw the relatively free and unregulated movement of Islamic capital away from state interference. 'Ubayd's financial connections certainly benefited the movement and helped it to expand its impact on society. 'Ubayd's success and the success of other businessmen like Khalid 'Auda, acted as a powerful form of 'propaganda by deed' about what the Brothers could achieve in the economic sphere without having to engage in financial practices not sanctioned by the *Shari'a* (e.g. the use of usury or *riba*). This added to the religious credibility of the Brothers.

Compared with their performance in professional syndicates, the Brothers' economic performance was not a major success story for the movement. Indeed, some economic ventures ended in failure, although many continued to provide a source of financial support for the movement. Many of the unemployed graduate Brothers found jobs in the 85 companies belonging to 'Ubayd. As many as 300 workers in one factory belonged to the Muslim Brothers.[77] Through 'Ubayd's network of contacts with other Islamist entrepreneurs, many more Brothers found employment in other companies. Many Islamist employees received higher wages than they would have done if they had worked in the state sector. Chapter Three showed how 'Ubayd used his contacts with the *tanzim* to draw large capital from inside Egypt and from Egyptians working in the Gulf into Al-Sharif's enterprises, and how this capital was later withdrawn once 'Ubayd had left Al-Sharif and established *Al-Hijaz* Investment Company. This happened not because the Brothers did not trust Al-Sharif (most did not know who he was) but because they preferred to deposit their savings with someone who they trusted and knew from the *tanzim*.[78]

Leaders of the Muslim Brotherhood tend to downplay the role of 'Ubayd and other entrepreneurs, such as Mohammad 'Elaiwa, in the financial gains made by the movement. I am not sure whether this was because of tactical reasons employed in order to evade the attention of the state and security services, which targeted the financial resources of Islamists in general, or whether it was indeed a fact. But the latter is unlikely since, even if 'Ubayd did work for his own financial interests as the Brothers claim, the movement continued to benefit from his fortunes.

Technically speaking, every member of the Brothers pays the movement a monthly subscription fee or *ishtirakat*, amounting to five per cent of his/her income (if unemployed then he/she is exempt or will pay a nominal fee). I have no exact figure for 'Ubayd's income from his 85 companies, but as far as his regular contribution to the *tanzim* is concerned, I would expect that it is significant.[79]

The movement also encourages its more able members to contribute generously to its budget, and one veteran Brother told me that 'Ubayd had once contributed around £E250, 000, which in the mid-1980s was a significant sum of money.[80] In addition, 'Ubayd's many companies and factories, located in different parts of Egypt, were sometimes used as spaces for religious education and political activism. During the 1984 elections and more so in 1987, workers at these factories helped to run the political campaigns of the Brothers' candidates; this involved talking to people, putting up posters, and distributing leaflets. *Al-Sharika al-'Aqariyya*, an investment company founded by the Shalabi family, employed between 200–300 workers, most of who were members of the movement. The company also contributed to the funding of the production of printed posters and leaflets at a subsidised cost.

Private Enterprises

The case of Khalid 'Auda who, as a business Brother, was outside the circle of Islamic investment companies, was not much different from the case of 'Ubayd. 'Auda paid his obligatory monthly dues to the movement in the form of *ishtirakat* (5 per cent of total income) and helped younger Brothers by employing them in his factories in Asyut. Chapter Three showed how some of 'Auda's factories benefited from Mubarak's spirit of tolerance in the early 1980s, and the impact this had on the progress and expansion of new ventures later in the decade. His clothing factory, *Al-Ribat*, established in 1980, flourished largely as a result of 'Auda's close contact with the Ministry of Supplies in providing cheap ready-made clothes to public sector retailers. His other factory, for making bricks, *Al-Buniyyan Al-Marsos*, was established in 1982 and soon developed into a tile-making factory.

In 1984, 'Auda set up a factory for manufacturing in wood. Called *Al-Fath*, it was run by one of his relatives and contained modern equipment worth hundreds of thousands of Egyptian pounds. According to 'Auda, *Al-Fath* was the second largest factory in Egypt for wooden items and furniture. It employed around 120 workers and could produce as many as one hundred doors and windows a day. 'Auda's fourth factory, *Al-Rashad*, manufactured plastics, and was soon flourishing with over 50 workers.

His fifth significant venture was the chain of Dar al-Salam groceries and supermarkets which opened up in five or more urban locations in Asyut. One branch, called *Al-Quds*, was located on the campus of Asyut University, where 'Auda worked as a lecturer in geography and where the Brothers controlled the student union and the teachers' faculty club. A second branch was located in *Al-Sadat* area, inhabited mostly by the lower middle classes and public sector employees, while another branch, *Al-Nil*, was located in a more modern area that was inhabited mostly by doctors, engineers, lawyers and police officers.[81]

'Auda acknowledged that Mubarak never intervened to obstruct his enterprises during the 1980s, but in fact tolerated their expansion, as was the case with the Islamic investment companies. He also made it clear that the regime was aware that all such ventures were owned by member of the Muslim Brothers and made a clear distinction between the Brothers and the more radical *Al-Jama'at Al-Islamiyya* in Asyut. *Al-Ribat* factory is an extreme case of Brother-state co-operation, where the Brothers utilised the public as well as the private sectors for investing their resources and broadening their impact. However modest 'Auda's ventures were, and even if the Brothers claimed they were limited in effect, such ventures certainly contributed to the 'propaganda by deed' by showing what the movement was capable of achieving in the financial sphere. 'Auda himself used his wide resources to build a public reputation which he later employed politically. In the 1990s he attempted to contest the elections for Asyut but was unsuccessful as a result of allegations of state intervention at the ballot box.

Conclusion

This chapter has showed how the 1984 elections turned legal legitimacy into a 'dominant mode' for both Mubarak and the Muslim Brothers. In the case of Mubarak, this was seen in his political discourse, which focused on political pluralism guided by the rule of law and commitment to the will of the people. Mubarak's political campaign might have succeeded with the political elites but failed with society at large. He lacked a vision and his regime seemed incapable of addressing the wider issues and concerns of society. The result was an increasing number of socio-religious disturbances, which in turn increased the role of the security services. The paradox between the regime's pursuit of legitimacy via consent and its reliance on coercion to offset dissent added to its predicaments.

In the case of the Brothers, the pursuit of legal legitimacy was seen in their desire to secure the recognition of the state and to restrict their role to being a political party. Meanwhile, and in order to participate in the political process, the Brothers agreed to form an alliance with the secular New Wafd Party, which showed the extent to which the movement was willing to go to normalise its relations with the state and society. But as this was happening in the political field, the Brothers were simultaneously making inroads into student unions and syndicates, where legitimacy was based not on recognition by the state but on that of the society. Provision of material benefits and services became just as, if not more important than, the use of political rhetoric and religious symbols. Political rhetoric was used in the political field and during election campaigns, while religious discourse was promoted primarily inside mosques and neighbourhoods, largely for recruitment purposes.

In all cases, the Brothers funded their activities and broadened their impact through their expanded finances, as could be seen in the gradual growth in the mid-1980s of Islamic investment companies and private enterprises. Mubarak tolerated the social and economic roles of the Brothers because they were compatible with his desire to show a democratic face, and because the Islamists seemed to be assisting the state in its efforts to carry the burden of the growing lower middle classes. The regime benefited formally from some of the Brothers' ventures, such as the *Al-Ribat* factory, as well as informally and on a personal basis from Islamic investment companies. Some senior officials were employed as 'consultants' to these investment companies (a notable example was the former Minister of Interior, Nabawi Isma'il, who worked for Al-Raiyyan company). The scandal behind what was called 'kushuf al-baraka' (a private list of names of senior Egyptian officials who were employed by Al-Raiyyan company as members of the board council in return for a huge sum of money) revealed the extent of the state's involvement in Islamist finances, an involvement that had, however, come to an end by the late 1980s.

Notes

1 See Mubarak's interview with *Arab Times*, 29–30 December 1984.
2 Personal interview with Hasan N af'a, Cairo, 9 July 2002.
3 Hassanain Ibrahim. *Al-Nizam al-siyasi wa al-ikhwan al-muslimun fi misr: min al-tasamuh ila al-muwajaha 1981–1996*, Beirut, Dar al-Tali'ah, 1998. p. 19. Also, see Jihad 'Auda, Istratijiat al-ra'is Mubarak fi al-ta'amul ma' al-mu'arada, 1981–87" (Mubarak's Strategy in Dealing with the Opposition) in Ali Hilal, ed., *Al-Nizam al-siyasi al-misri: al-tagiur wa al-istimrar* (The Egyptian Political Regime: Change and Continuity), Cairo University, Egypt, 1988, pp. 165–210.
4 *Al-Mujtama'*, 9 September 1994, pp. 34–35.
5 According to the Constitution, the president has the right to appoint ten members, usually selected from a wide range of public figures and politicians. Some were actually selected from the Tajammu' and the 'Amal.
6 Nazih Ayubi, "Government and the State in Egypt Today" in Charles Tripp and Roger Owen, *Egypt Under Mubarak*, London, Routledge, 1989, p. 13.

7 In practice this meant that a particular party wishing to run for all 48 districts was obliged to nominate 899 candidates for the 448 Assembly seats.

8 Personal interview with Hasan Naf'a, Cairo, 9 July 2002.

9 Personal interview with Abdul Mun'em Abu al-Futuh, Cairo, 23 July 2002.

10 Ali Hilal, ed., *Intikhabat majlis al-sha'b: dirasa wa tahlil* (The Elections of the National Assembly: A Study and an Analysis), Cairo, Al-Ahram Centre for Political and Strategic Studies, 1986, p. 36.

11 *Al-Qisa al-kamila Ii ekhtiyyar al-iIkhwan al-muslimin al-tarshih dimn qwa'im hizb al-wafd* (The Complete Story about Choosing al-Ikhwan al-Muslimin to Contest the Elections with the Wafd), internal private document, undated.

12 *Ibid.*, It is interesting to note how the Muslim Brothers decided in the 1987 elections to forge alliances with the 'Amal Party.

13 Personal interview with Badr Mohammad Badr, Cairo, 14 January 2001.

14 See Alexander Flores, "Secularism, Integralism and Political Islam: The Egyptian Debate", in Joel Beinin and Joe Stork, *Political Islam: Essays from Middle East Report*, London, I.B. Tauris, 1997, pp. 83–94.

15 Personal interview with Abdul Mun'em Abu al- Futuh, Cairo, 23 July 2002.

16 See Rif'at al-Sa'id, *Hasan al-banna, mw'asis jamat al-ikhwan al-muslimin: mata, kaifa, wa limaza?* (Hasan al-Banna: the Founder of the Muslim Brothers, When, How and Why?), Cairo, Dar al Thaqafa al-Jadida, 1984; and Rashid Ghannoushi, *Al-Huriyyat al-'amma fi al-dawla al-islamiyya*, Beirut, Centre for Arab Unity Studies, 1993.

17 Ibrahim Biyyumi Ghanim, *Al-Fikr al-siyasi lil imam hasan al-banna* (The Political Thinking of Imam Hasan al-Banna), Cairo, Dar al Tawzi' wa al-Nashr, 1992.

18 Personal interview with Abdul Mun'em Abdul al-Futuh, Cairo, 23 July 2002.

19 Roel Meijer, *From al-da'wa to al-hizbiyya: Mainstream Islamic movements in Egypt, Jordan and Palestine in the 1990s*, Amsterdam, Middle East Research Associates, Occasional Papers, no. 10, August 1997, p. 6.

20 *Al-Ittihad*, 14 June 1986.

21 Hassanain Ibrahim, *Al-Ikhwan al-muslimun wa al-ta'adudiyya al-hizbiyya: qira'a fi ru'iat hasan al-banna* (The Muslim Brotherhood and Multiparty: A Reading into the Stance of Hasan al-Banna), Centre for Political Research and Studies, Cairo University, Egypt, 1996, p. 71; and Abdul 'Ati Abdul Halim, *Al-Harakat al-islamiyya fi misr wa qadiat al-ta'adudiyya al-siyasiyya 1976–1986* (The Islamic Movements in Egypt and the Issue of Political Pluralism 1976–1986), unpublished PhD thesis, Cairo University, Egypt, 1994, p. 133.

22 *'Akhir Sa'a*, 6 February 1985.

23 Personal interview with Mohammad Fuda, Cairo, 13 January 2001.

24 Neither party was ever submitted to the Parties Committee (*lagnat al-ahzab*) because, according to the Muslim Brothers, "the political circumstances were never appropriate."

25 *Barnamij hizb al-Shura* (The Programme of *al-Shura* Party), unpublished, n.d., p. 1.
26 *Ibid.*
27 See Ma'mun al-Hudaybi's election programme for 1995.
28 The Islah Party's manifesto was around 190 pages long. See *Barnamij hizb al-Islah* (The Programme of *Al-Islah* Party), unpublished, undated, p. 13.
29 *Ibid.* p. 22.
30 See, for instance, Janine Clark, "Democratisation and Social Islam: A Case Study of the Islamic Health Clinics in Cairo", in R. Brynen, B. Korany and P. Noble, (eds.) *Political Liberalization and Democratisation in the Arab World*, vol. 1, Boulder CO and London, Lynne Rienner Publishers, 1995, pp. 167–186.
31 Personal interview with Hamid Abdul Majid, London, 13 September 2001.
32 *Ibid.*
33 Personal interview with Fu'ad 'Alam, Deputy Director of State Security, Cairo, 8 July 2002.
34 See Hamid Ansari, "The Islamic Militants in Egyptian Politics", *International Journal of Middle East Studies*, vol. 16, no. 3, 1984, pp. 123–144.
35 A. Ayalon and H. Shaked, (eds.), *Middle East Contemporary Survey*, Boulder, The Moshe Dayan Center for Middle Eastern and African Studies, The Shiloah Institute, Tel Aviv University, Westview Press, 1986, p. 266. The Central Security forces (*al-'amn al-markazi*) consisted mostly of illiterate youths from the countryside; their service conditions were extremely poor, as was their public image.
36 *Ibid.*, p. 266.
37 Personal interview with Fu'ad 'Alam, Deputy Director of State Security, Cairo, 8 July 2002.
38 Hasan Abu Basha, *Mudhukrat Hasan Abu Basha* (Memoirs of Hasan Abu Basha), Cairo, Dar al-Hilal, 1990, p. 181.
39 *Ibid.*, p. 149.
40 Personal interview with Ibrahim Munir, London, 10 September 2001.
41 Personal interview with Amani Qandil, Cairo, 2 July 2002.
42 Knowledgeable informants claim that Makram occasionally writes some of Mubarak's speeches.
43 Personal interview with Salah Abdul Maqsud, Cairo, 2 July 2002.
44 Personal interview with Hilmi al-Jazzar, 5 August 2002.
45 *Ibid.*
46 Personal interview with Salah Abdul Maqsud, Cairo, 2 July 2002.
47 Personal interview with 'Amr Abu Khalil, Alexandria, 10 July 2002.
48 I am very much indebted to 'Amr Abu Khalil, a leading student activist in Alexandria University in the late 1970s, who provided me with unpublished documents on the Islamic student movement in Egypt's universities during the 1980s and 1990s. I am also indebted to Mahmoud Hussein, a leading Ikhwan in the Teachers' Club in Asyut University, for the help he provided on the Ikhwan student movement in Asyut University during the 1980s.

49 Personal interview with 'Amr Abu Khalil, Alexandria, 10 July 2002.

50 Personal interview, Asyut, 6 July 2002.

51 On *Al-Jama'at Al-Islamiyya*, their ideas and practices, see Tal'at Fu'ad Qasim's interview with Hisham Mubarak in "What Does the Jama'at Islamiyya Want?" in J. Beinin and J. Stork (eds.), *Political Islam: Essays From Middle East Report*, London, I. B. Tauris, 1997, pp. 314–326.

52 Personal interview, Asyut, 6 July 2002.

53 This was especially with regard to the companies of 'Uthman Ahmad 'Uthman, the late President or *naqib* of the engineers' syndicate, which were making great losses. Personal interview with Abu al 'Ila Madi Cairo, 7 January 2001.

54 Personal interview with Amani Qandil, 2 July, 2002.

55 Personal interview with Ahmad Al-Nahas, Alexandria, 10 July, 2002.

56 Personal interview with Abu Al-'Ila Madi, Cairo, 7 January 2001.

57 For an account of the accession of the Brothers to syndicates, see Ninette Fahmy, "The Performance of the Muslim Brotherhood in the Egyptian Syndicates: An Alternative Formula For Reform?", *Middle East Journal*, vol. 52, no. 4, autumn 1998, p. 552.

58 Personal interview with Ahmad al-Nahas, Alexandria, 10 July, 2002.

59 Personal interview with Ahmad al-Nahas, Alexandria, 10 July, 2002.

60 Personal interview with Ahmad al-Nahas, Alexandria, 10 July, 2002.

61 Personal interview with Anwar Shihata, Cairo, 20 December 2000.

62 Mubarak's May Day Speech, 15 May 1984.

63 *Ruz Al-Yusuf,* 16 July 1984, p. 23.

64 See Mohammad Sidiqi, "Al-Siyasat al-iqtisadiyya wa al-qita' ghayr al-rasmi" (Economic Policies and the Informal Sector) in Al-Saiyyd al-Hussyni (ed.) *Al-Qita' ghayr al-rasmi fi hadar misr* (The Informal Sector in Urban Egypt), Cairo, Markaz al-Buhuth al-Ijtima'iyya wa al-Jina'iyya, 1996, pp. 345–401.

65 Personal interview with Rodney Wilson, Exeter, 25 September 2002.

66 See Daniel Brumberg, "Survival Strategies vs. Democratic Bargain: The Politics of Economic Reform in Contemporary Egypt", in Henry Barkey (ed.), *The Politics of Economic Reform in the Middle East*, New York, St. Martin's Press, 1992, pp. 73–104.

67 *Ibid.*, p. 88.

68 Hassanain Ibrahim, *Mushkilat al-shar'iyya al-siyasiyya fi al-duwal al-namiyya* (The Problem of Political Legitimacy in Developed Countries), Unpublished MA Dissertation, Cairo University, Egypt, 1985, pp. 404–406.

69 Mubarak's speech to the NDP Congress, 20 July 1986, reported in *Al-Ahram*, 21 July 1986.

70 Mubarak's speech, 6 November 1983, reported in *Al-Ahram*, 7 November 1983.

71 Mubarak' speech, 13 November 1985. Quoted from Ayalon, A., and Shaked, H., (eds.), *Middle East Contemporary Survey*, Boulder, The Moshe Dayan Center for Middle Eastern and African Studies, The Shiloah Institute, Tel Aviv University, Westview Press, 1985, p. 348.

72 A. Ayalon and H. Shaked, *Middle East Contemporary Survey, op.cit.* 1985, p. 350.

73 Clement Henry Moore, "Islamic Banks and Competitive Politics in the Arab World and Turkey", *Middle East Journal,* vol.44, no.2, 1990, pp. 322–43.
74 Personal interview with Mohammad Shalabi, Cairo, 8 January 2000.
75 *Ibid.*
76 *Ibid.*
77 Personal interview with 'Asim Shalabi, Cairo, 25 December 2000.
78 *Ibid.*
79 It should be noted, however, that a significant quantity of 'Ubayd's assets were not his own but belonged to partners and investors.
80 Personal interview with Hassanain Shihata, Cairo, 12 January 2001.
81 Sharaf al-Din, N. *Umara' wa Muwatinun* (Princes and Citizens), Cairo, Maktabat Madbuli, 1998, 108.

5

THE POWER OF THE *TANZIM*

Mubarak remained concerned with his public image as a ruler who abided by law and order, but his coercive policies against religious dissent against the state grew harsher and ultimately this had a negative impact on the state's attitude to society. At the same time the regime was suffering from the impact of Egypt's economic crisis, which added further to the public's disenchantment and anger. The period after the mid-1980s saw the rapid deterioration of foreign currency resources, increased inflation, decreased savings and investments, and intensified IMF pressure on the government to introduce serious restructuring and reform. Although the late 1980s saw the confiscation of Islamic investment companies and the regulation of the movement of capital, Mubarak remained, on the whole, tolerant to the Muslim Brothers. The movement was allowed to participate in the 1987 parliamentary elections, but an air of distrust was developing between the two as a result of the growing influence of the Brothers and their reluctance to support the regime's campaign against *Al-Jihad* and *Al-Jama'at Al-Islamiyya.*

The Brothers were by now an undeniable power in Egyptian politics and society, even if the state continued officially to deny their existence. In parliament, they constituted the largest opposition group, not only initiating serious debates on reform and the establishment of *Shari'a* but also, and more dangerously, having a say in the political fate of Mubarak himself when he was nominated for a second term as president in 1987. Their political success was paralleled by their swift and remarkable rise to positions of authority in major professional syndicates, student unions and teachers' faculty clubs, and their ability to provide lower middle class constituencies with impressive services. More crucially, they employed the *tanzim* and its organised networks to connect and co-ordinate between the various institutions they controlled. The *tanizim*'s networks operated in a manner that was counter to the regime's corporatist controls and thus came to constitute a source of threat to the regime and to its authority over civil society.

The growing impact of the Islamists in Egypt in the late 1980s presented Mubarak with the dilemma of legitimacy that faces most authoritarian regimes when they are not prepared to go all the way with what their pursuit of legitimacy entails. Mubarak was confronted with a paradoxical reality when he realised that what he had tolerated in the past and what had led him to open up political and social spaces, had soon turned out to be the source of threat to his legitimacy. Mubarak was caught between the spaces which he had maintained to enhance his public image, and the Islamist competitors who sought to challenge this image and instead to enhance their own.

Mubarak and the 1987 Elections

Mubarak's troubles with Islamist violence gradually radicalised his overall policies towards society, but he continued to be moderately responsive towards the political opposition. The 1987 elections, which coincided with his presidential elections, made sure that the pursuit of legal legitimacy was a worthwhile endeavour. Following the outcome of the 1984 elections, the political opposition had protested against the results and against the constitutionality of the electoral law (No. 114 of 1983) that unfairly banned independent candidates from participating in the elections. This caused serious embarrassment to Mubarak, especially when the opposition took the case to the Supreme Constitutional Court and demanded that the Assembly should be dissolved and a date set for new elections to take place.

Hoping to avoid further embarrassment, Mubarak decided to supersede the Court's ruling and in December 1986 agreed to introduce some amendments to the electoral law. As a result the Assembly was dissolved in February 1987 and the date for the elections was set as April of the same year.[1] The new electoral law (No. 188) recognised the right of independent candidates to contest the elections, and gave them 10 per cent of the seats. It also stipulated that the votes of the parties that failed to secure the eight per cent needed to be in parliament were to be added to the winning parties in accordance with their respective share of the votes. This was in contrast to the previous law which had simply added the total of the unused votes to the winning party with the largest number of votes, in a clear attempt to bolster the position of the ruling NDP party.

In his public speeches Mubarak encouraged all the political parties to participate in the 1987 elections, while in reality making sure that the legislature remained under the control of the NDP. The outcome of the elections was once again as expected, and the NDP won a majority of 309 out of 448 seats in the National Assembly. However, the NDP turned out to be the biggest loser this time, since its 70 per cent share of the vote was the lowest for any ruling party since 1952, and certainly lower than the number of seats it had secured in 1984 (390 seats). Furthermore, the number of voters in the elections was only 7 per cent higher than it had been in 1984. Both these figures were rough indicators of what people thought of the government and about the ability of parliament to bring about real change.[2]

Nonetheless, Mubarak did what was necessary to secure a legitimate second-term presidency after the first had expired on 13 October 1987. As noted earlier, his responsiveness to the demands of the political opposition for a new assembly stemmed from his desire to secure a constitutional parliament that would then evade questions on the constitutionality of his renewed right to rule. In November 1987, the Parliament, including the largest opposition block, the Islamic Alliance headed by the Muslim Brothers, nominated Mubarak for a second-term presidency. He obtained the votes of 420 of the 448 deputies in the Assembly, which was far more than the two-thirds majority required by the constitution.

As much as this was good news for Mubarak, it was also a source of uncomfortable reality. What Mubarak had intended would be a 'constitutional parliament' was now dominated by an unconstitutional opposition (i.e. the Muslim Brothers) which, if nothing else, suggested something of a critical attitude towards Mubarak's political system and its commitments to real pluralism. This uncomfortable reality was another significant manifestation of Mubarak's dilemma of legitimacy.

The Brothers in Parliament

In the 1987 Assembly, the Brothers, who were now allied with the

'Amal and the Ahrar parties,[3] won 36 seats compared with the eight seats they had taken in 1984. For the first time in Egyptian politics this made the movement the largest opposition group in parliament.[4] This was a significant development that renewed hopes among many of the Ikhwan that the Parties' Committee might now recognise them as a political party. (According to the constitution, a political force that secured 20 seats was entitled to establish its own party, a scenario that certainly frightened the regime.)

Mubarak and his security apparatuses were already aware of the growing impact of the Ikhwan, whose influence was undeniably visible in mosques, urban neighbourhoods, student unions and professional syndicates. The Brothers claimed that in the 1987 Assembly their share of the seats had exceeded 36 in number, and that the real number of successful candidates had been concealed by interference on the part of the security services as well as by rigged election results (a charge made by almost all members of the opposition). Abdul Hamid Al-Ghazali, an Ikhwan candidate who claimed that blatant rigging had prevented him from winning the elections in his small Munufiyya constituency, noted that:

> In this small hometown in Munufiyya, two thirds of the people were related to me, either through my mother or on my father's side. Can you imagine that the final election results showed that 100 per cent of the people voted for the NDP? This means not only that my own relatives voted against me, but also that I voted against myself![5]

Al-Ghazali maintains that had the election results been fair, the Brothers would have secured more than 150 seats (controlling 33 per cent of the Assembly), although he gives no evidence to substantiate this figure.

The composition of the 36 Islamist members of the 1987 Parliament was different from that of 1984, which had been made up of younger and more educated cadres. In 1987, these young cadres, like their fellow Brothers in syndicates and in student unions, were more familiar with the contemporary needs of their constituencies.[6] This, combined with the significant number of the Brothers in parliament (supported, of course, by the Islamic Alliance) enabled the movement to play a more active role in the Assembly, compared to 1984, when their presence had been symbolic more than practical. The 1987 Assembly gave the movement a platform from which to lobby for its right to be recognised as a legitimate power in Egyptian politics and society, voiced in the context of its demand that the regime should maintain the freedoms of political groupings, unions, syndicates and parties. Related to this were the criticisms levelled by the movement at the repressive practices of the state's security apparatuses against society (and particularly the Islamists), which they used to question the regime's claims to respect the law.[7] The movement also attacked the way the regime resorted to the Emergency Law, arguing that this defied the logic of promises to introduce real reforms.[8]

The Brothers in the Assembly did not succeed in introducing new laws into a legislature dominated by the NDP, but they certainly succeeded in 'normalising' their presence in formal politics, and in turning the prospects for their future into a public debate. Thus the Brothers' call to the state to recognise them was no longer a private matter for the movement. Instead, and as a result of their successful performance in parliament and in society, it became also a public concern for those who aspired to see real political pluralism in Egypt. Sa'd Eddin Ibrahim, an influential secular figure, is one among many Egyptians to support the right of the outlawed movement to be officially recognised by the state.[9]

According to Ibrahim, the performance of the Brothers in parliament was "markedly felt by their articulateness and parliamentary skills, which the majority or for that matter most other opposition deputies cannot match".[10] This was partly because the Brothers went beyond the stereotypical expectation that once in parliament they would talk of nothing but the need to establish the *Shari'a* and ignore issues of more relevance to most Egyptians. The Islamists did, of course, address the subject of *Shari'a*, as part of their discourse and concern to stress their religious credibility, and condemned what they saw as the "un-Islamic" practices sanctioned by the regime. These practices included dealing with *riba* or interest, permitting the consumption of alcohol, and broadcasting inappropriate material.[11] At a point when the regime was struggling to confront the growing effect of Islamist violence, the Brothers' criticisms helped undermine the state's religious credibility, [12] with the result that the regime and other major parties, except the Tajammu', found it necessary to espouse elements of religious rhetoric to safeguard this credibility. Thus, while Mubarak often stressed his personal commitment to "noble religious values",[13] the

NDP reiterated that the majority of laws in Egypt were in accordance with the *Shari'a*.

However, the Brothers in parliament went beyond religious concerns and began to discuss broader issues that were of concern to the general public. As well as criticising the regime's human rights record in dealing with dissenters, the movement criticised the government's policies in health, in the media, and especially in education, where the authorities had failed to improve the general infrastructure and facilities of schools or Egypt's growing problem of illiteracy. The Islamists also raised serious questions about the regime's attitude to the growing problems of unemployment, inflation, debts, massive consumption and the privatisation of major parts of the public sector infrastructure.[14] These were real contemporary problems, and all Egyptians, whether Muslim or Copt, religious or secular, wanted to see immediate practical action being taken to resolve them.

The Islamists Nominate Mubarak

In making their criticisms, the Brothers were careful to distinguish clearly between attacking the performance of the government and appearing directly to undermine the legitimacy of the president of the regime. Their expansion into politics and society was still taking place, and at this stage the Brothers were careful not to jeopardise their progress by creating friction between themselves and Mubarak. This was one reason why the Brothers decided to run in the elections as candidates on the Islamic Alliance's list, rather than as independents. In this way they avoided having to confront the NDP candidates who were contesting the same seats (and could also sidestep the need to limit their maximum representation to only 48 seats).[15] More importantly, though, and notwithstanding their pronounced reservations against the regime, they were eventually prompted by their desire to avoid confrontation with the regime to nominate Mubarak for a second presidential term (i.e. a further period of six years). Gratifying as this was, the regime was well aware that the nomination represented a tactical move by the Brothers, and this increased its worries about the consequences of Islamist participation in future parliamentary elections.

Mohammad Fu'ad, a leading Ikhwan veteran now living in London, believes that the tactical element of the movement's

nomination was revealed to the regime by the controversial discussions inside the *tanzim* as to whether or not it was right to
nominate Mubarak. These confirmed that support for the regime
was not a matter of consensus among the movement's membership.[16] Abdul Mun'em Abu Al-Futuh, too, admits that many
Brothers, including the deputies in parliament, were against
nominating Mubarak because of his poor performance during his
previous six years in office, and because of the impact that
supporting the regime would have on the movement's credibility
with the public.[17] The Islamist students of 'Ayn Shams University in
Cairo also issued a strongly-worded statement accusing Mubarak of
repressive policies that were not much different from those of his
two predecessors, and voted against his nomination.[18] However, the
calculations of the leadership in the Guidance Bureau or *maktab al-
irshad* were different. According to Abu Al-Futuh, the *maktab*
wanted to avoid unnecessary confrontation with the regime since,
even if they decided not to nominate him, the NDP's dominance
over the Assembly would still guarantee Mubarak a second term
presidency.

These kinds of calculations made Mubarak even more aware of
the potential risks involved if the Islamists were allowed to
participate freely in future elections, and of the impact this would
have on his political fate and on the state itself. The Constitution
states that two-thirds of the Assembly's seats will be needed to
nominate the president, whose nomination is then formally
confirmed by a referendum. Theoretically this could mean that if
the Brothers were able in the future to secure more than third of
the seats (i.e. around 140), they would be then in a strong position
to disturb the balance of power which the NDP struggles to
maintain. Added to this, a significant rise in the number of
Brothers in parliament would strengthen their case in the Parties'
Committee, or in the courts, for the right to establish a political
party (a right that is recognised by the law for any political power
that secures at least 20 seats in parliament).[19]

The Rise of Islamist Violence

The regime was angered not only by the Brothers' reluctance to
nominate Mubarak but also their reluctance to support the regime
in its campaign against Islamist terrorism, which had become a
recurrent phenomenon by the late 1980s. In 1987, Islamists began

to rage war against the state and on its public and official figures, including the former interior ministers Hasan Abu Basha and Muhammad Al-Nabawi, and the editor of *Al-Musawwar* Magazine, Makram Muhammad Ahmad. In 1988 there were nine violent incidents between *Al-Jama'at Al-Islamiyya* and the police with people killed and injured on both sides, as well as 16 riots and five insurgencies by the same group, using knifes and grenades.[20] In 1989, the tide of violence escalated to 19 riots, three major insurgencies and 14 bloody clashes with the police. There were 8,000 arrests and five hidden weapons caches were discovered.[21]

The rise of this coercive behaviour was regarded as an alarming indicator of the regime's legitimacy, which was already in question because of various issues related to the absence of genuinely representative political institutions, serious breakdowns in respect of the rule of law, and failure to bring about satisfactory economic progress.[22] To counter the impact of violence, the regime began to pursue contradictory policies, which, as the 1990s revealed (see Chapters Six and Seven), exacerbated rather than solved the problems of the state. On the one hand, the security services were given a more prominent role by the regime in intimidating Islamists and those who sympathised with them on the basis of ideology and family loyalties. On the other, the regime was forced to broaden its efforts to legitimise itself by accommodating the previously neglected and more disenchanted sectors of society. In order to gain public credibility against the propaganda of its local opponents, it had to pay greater attention to the role of religion and to its official institutions and representatives. It also needed somehow to redefine its approach to eudaemonic legitimacy to ensure that the beneficiaries of its performance included the frustrated lower middle classes, who were seen as having in the short term the most to lose through reform.

The Use of Coercion

The prominent role given to the security services to counter Islamist violence was confirmed when Zaki Badr was appointed as Interior Minister in 1986. A former governor of Asyut, which was regarded as the stronghold of extremism, Badr was notorious for his brutality, and his appointment, which followed the imposed resignation of Rushdi after the central security riots in 1986, marked a turning point in the relationship between the state and the Islamists. By appointing Badr as Minister of Interior (followed in the 1990s by Abdul Halim Musa and Hasan Al-Alfi, both of whom were also former governors of Asyut), the state effectively transformed its coercive regional policies against the Islamists in Asyut (and in Upper Egypt generally) and made it into a national policy that affected the whole country. The new figures who became the directors of domestic security in the late 1980s were different from the generation of Abu Basha and Rushdi, since their professional background and their experiences with troubled Asyut made them more inclined to use force rather than negotiation as an option when dealing with dissenters.

Badr's coercive policies were felt everywhere, especially on university campuses. At Asyut University, for example, an *Al-Jihad* member was shot by a security official while putting up posters of a talk to be delivered by Shaikh 'Umar Abdul Rahman.[23] Embarrassed by this incident, Mubarak hastened to distance himself from the atrocity and ordered a special plane to take the wounded student from Asyut to a private military hospital in Cairo for treatment (the student died). However, such incidents have recurred ever since.[24]

The increasing intervention of the security services on campuses was also a nervous response to the successes being achieved in student elections by the Islamists. Asyut University, which was controlled by the Brothers as opposed to *Al-Jama'at Al-Islamiyya*, witnessed an organised interference in the election results and the removal of names of candidates suspected of having Islamist tendencies. The Brothers later learned that the best way to avert this was to put forward the names of new candidates who were not known to have affiliations with Islamists – a strategy they also used in the elections of the assembly and syndicates. Candidates were also frequently threatened and sometimes physically abused to deter them from running in student elections. In 1988, the security forces arrested 27 Islamist students during an election campaign at Asyut University, thrashed them and threatened them with sexual abuse.[25]

In 1988, following the statement by the Student Unions against Mubarak's re-election, the security forces entered the campus of 'Ayn Shams University in Cairo, and arrested and injured hundreds of students who had gathered inside the prayer room to commemorate a religious event.[26] Many of these incidents were reported in the press and were used in parliament by the Brothers as evidence against the radical policies of the regime.

In Pursuit of Religious Legitimacy

While employing coercion in dealing with dissenters, the regime was, paradoxically, appealing to religion and to its official institutions as a way of gaining credibility over its opponents. To various degrees, 'Islam' has always been a source of legitimacy for all Egyptian regimes, from King Farouk and Nasser to Mubarak. According to Rif'at Al-Said, General Secretary of the leftist Tajammu' Party, "its level in the public discourse of the state increases with the increase in Islamist violence".[27]

From the late 1980s onwards, the state-controlled press and media saw a gradual Islamisation, which was intended to counter the growing impact of Islamists in general. The regime launched Islamic newspapers such *Al-Liwa' Al-Islami* and *'Aqidati* that aimed to present its own version and interpretation of Islam and of Islam's role in society and politics. The hours allocated by the state to religious programmes on national television and radio increased with time, reaching 14,500 hours annually compared with the 8,000 hours given over to entertainment programmes, which gradually became more conservative.[28] Abu-Lughod, who studied the impact of Islamists on the cultural production of the Egyptian media, offers an example of the shift in official discourse and appearance with regard to social morality:

> Minster of Information Safwat Al-Sharif had given instructions that television announcers were to wear subdued make-up and to refrain from wearing brightly coloured or flashy clothing. This, he informed the television staff, was to show the broadcaster's sympathy for the families of the victims of terrorism.

Al-Sharif also announced that the subjects discussed on television programmes during the coming months should be in keeping with "the mood of the Egyptian street".[29] His remarks confirm the Islamists' impact on the state and the necessary shifts that the government had to undertake in order to avert the effect of the Islamists and to bolster its own credibility.

Moreover, the regime continued to court Al-Azhar as an essential institution representing Sunni Islam in Egypt and worldwide. Chapter Two has shown how the regime used Al-Azhar and its *'ulama* during the early 1980s to refute the religious arguments presented by the radicals to justify the use of armed struggle against the state, and to approve the way the organised debates were aired on national television and reported in the press. However, the state's radicalised policies against Islamists made it difficult for Al-Azhar to continue to give its religious endorsement to what the state was doing, since this had a negative impact on the its own institutional credibility. In his final years in office the Shaikh of Al-Azhar, Gad Al-Haqq Ali, who had initially supported the state, became loudly critical of the regime's repressive attitude to the radicals, arguing that such policies back-fired and that the speared of extremism was also the result of corrupt behaviour sanctioned by the state.[30]

Al-Azhar's shift was also related to the growing number of young Azharites who were affiliated to the Brothers and who thus objected strongly to participating in the state's campaign. More senior Azharite shaikhs, some of whom (such as Abdul Hamid Kishk, Mahallawi and Salah Abu Ismail) were also affiliated to the Brothers, also had a tremendous effect in shaping Al-Azhar's policies towards the issue of religious extremism. Other Azharites exploited the regime's need for religious credibility and exerted pressures for Islamic reforms in return for their institution's sup-port: on many occasions, the regime was forced to concede.[31] This gradually helped bring forward the process of the Islamisation of society, as could be seen in the case of the official media.

However, the growing rift between Al-Azhar and the regime led the latter to rely more on Dar Al-Ifta' (the second most important religious institution in Egypt after Al-Azhar), which was headed by the Azharite *mufti* Mohammad Sayyid Tantawi.[32] Tantawi, who had been appointed to Dar Al-Ifta' in 1986, was perceived by the regime to be "more political, flexible and realistic" than Gad Al-Haqq and therefore more prepared to support the policies of the state.[33] This was seen in the controversial *fatwa*s put out by Tantawi in relation to the use of savings certificates issued by the state-owned banks. According to Tantawi, such certificates (*shahadat al-istithmar*) were not against the commands of the Qur'an and its prohibition of usury.[34] Tantawi's *fatwa* was widely seen as an orchestrated attempt to undermine the religious credibility of Islamic banks and investment companies, and to restore public confidence in state banks.

An Islamist Social Legitimacy

The regime expected the Brothers to join in supporting its

campaign against radical Islamists, and tolerated them largely on this basis of this expectation. However, the Brothers were not prepared to forsake their own religious legitimacy to rescue that of the regime, and therefore made sure that whenever they did condemn acts of violence by the radicals, they did the same towards state-initiated violence.[35] In order to show that they had a different solution to how the state could avert terrorism,[36] the Brothers exploited the escalating violence as a way of exerting more pressure on the regime to grant official recognition to the movement. Mustafa Mashhur, former *murshid* of the Brothers, argued more than once that if the Brothers were permitted to function properly, it would be easier for them to restrain the angry youngsters who otherwise had nothing to turn to except the radical groups.[37] This attitude angered Mubarak, and according to Mohammad Fu'ad, a senior Brother, prepared the ground for a change of state policy against the *tanzim*.[38] The regime's fury was confirmed by Makram Mohammad Ahmad, a source well connected to official circles, who admits that the mistrust between the two was deepened by the Brothers' refusal wholeheartedly to condemn Islamic violence.[39]

Even so, this development did not obstruct the progress being made by the Brothers in society. Because the movement continued to provide its constituencies with better services than those provided by the regime, this bolstered its eudaemonic legitimacy. The late 1980s witnessed not just the development of an Islamist social contract, alternative or parallel to that of the state, but more importantly the development of a contract that was conducted in a highly organised manner, due to the powers of the *tanzim* and its networks. Below we examine both developments in relation to campuses, teachers' faculty clubs and professional syndicates.

University campuses

Despite increasing interventions by the security services, the Brothers continued to win student elections. In 1987 they won a majority of seats in the student unions of Cairo, Alexandria and Zaqaziq,[40] and in 1988 and 1989 they extended their control over the major universities of Al-Mansura and Al-Azhar.[41] Most of the progress achieved was based on the Brothers' ability to provide students with services which transcended political and ideological rhetoric and which therefore appealed to broader sectors of students. Such services built the reputation of the Brothers as credible representatives of student interests, and on the strength of this legitimacy their candidates contested the elections. During election campaigns, the Islamist candidates reviewed their past records of achievements and promised better services when re-elected.

In 1988, first-year students at Mansura University were presented with welcome packs from their Islamist-controlled union and were introduced to a list of the services provided by the union, which also pledged its commitment to "provide *any* student with *any* help".[42] The services listed included regular sales of cheap study books and revision aids, as well as expensive medical and engineering equipments (which were sold at a 30 per cent reduction). This campaign was repeated at other universities, such as at Alexandria where the candidates made it clear to their constituents that "the objective of listing our achievements" was not to show off, but "to fulfil our responsibility".[43]

Not only were existing services improved but many others were inspired and negotiated by the students themselves through the use of feedback assessment questionnaires which became a popular means of engaging students on campuses during the late 1980s. Students were asked in the questionnaires to evaluate the services provided by the union and to suggest new ways of improving them.[44] In an authoritarian political structure, where almost all social and political spaces were controlled by the state, campuses became important spaces for students to voice their specific concerns and to make their own decisions about what they needed.

The Teachers' Faculty Clubs

As well as making inroads on university campuses, the Brothers began to gain access to the teachers' faculty clubs (*hay'at al-tadris*), which resemble the senior common rooms in British universities. They also secured control of these clubs in the major universities of Cairo, Alexandria and Asyut.[45] The teachers' faculty club at Asyut University was the first teachers' body to come under the control of the Brothers in 1985, and was followed by the teachers' faculty at Cairo University in 1986, where they won 8 out of 12 seats.

During their election campaign in 1986, the Brothers in the faculty clubs promised their electorates to increase their salaries, organise housing for young teachers and improve the health care services. Prior to the advent of the Islamists, the clubs had been controlled by nationalists and leftists who did not really address such issues seriously, which meant that the Brothers' campaigning on improved services struck a chord among most teachers. According to Badr Ghazi, lecturer in chemistry and President of the Faculty Club at Cairo University during the early 1990s:

> In our campaigns we did not speak about politics. Instead we focused on the real concerns of people. Salaries, accommodation and health treatment constituted the concerns of many young teachers who made up 25 per cent of the club, and it is they who have voted for us regularly since. [46]

Like the majority of employed Egyptians, the teachers were dissatisfied with the rapid rise in living costs while their incomes remained fixed. Most teachers looked for extra income sources, mainly from private tuition which, in many cases, earned them more than their basic salary from the university.[47] Once they were on the governing board Cairo University's faculty club, the Brothers set out to solve this problem, and to overcome the side-effects of private tuition on the quality of education. Their first move was to hold a meeting with Fathi Suroor, Vice-Chancellor of the university (and Speaker of the Parliament at the time of writing), at which they succeeded in persuading the university to introduce certain additional allowances to the basic salary that covered time spent on academic supervision and research. By the 1990s the net salary of teachers had increased threefold since 1986.

Decent accommodation in crowded Cairo was a second major concern for most teaching staff, especially the assistant professors, most of whom were young, unmarried graduates who, unless they had inherited wealth, had to rely on their savings and salaries to buy a flat and get married. On the low salaries they were receiving, this was almost impossible. The Brothers held another meeting with the Education Minister, Fathi Mohammad, demanding cheap flats for young teaching staff. According to Badr Ghazi, a Brother who was present at the meeting:

> The minister was surprised to see us raise such an issue. He said to us: I thought you were Islamists with beards and *galabiyyas* and that you were coming to make demands about

religious matters. We told him: we are what you see: a group of teachers wanting to be of service to our colleagues. He asked: how could we help? We suggested that he should speak to the minister of housing and ask him to provide us with some flats in the newly developed Sixth of October City and he agreed.[48]

The Ministry of Housing agreed to give the club 208 flats, which the Brothers used exclusively to accommodate young assistant professors.

The third major problem was providing teachers with decent health care. This was not always provided in public hospitals and had therefore to be obtained in private hospitals at a high cost that could not be met out of the salaries earned by teachers. Lower middle class assistant professors had in most cases to rely on public treatment, which was less than satisfactory. Before the Islamists became involved, the faculty club at Cairo University had lacked a proper health care service, and teachers had to pay the full costs of their treatment. If the teacher needed an operation and the costs were significantly high, he/she would submit a formal request to their faculty head asking for a refund. The request would be passed on to the chancellor, and would then be assessed by a medical committee who decided whether to approve the amount. This long-winded and time-consuming process excluded assistant professors who, because they were not counted by the faculty club as full members of staff, had to search for private funds. The Brothers' achievement was that they lobbied for all teachers, including the assistant professors, to be given a medical card that entitled them to private hospital treatment, paid for by the university.[49]

In addition to the above services, the Brothers also organised an annual sale of consumer durables, a popular occasion for young teachers, as well as a profitable one for the organisers. According to Ghazi, the profits of the first sale, which was organised in 1986 at Cairo University's faculty club, reached round about a million Egyptian pounds. Ahmad Lutfi, a lecturer in economics at Cairo University and a Brother who was also the faculty administrator, showed me the annual financial reports of the faculty from 1984, when it had been controlled by the leftists, to 1994, by which time it had been in the hands of the Brothers for eight years (since 1986). Based on these reports, it could be established that the Brothers had secured a basis for social legitimacy, based on their successful performance in services. This success was indicated by the general increase in the faculty's revenues through profits from the projects they had initiated and developed (Figure 5.1):

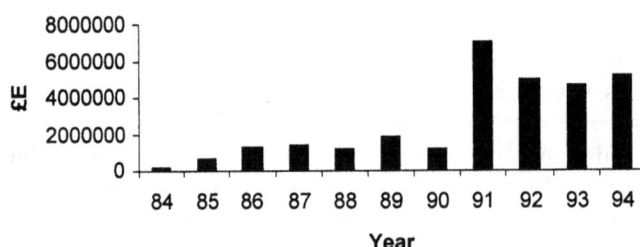

FIGURE 5.1. Revenues from the
Cairo University Teachers' Faculty Club.

Professional Syndicates

The Brothers continued to make progress in syndicates throughout the late 1980s, largely as a result of their superior administrative and financial management, and the improved welfare services that they offered. The achievements of Islamists in syndicates are well-documented elsewhere, and it is not my intention to produce a detailed account of them here. Rather, I wish to emphasise the role of these services in conferring legitimacy on the Brothers over that of the regime.

The most appreciated, and popular, service was that of health care. Formerly, professionals received free but poor treatment in the government's public hospitals, but if they preferred to be treated privately they had to pay considerable sums of money. For young and/or lower middle class graduates both options were impractical. In 1988, the Islamists introduced their health care scheme into the medical syndicate. It offered subsidised treatment in private hospitals and clinics to members and their families[50] and in 1988 the beneficiaries of the scheme included more than 17,600 doctors and 43,960 dependents. The popular project was extended the following year to the engineers' syndicate where the number of beneficiaries reached 72,000.[51] Both cases showed the extent to which this kind of service was needed, despite the existing state system of health insurance.[52]

The Brothers also organised massive sales of furniture, washing machines, gas cookers, refrigerators and other items that young professionals needed for their flats, at subsidised costs or through interest-free instalments.

Organised Legitimacy

The impact made by the Islamists on the regime and on its legitimacy was not simply related to their performance in terms of the services they provided to society, but to the organised way in which those services were provided. Chapter Two outlined the main sections within the *tanzim* that were rebuilt and developed during the 1980s to facilitate and empower the Brothers' role in society. It is easier to explain the link between the *tanzim* and how the Brothers influenced society through an example that I encountered during my research in Egypt. In 2002, I was allowed to participate as an observer or 'guest' at a private meeting of the Brothers in Alexandria, which included members of parliament, syndicates and teachers' faculty clubs. One of the issues discussed was how to mobilise Egyptians to boycott imported American goods as a way of supporting the Palestinian *intifadah*. The pharmacists' syndicate, controlled by the Ikhwan, was expected to organise a series of lectures on the subject of boycotting American medicine, to which speakers from different ideological and political backgrounds would be invited, rather than Islamists who were known for their affiliation to the movement.

Those who participated in the meeting agreed that in order to engage the broader public, and to mobilise pharmacy owners, most of whom were Copts, the campaign's discourse should be nationalist rather than religious. A nationalist campaign was unlikely to anger the regime, and would thus avoid security harassment, especially if it declared its aim as being to promote Egyptian products and strengthen the local economy rather than simply opposing American products.

The Brothers utilised the powers and resources of the *tanzim* to improve the efficiency of their services and to make connections between the spaces they occupied as a way of furthering their impact on society and politics. Organised links enabled the Ikhwan in particular spaces to mobilise their particular constituencies in support of the movement's objectives elsewhere, and to use the spaces as platforms from which to address the *tanzim*'s concerns. The Brothers on university campuses used their legitimacy to mobilise students to participate in the 1987 parliamentary elections and vote for the Islamist candidates. 'Amr Abu Khalil, a Brother and former President of the Alexandria University Student Union, confirmed that students were usually sympathetic to the Islamists because of the way they functioned on campuses and would therefore vote for their candidates in parliament.[53]

Organised links were also evident between campus and syndicate, and university students were encouraged and mobilised to develop links with the syndicates of their future professions. At Alexandria, for example, the engineers' syndicate organised regular lectures and graduation ceremonies for engineering students who were still at university. The obvious intention of the syndicates was to engage the students as early as possible, and others set up special committees. The medical syndicate, for example, had a unit for future young doctors, in which medical students in their third or fourth year were given informal membership and access to some of the syndicates' facilities and clubs.[54] The practical outcome of this process was that students who voted for the Muslim Brothers on campuses were skilfully persuaded to continue to do so.

The Brothers also used these organisations to articulate the political views of the *tanzim*, which otherwise would not have been articulated elsewhere. The teachers' faculty clubs in Cairo and Alexandria held joint conferences with the student unions in the same universities in support of the *Intifadah* and the *mujahadeen* in Afghanistan. This co-operation between the unions and the clubs continued until the 1990s, reflecting the views of the *tanzim* on the issues of the decade, including the Gulf War in 1991.[55] At one joint conference, the Cairo University clubs and unions stressed the need to abolish restrictive measures, such as the Emergency Law, and to allow people the freedom to establish political parties. Significantly, one of the main speakers at this conference was 'Esam Al-'Aryan, representing the medical syndicate.

Teachers' faculty clubs also co-ordinated their activities with syndicates, in order to exchange ideas and experiences on health care programmes and sales of consumer durables in order to improve the performance of both. Organised co-operation between powerful syndicates, prompted by the *tanzim*'s networks, was also evident. Anwar Shihata, treasurer of the medical syndicate, confirmed the existence of the organised co-operation between the Brothers in different syndicates:

> I think this is normal for any group of people who share the same views and aspirations to co-ordinate among themselves on everything. It would be strange if there were Ikhwan in the engineers' syndicate and in the lawyers' syndicate and they never discussed anything with each other. The lawyers have to benefit from the projects I did in the medical syndicate, in the same way that I have to benefit from the projects of the engineers.[56]

The Gulf War in 1990 prompted the Islamists, through their creation of the Committee for Co-ordinating Syndicates' Action (*lagnat tanseeq al-'amal al-niqabi*) to rouse the syndicates and transform them into a unified front. Such organised connections were seen as a counterweight to the corporatist links used by the regime to control the various spaces and prevent them from expanding beyond their predetermined limits. The encounter between the *tanzim*'s links (with the syndicates, student unions and the teachers' staff clubs) and the regime's links (with the relevant spaces) is illustrated in Figure 5.2:

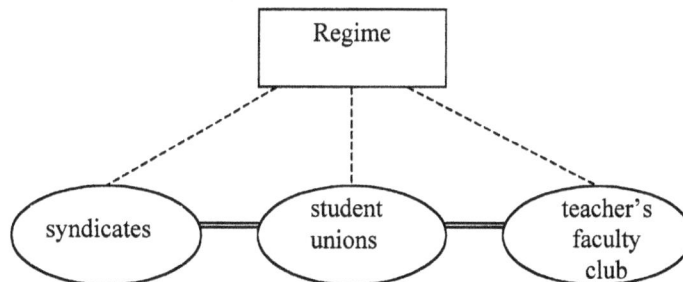

FIGURE 5.2: The Organised Links between the Ikhwan and the Regime.

The model explains the development of the Brothers' progress in society during the 1980s and the impact this has had on the regime. During the early 1980s, as explained in Chapter Two, the regime opened up social spaces, such as the professional syndicates, student unions and teachers' faculty clubs, as a way of self-legitimation. However, its tolerance of these spaces was not absolute, being restricted through authoritarian corporatist controls (represented by the dotted lines) that made sure the spaces were not totally autonomous. Meanwhile the Brothers occupied these spaces and developed an Islamist social contract that gained them a basis of legitimacy. This legitimacy had a particularly strong impact on the regime when the Brothers began to use these networks and those of the *tanzim* to connect between the spaces they occupied (represented by the double lines), since this development challenged the controls of the regime. What this meant in practice was that the Brothers could later mobilise the constituencies and the resources inside these spaces outside their predetermined boundaries in service of the *tanzim*'s wider gaols (as was seen in syndicates).

According to Amani Qandil, who has closely examined the activities of Islamists in major syndicates:

> Syndicate activism went beyond the syndicate walls, where Islamists began to organise open functions that intended to appeal to a wider audience who were not members of syndicates. As well as forming active alliances with each other, syndicates also began to form alliances with political parties.[57]

In Pursuit of Social Legitimacy

Growing social and religious turmoil was in a part a response to the continued deterioration of Egypt's economy, which was evident in the rapid decline in foreign currency resources, increased inflation, and decreased savings and investment. The IMF and the World Bank increased their pressure on the government to introduce serious restructuring reforms, but Mubarak was reluctant to do this, fearing that such actions would exacerbate social tensions. Many Egyptian economists were warning that rapid structural reforms would have considerable side effects on the poorer Egyptians who depended on the public sector to keep them placated. Initiating economic reforms might prove to be an incentive for some of them to participate in terrorism.

An official study commissioned by the Egyptian Consultative Council (*majlis al-shura*), acknowledged that the majority of extremists were young Egyptians, aged between 16 and 25, who came from humble backgrounds and were unemployed.[58] Most lived in poorly urbanised conditions, lacking electricity, water and sanitation facilities. Certainly many of the Upper Egypt governorates, such as Asyut and Minya, from which members of *Al-Jihad* and *Al-Jama'at Al-Islamiyya* were recruited, lacked proper housing arrangements and basic public services.[59] Basing its findings on interviews with former members of these groups, the Consultative Council study called on the state to invest in welfare services, and warned that economic reform should not impact on the lives of the lower classes in Egypt, but should instead focus on building a proper infrastructure in the poorer districts and solving problems of unemployment.[60]

Ibrahim Aoude confirmed the results of the study, arguing that slow growth in the economy and the misdistribution of social production provided fertile ground for the rise of Islamist extremism in Egypt.[61] His comments reflected the wider national and official mood that the state had to play a more aggressive role in improving the domestic economy if it wanted to bolster its legitimacy among the less privileged.[62]

The late 1980s saw rapid developments in Mubarak's attempts to improve his country's economic performance, as part of his basis for eudaemonic legitimacy. First, he dismissed Ali Lutfi, his Prime Minister, for failing to improve the economy, and instead appointed Atif Sidqi. He justified the move as part of mobilising "all domestic and foreign resources to effectively tackle the economic situation", arguing that this was his top priority.[63] Secondly, he continued to appeal to international donors and creditors (e.g. the U.S., West Germany, France, England, Italy and the IMF) for more aid to counter the impact of inflation and the decline in oil prices. Third, the regime reluctantly signed an agreement with the IMF in which it agreed to lower subsidies on popular consumer items, such as cigarettes and tobacco (a move that later resulted in a 20 per cent price increase).[64]

The agreement ended partly because the Egyptian deficit remained unchanged at around £E10 billion, and partly because the regime was still not prepared to go all the way with reform and to endure the consequences, including the impact on its stability. Thus, whenever the regime announced a price increase for certain items, it made sure that this did not affect the prices of the essential goods (oil, rice, sugar, etc.) that were subsidised by the government and a burden on its budget. Mubarak revealed that in 1987 government revenues amounted to £E18 billion, of which almost £E11 billion (61 per cent) went to cover these subsidies.[65]

In addition, the regime also made sure that a price increase was usually (but not always) followed by some kind of increase in wages, to help in narrowing the gap between salaries and increased living costs. Following the signing of the 1987 agreement with the IMF, the regime declared a 20 per cent rise in wages for all civil service and public sector employees. However, the regime failed to appease the majority of Egyptians, who regarded these moves as palliative gestures rather than serious changes to improve their living standards. Constraints such as mismanagement, bureaucratic sleaze, rapid population increase and conflict between private and public sector elites hampered efforts to improve the economy.[66] In the end, the regime had to accede to the IMF's demands, and in 1991 another agreement was signed with the organisation.

The Clampdown on Investment Companies

The year after the 1987 agreement with the IMF, the regime launched an aggressive action against Islamic investment companies (Law 146 of 1988) as part of its wider campaign to reform the economy and resume control over resources and movement of capital.[67] The spread of Islamic investment companies during the 1980s and the high returns of profits offered to creditors prompted many people to withdraw their capital from public sector banks and transfer it into the control of the Islamists. From 1983 to 1986, more than £E8 billion worth of accounts in the official banking system were closed. According to a "secret report", most of the funds in these accounts were then directed to the Islamic investment companies for a larger profit.

This added to the weakness of the state economy and prompted the state to take serious action against the expansion of the investment companies as a step towards reversing the movement of capital from the Islamists to its own financial institutions. At the same time the clampdown on the investment companies was part of a wider scheme to curb the growing power of the Islamists, starting with a plan to dry up their financial resources. *Al-Ahali* newspaper, the mouthpiece of the Tajammu' Party, along with other state-owned newspapers, played a significant role in heightening the regime's fears that the investment companies constituted a source of funding for militant groups and for political campaigns to contest elections.[68] In the late 1980s, Al-Raiyyan had ideas to invest in public transport in an attempt to solve the problem of Cairo's crowded roads and had put forward a proposal to the Ministry of Transport to provide the capital with mini buses. The proposal was accepted and Al-Raiyyan obtained the necessary permits to set up his bus company. However, the agreement between the Ministry of Transport and Al-Raiyyan was seen as a sign of the government's subordination to the growing Islamist influence, and the regime was forced to intervene and cancel the project.[69]

The Islamists' financial companies were also seen as a threat to the state's intentions of embarking on structural reform, and of its wish to protect private investors.[70] The latter were closer than the Islamists to the regime,[71] and did not challenge the state's dominance in controlling resources in the way that the Islamic investment companies did.[72] The late 1980s saw the end of the investment companies and the emergence of a new breed of entrepreneurs and businessmen who would play a role in the process of economic reform.

The Weakening of Islamist Finances

According to one reliable Islamist source, more than 40 per cent of the Islamic investment companies belonged to owners who were either from the Muslim Brotherhood or who sympathised with this cause, with the result that the regime's clampdown on the companies dealt a huge blow to one of their most powerful sources of finance.[73] Other sources included the regular subscriptions (*ishtirakat*) paid to the *tanzim*, and donations from Brothers working in the Arab Gulf, who were able to exploit the *tanzim*'s transnational affiliations and connections with Islamist entrepreneurs and organisations and to raise money for the movement's activities in Egypt. A Brother who had previously lived in the United Arab Emirates and who was well connected there told me that at one point, following the regime's clampdown on Islamic investment companies, Zaki Badr, the Egyptian Interior Minister, had toured the Gulf States. During meetings with security officials, he warned them of the dangers of funding the Brothers, alleging that they had used such money for funding terrorism.

As with the investment companies, the Islamic banks, in whose development the Brothers had played a role, were also exposed to government harassment. Their religious credentials were discredited by Shaikh Mohammad Tantawi's controversial *fatwa*s, which denied the existence of such things as 'Islamic' banks and argued that the interest received by the state banks was lawful. It is, however, difficult to establish what impact the *fatwa*s had on depositors. Islamic banks were also discredited through their own performance and internal struggles and disputes, circumstances which the regime utilised as an excuse to intervene in their affairs.

The successful early 1980s growth of the International Islamic Bank also came to a halt in 1988 when a row broke out between Ahmad Amin Fu'ad, president of the board of the bank's council, and the council members who were dominated by the Brothers. The quarrel concerned Fu'ad's excessive spending and allowances. According to Abdul Hamid Al-Ghazali, a Brother and a member of the council board, Fu'ad's net monthly salary was US$1,760, while his yearly allowances for travelling and other unspecified expenses reached US$20,244, making an overall salary of US$22,000 annually.[74] What Al-Ghazali and his Islamist colleagues in the council were implying was that Fu'ad was exploiting his senior position at the Bank to make unlawful profits for himself, while Fu'ad claimed that behind the spreading of their false accusations the Islamists had sinister intentions to consolidate their control over the Bank.

Relations between the board of council and their president deteriorated, and the Central Bank had to intervene to dissolve the council and to appoint one of its representatives, Ismail Hasan, as the International Islamic Bank's new president. Although this undermined the authority of the Islamists, it did not entirely mean the end of their influence. Soon after Hasan's appointment, Al-Sharif exploited the financial difficulties of the Bank and bid for the purchase of a significant share of its assets; this also gave him the right to appoint three persons to the board of council. Al-Sharif duly chose to appoint Khairat Al-Shatir, Salih Al-Hadidi and Ismail Al-Hudaybi (brother of the late *murshid* Ma'mun Al-Hudaybi), all of whom were members of the Brotherhood. However, in practical terms this did not mean much, since Al-Sharif's financial situation was already hampered by the fall of his investment companies and the big losses being made by the Bank. Eventually the Central Bank intervened again, and this time decided to sell most of the Bank's shares to the public sector banks.

Conclusion

The late 1980s witnessed new approaches and trends in the pursuit of legitimacy by Mubarak and the Brotherhood. Although Mubarak continued to build a basis of legal legitimacy, driven by the need to establish a constitutional Assembly that would nominate him for a second term presidency, the rise in Islamist terrorism as part of a wider public frustration emphasised the regime's need to focus on its economic performance. In parallel with partial concessions to IMF's pressure to embark on structural adjustments, the regime continued to court its public sector employees with increased wages and through the maintaining of subsidies intended to offset social reactions to stabilising the economy. The regime also appealed to the religious basis of legitimacy by making further concessions to religious institutions such as Al-Azhar and Dar Al-Ifta', and to popular movements such as the Muslim Brothers, in the hope that they would join in supporting the regime's campaign against Islamist violence.

As well as pursuing legitimacy, the regime also began to emphasise the use of coercion against society. This was seen in the way it chose to appoint as Ministers of Interior certain figures who were notorious for their brutality (e.g. Zaki Badr). While this contributed to the radicalisation of the regime's social policies, the use of coercion failed to solve the regime's problems with terrorism, which became a rampant phenomenon in the 1990s.

The Brothers, on the other hand, continued to consolidate the social basis of their legitimacy by improving their social services and developing an Islamist social contract which paralleled that of the state. Although it was not comparable to the state's social contract, since its benefits and resources were limited, it was nevertheless powerful. The *tanzim* and its highly-developed internal sectors and networks were employed in the process of connecting and co-ordinating action among the Brothers who were located in the middle-class institutions of syndicates and campuses, and this increased the significance of the services that they provided. The networks helped to improve the Brothers' services, deepened the sympathy of the recipients towards moderate Islamists, and threatened the corporatist controls of the regime.

Mubarak's dilemma of legitimacy was increased by the significant progress of the Brothers in society and politics (36 seats in the 1987 Assembly), but he did not revoke his tolerant policies since this would have had a negative impact on his image inside Egypt and abroad. Mubarak restrained the spirit of his tolerance, but continued to accommodate a substantial portion of the Brothers' activities (which excluded Islamic investment companies). He also tolerated the unofficial social legitimacy which they gained from this, as long as such legitimacy was neither politicised nor mobilised against the regime's strategic polices. Such a development was to occur in the 1990s and predictably prompted the regime to revoke its tolerance.

Notes

1 Three months after Mubarak had dissolved the 1984 Assembly, the Court confirmed in its juridical ruling that the electoral law No.114 was indeed unconstitutional.
2 Mustafa Kamel Al-Sayyid, *Intikhabat majlis al-sha'b fi ibril 1987: dilalat nata'ij al-intikhabat* (The Elections of the National Assembly in April 1987: Indications of the Elections' Results), Cairo, Al-Ahram Centre for Political and Strategic Studies, 1988, p. 130.
3 Negotiations between the Labour Party and the Muslim Brothers began in 1986, when Ibrahim Shukri, the leader of the Labour Party decided to make his party more Islamic. In addition to this shift, Salah Abu Ismail, a close associate of the Brothers, was able to form an alliance between the Brothers and the Liberal Party.
4 Ali Hilal (ed.), *Intikhabat majlis al-sha'b: dirasa wa tahlil* (The National Assembly Elections: A Study and an Analysis), Cairo, Al-Ahram Centre for Political and Strategic Studies, 1988, p. 133.
5 Personal interview with Abdul Hamid Al-Ghazali, Alexandria, 2 August 2002.
6 Personal interview with Badr Mohammad Badr, Cairo, 14 January 2001.
7 Tawfiq Al-Wa'i, *Al-Fikr al-siyasi al-mu'asir 'ind al-ikhwan al-muslimin* (The Contemporary Political Thought of the Muslim Brothers), Kuwait, Al-Manar Al-Islamiyya, 2001, pp. 147–149.
8 Hassanain Ibrahim and Huda 'Awad, *Al-Ikhwan al-muslimun wa al-siyasa fi misr* (The Muslim Brothers and Politics in Egypt), Cairo, Markaz Al-Mahrusa, 1996, p. 371.
9 Personal interview with Sa'd Eddin Ibrahim, Cairo, 8 July 2002.
10 Sa'd Eddin Ibrahim, "Islamic Alternative in Egypt: The Muslim Brotherhood and Sadat" in *Egypt, Islam and Democracy: Twelve Critical Essays*, Cairo, AUC Press, 1996, p. 58.
11 Hassanain and Huda, *Al-Ikhwan al-muslimun, op.cit.*, p. 364.
12 Maha Azzam, "Egypt: The Islamists and the State Under Mubarak", in Abdel Salam Sidahmed and Anoushiravan Ehteshami (eds.), *Political Fundamentalism*, Boulder, Colo.: Westview Press, 1996, p. 111.
13 *Al-Ahram*, 7 July 1987.
14 Mohammad Al-Tawil, *Al-Ikhwan fi al-barlaman* (The Ikhwan in Parliament), Cairo, Al-Maktab Al-Misri Al-Hadith, 1992, pp. 22–65.
15 Noha El-Mikawy, *The Building of Consensus in Egypt's Transition Process*, Cairo, AUC Press, 1999, p. 92.
16 Personal interview with Mohammad Fu'ad, London, 11 September 2001.
17 Personal interview with Abdul Mun'em Abu Al-Futuh, Cairo, 23 July 2002.

18 See *Al-Mukhtar Al-Islami*, no 56, September 1987, pp. 66–68.

19 *Al-Mujtama'*, 19 July 1994, pp. 40–41.

20 The figures are quoted from Mubarak, Hisham., *Al-Irhabiyun qadimun: dirasa muqarana bayna mawqif al-ikhwan al-muslimin wa jama'at al-jihad min qadiyat al-'unf* (The Terrorists are Coming: A Comparative Study of the Position of the Muslim Brotherhood and the Jihad Groups from the Question of Violence), Cairo, Dar Al-Mahrusa, 1995, p. 394.

21 *Ibid.*, p. 402.

22 Maha Azzam, "Egypt: The Islamists and the State Under Mubarak", in Abdel Salam Sidahmed and Anoushiravan Ehteshami (eds.), *Political Fundamentalism*, Boulder CO, Westview Press, 1996, p. 113.

23 *Arabia* (English), July 1986, p. 26.

24 His death provoked wide protests in Asyut and nearby cities like Minya and Aswan. In Minya, north of Asyut, demonstrators were forced into the mosque by security forces that used tear gas to disperse and arrest many members of Islamic groups. In Aswan, students were injured in clashes with the police.

25 Personal interview with Mahmoud Hussein, Asyut, 6 July 2002.

26 See *Liwa' Al-Islam*, no. 168, September 1988, pp. 28–29.

27 Personal interview with Rif'at Al-Sa'id, Cairo, 18 July 2002.

28 This subject is discussed by Lila Abu-Lughod, "Dramatic Reversals: Political Islam and Egyptian Television", in J. Beinin, and J. Stork (eds.), *Political Islam: Essays from Middle East Report*, London, I. B. Tauris, 1997, pp. 269–282.

29 *Ibid.*, p. 281.

30 Tamir Mustafa, "Conflict and Cooperation Between the State and Religious Institutions in Contemporary Egypt", *International Journal of Middle East Studies*, vol. 32, no. 1, February 2000, p. 9.

31 Malika Zeghal, "Religion and Politics in Egypt: The "ulama" of Al-Azhar, Radical Islam, and the State (1952–94)", *International Journal of Middle East Studies*, vol. 31, no. 3, August 1999, p. 385.

32 J. Skovgaard-Petersen, *Defining Islam for the Egyptian State: Muftis and Fatwas of Dar Al-Ifta*, Leiden, Brill, 1997, p. 295.

33 Personal interview with Mustafa Al-Fiqi, the former Information Secretary of Mubarak, Cairo, 28 June 2002.

34 Skovgaard-Petersen, p. 296.

35 See some of the Ikhwan's statements in *Al-Ahram*, 8 May 1987 and 20 August 1993; also in *Al-Sha'b* 18 December 1992, 2 April 1993, 23 April 1993, 22 June 1993, 22 July 1993 and 20 May 1994.

36 See Amin Jum'a, *Qadiyat al-irhab: al-ru'iya wa al-'ilaj* (The Issue of Terrorism: the Vision and the Solution), Cairo, Dar Al-Tawzi' wa Al-Nashr Al-Islamiyya, 1998.

37 See Mustafa Mashhur, *Al-Taiyyar Al-islami wa dawruhu fi al-bina'* (The Islamic Trend and Its Role in Building), Cairo, Dar Al-Tawzi' wa Al-Nashr, 1987, pp. 45–46.

38 Personal interview with Mohammad Fu'ad, London, 11 September 2001.

39 Personal interview with Makram Mohammad Ahmad, Cairo, 17 July 2002.

40 *Al-Taqrir al istratiji al 'arabi, 1987* (The Arabic Strategic Report, 1987), Cairo, Al-Ahram Centre for Strategic and Political Studies, 1988, p. 380.

41 *Al-Taqrir al istratiji al 'arabi, 1988* (The Arabic Strategic Report, 1988), Cairo, Al-Ahram Centre for Strategic and Political Studies, 1990, p. 433.

42 *Welcome*, (A Welcome Pack), Mansura University, the Student Union, 1988.

43 *Rapana taqabl mena* [Oh Our Lord, Accept from Us], Alexandria University, 1989.

44 One of these questionnaires included such questions as: "Do you think student services, like text books, study aids, model exam answers, financial support, student support to cope with personal problems, selling of discounted materials, are sufficient or insufficient?"; "To what extent do you feel that we are introducing improvements and new initiatives in our functions?"; "Do you feel that the student union is close enough to you, and do you feel that its members feel your pains and share your concerns?"; and "Mention functions that the union performed which you liked? or disliked? and suggest new functions or services". While the name of the university and/or student union for this questionnaire was not given, the academic year was 1987–88.

45 Sana Abed-Kotob, "The Accommodationists Speak: Goals and Strategies of the Muslim Brotherhood of Egypt", *International Journal of Middle East Studies*, vol. 27, no. 3, 1995, p. 329.

46 Personal interview with Badr Ghazi, Cairo, 20 July 2002.

47 Fees for private tuition vary according to specialisation, teacher's reputation, and region. On average, however, a science teacher could earn as much as £E100 an hour per student, and a humanities teacher £E60 an hour per student on average, compared to a teachers' average net salary, which could be as modest as £E300–400 per month, this represented a significant source of income.

48 Personal interview with Badr Ghazi, Cairo, 20 July 2002.

49 Personal interview with Badr Ghazi, Cairo, 20 July 2002.

50 According to Shihata, involvement in this project was initially voluntary but was then made obligatory "to train our members to make full use of the services provided by the Syndicate". Personal interview with Anwar Shihata, Treasurer of the Doctors Syndicate, Cairo, 20 December 2000.

51 Ahmad Hussein Hasan, *Al-Su'ud al-siyasi al-islami dakhil al-niqabat al-mihania* (The Islamic Political Ascent to Professional Syndicates), Cairo, Al-Dar Al-Saqafia li Al-Nasher, 2000, p. 235.

52 Amani Qandil, "Taqyeem ada' al-islamiyyin fi al-niqabat al-mihaniyya'" (Assessing the Performance of the Islamists in Professional Syndicates), paper presented to the 5th Franco-Egyptian Symposium on *The Phenomenon of Political Violence*, (Published Proceedings), Cairo University, Research Centre for Political Studies, 1993, p. 451.

53 Personal interview with 'Amr Abu Khalil, Alexandria, 10 July 2002.

54 Personal interview with Ahmad Al-Nahas, Alexandria, 10 July 2002.

55 See *Liwa' Al-Islam*, 12 September 1990, pp. 44–45.

56 Personal interview with Anwar Shihata, Cairo, 20 December 2000.

57 Personal interview with Amani Qandil, Cairo, 2 July 2002.

58 Arab Republic of Egypt, Consultative Council (*majlis al-shura*),

Muwajhat al-irhab [Confronting Terrorism], Report 14, Cairo, 1994, pp. 37–39. I am indebted to Mohammad Ragab, Leader of the Consultative Assembly, for providing me with a copy of this study.

59 *Ibid.*, pp. 39–40.

60 *Ibid.*, pp. 86–87.

61 Ibrahim Aoude, "From National Bourgeois Development to Infitah: Egypt 1952–1992", *Arab Studies Quarterly*, vol.16, no.1, winter 1994, p. 18.

62 Karima Korayem, *The Egyptian Economy and the Poor in the Eighties*, Cairo, Institute of National Planning, 1991, p. 33.

63 Mubarak's speech to his new government, 9 November 1986, reported in *Al-Ahram*, 10 November 1986.

64 Posusney, Marsha, *The Political Environment of Economic Reform in Egypt: The Labour Movement vs. Privatisation Revisited*, Amsterdam Middle Eastern Papers, University of Amsterdam, 1995, p. 3.

65 According to Iliya Harik, these subsidies covered "Bread, flour, sugar, tea, coffee, oil, soap, rice, fats, meat, imported and state-produced chicken, milk, medicine, clothing, gasoline, natural gas, diesel, electricity, water, telephones, housing, rents, transportation, movie theatre tickets, automobiles, air conditioners, refrigerators, education and health services, interest rates and exchange rates. Through the last two, one can easily see that almost all products of the public sector are indirectly subsidised". See Iliya Harik, "Subsidization Policies in Egypt: Neither Economic Growth nor Distribution", *International Journal of Middle East Studies*, vol. 24, no. 3. 1992, pp. 485–6.

66 See Samir Youssif, "The Egyptian Private Sector and the Bureaucracy", *Middle Eastern Studies*, 30, no.2, 1994, p. 369.

67 Giacomo Luciani, "Economic Foundations of Democracy and Authoritarianism: The Arab World in Comparative Perspective", *Arab Studies Quarterly*, vol. 10, no.4, 1988, p. 460.

68 *Al-Ahali* newspaper, the mouthpiece of the Tajammu' Party, played a vital role in circulating information on such accusations. See samples of *Al-Ahali*'s articles in R. Springborg, *Mubarak's Egypt*, Boulder CO, Westview Press, 1989, pp. 45–93.

69 Personal interview with 'Asim Shalabi, Cairo, 25 December 2000. These were in addition to promises by the investment companies to solve the problems of housing and food.

70 Maha Azzam, "Egypt: The Islamists and the State Under Mubarak", in Abdel Salam Sidahmed and Anoushiravan Ehteshami (eds.), *Political Fundamentalism*, Boulder CO, Westview Press, 1996, p. 117.

71 Eberhard Kienle, "More Than a Response to Islam: The Political Deliberalization of Egypt in the 1990s", *Middle East Journal*, vol. 52, no. 2, spring 1998, p. 235.

72 Fakhri Al-Hawari, "Dawr rijal al-a'mal fi al-nizam al-siyasi" (The Role of Businessmen in the Political Regime), *Qadaiyya Barlamaniyya*, Cairo, Al-Ahram Centre for Political and Strategic Studies, Issue 4, July 1997, p. 43.

73 Personal interview with 'Asim Shalabi, Cairo, 25 December 2000.

74 Personal interview with Abdul Hamid Al-Ghazali, Cairo, 2 August 2002.

6

THE POLITICISATION OF LEGITIMACY

The regime did not abandon its tolerant attitude towards the Muslim Brothers or launch its aggressive campaign against them until ten years after Mubarak had assumed power. From the 1990s onwards, the Brothers began increasingly to politicise their achievements (or social legitimacy) in society, and to mobilise their lower middle class supporters (or beneficiaries) against the regime's strategic policies, including the policy that continued to deny them legal legitimacy. The politicisation of legitimacy acquired from syndicates, university teachers' clubs and student unions had developed as a gradual process to compensate for the failure of the movement to secure recognition from the courts or the Assembly, and as an alternative platform from which to pursue its long-awaited ambitions. Unlike the courts (which are subservient to the will of the state) or the Assembly (which is dominated by the NDP), the constituencies of the syndicates, university teachers' clubs and student unions were the recipients of the Brothers' social services, and were therefore mobilised, not necessarily in support of the Brothers organisational demands, but certainly in support of greater political freedoms to be given to the opposition in general. This process of conscious politicisation was thus intolerable.

The dramatic shift in the attitude of the Egyptian regime towards Islamists was also a response to local, regional and international developments that influenced the state's perceptions and made it rely increasingly on coercion rather than reconciliation. The 1990s saw the end of the Cold War and the emergence of the United States as the only superpower in the Middle East and in the world in general. In one way or another America applied pressure on many

Arab regimes to conform to the new geopolitical arrangements.
Since the Islamists were seen as powerful opponents of most of these
arrangements, particularly the need to normalise Arab relations with
Israel (manifested partly in the Israeli-Palestinian agreement in
September 1993), they needed, therefore, to be coerced.

As far as the Egyptian regime was concerned, its apprehension
about the Brothers was exacerbated by the movement's organisational connections with the Palestinian *Hamas* movement, and
the unexpected victory of Islamists in Algeria in the1992 elections.
Along with the Gulf War in 1991 and the earthquake in Egypt in
1992, such developments represented a strong context within
which the Brothers could politicise their legitimacy. Certainly in
case of the earthquake, where the relief efforts of the Brothers surpassed those of the state, the regime's image abroad was greatly
impaired, which made Mubarak even more sensitive to the attempts
of the Islamists at politicisation.

The image of the regime had already been shaken by the rise of
Islamist radicalism, which targeted Western tourists and state
officials. The regime's inability to maintain its social contract with the
middle class, and its failure to counter public dissent prompted it to
focus more on its economic performance instead of making political
concessions to the opposition. During the 1990s, eudaemonic
legitimacy became the 'dominant mode', as opposed to legal and
populist modes, which receded in importance. The regime
anticipated that its concessions to the IMF would enable it to reform
the economy, and that in the long term this would generate advan-
tages for all Egyptians, thus restoring their confidence in the state.[1]
However, in order to embark on reform, the regime needed to consolidate its alliance with the business sector, which had been gaining
increasing prominence in the economic and the political spheres
since the early 1990s. Businessmen, rather than political parties and
Islamists in syndicates or investment companies, became the new
forces of the decade and were exploited by the regime in its pursuit
of legitimacy. The result of this shift was economic liberalisation and
political repression.

Mubarak and the 1990 Elections

Once again, and in circumstances similar to those of the 1984
elections, the regime accepted the Supreme Constitutional Court's
ruling that the electoral system adopted in the 1987 elections had

been unconstitutional (since full equality between individual candidates and those on party lists was not guaranteed). The Assembly was dissolved and new elections were called for 1990. The regime reacted to the ruling by replacing the list-based electoral system that had been in use in 1984 and 1987 with a new system of independent candidates. This meant that elections were contested on an exclusively individual basis. Parties could present and promote their candidates, but the candidates would then run as individuals in their respective constituencies, though their party affiliations would still be pronounced. This change automatically cancelled the previous 8 per cent minimum of votes required for parties to be presented in the Assembly. Furthermore, and as had been stipulated in the earlier electoral law, the number of constituencies was increased from 48 to 222, and each constituency was entitled to elect two candidates, at least one of whom had to match the official description of a worker or peasant (*'amil*). By accepting the Court's judgments, the executive appeared to respect the principle of separation of powers, thereby giving proof of its own evolution towards post-authoritarian government.[2]

Though many of the reforms coincided with previous demands by the opposition, they were nevertheless still regarded as favouring the government's interests. The Muslim Brothers and major opposition parties including the New Wafd, *Al-'Amal* and *Al-Ahrar*, were sceptical of the regime's intentions and decided to boycott the elections, arguing that they had not been consulted on the reforms and the Emergency Law, and that elections continued to be held under the supervision of the Ministry of Interior instead of the Ministry of Justice, all of which pre-empted fair results.[3] Furthermore, the division of constituencies was seen as another of the regime's strategies for securing greater successes for the NDP candidates, who would run as individuals supported and funded by the government.[4]

Whereas the regime had accommodated the opposition in 1984 and 1987, and had responded to many of their criticisms, in 1990 it was prepared to alienate the opposition and ignore their demands and threats of boycott. Mubarak no longer seemed eager for the opposition to participate in the political process as he was in the 1980s, nor did he seem to be worried about the implications of their boycott with regard to his political legitimacy. In the 1990 Assembly elections, the NDP won a an expected but nonetheless remarkable majority of 360 of the 444 seats (compared to 309 in

1987), while the number of opposition seats fell from the 1987 figure of 96 to 29; these were occupied mainly by leftists and Nasserists, who had decided not to boycott the elections. Official estimates tended to exaggerate the turnout of voters, arguing that the figure had reached 45 per cent in 1990, but independent estimates indicated that only 20 per cent of those eligible to vote had done so (compared with 50 per cent in 1987). This was a strong indicator of the legitimacy of the entire political process.

The change in the attitude of the regime was the result of changing contexts over two decades. Mubarak came to power in the 1980s in troubled circumstances and needed to calm state-society relations and court the opposition. But as with most Arab leaders who remain in power for some time and are able to consolidate their position in the army and the security apparatuses, his views began to alter and his priorities changed. The 1990s saw deteriorating economic conditions that needed greater state intervention and management, even if this had to be done at the expense of political and social liberties. The regime was on many occasions disappointed with the opposition, which it expected would have been more grateful for, and supportive of its social and economic policies. Already weak and divided, the opposition was seen as exploiting the limited freedom given to them by the state to undermine and criticise the state's performance. This simply played into the hands of the extremists and deepened public frustrations.

Accommodating the Islamists and the rest of the opposition within the political process failed to prevent the rise of violence against the state, nor did it improve economic conditions. The New Wafd and the Muslim Brothers used the Assembly as platform to warn against Egypt's negotiations with the IMF, arguing that economic reform had to be preceded by political reform. Thus while Mubarak was warning his people that with every increase in population, consumption subsidies would increase until eventually there would be "absolutely no funds for anything",[5] the New Wafd was organising public rallies and telling its supporters that "only a legitimate parliament, rather than an illegitimate one" would be able to get the country out of its economic crises.[6] If the shift to economic reform was to be feasible, the executive and the legislature needed to ensure a greater degree of harmony, with minimum opposition and obstructions. Only with a weak political opposition and an increased presence of loyal businessmen in the Assembly would the regime be able to accelerate its negotiations with the IMF and secure the legislation needed for the process. The presence of a leftist opposition headed by the Tajammu' (with only six seats in the Assembly), and critical of privatisation, would serve as proof of a continued democratic margin in the political process, and public frustration would be alleviated by "letting off steam".[7]

The Brothers Boycott Elections

The Muslim Brothers also decided to boycott the 1990 elections for reasons that were unclear, despite its assertion that the boycott was a statement against political corruption and the continuation of the Emergency Law.[8] Hassanain Tawfiq, an independent researcher, argues that the boycott indicated their frustration both with parliament and with their ability to introduce changes in respect of rule by *Shari'a*.[9] Nevertheless, the fact that the Brothers decided vigorously to contest the elections in 1995 and in 2000 shows that the movement continued to be open to all platforms of influence. Others have argued that, according to an agreement with the New Wafd and the Islamic Alliance, the Brothers decided to boycott the elections after they had realised the impossibility of covering all 222 districts as stipulated by the new electoral system.[10]

However, quite apart from the reasons behind the boycott, the decision itself was an indication of the strength that the movement had built up, by comparison with the weak status that had determined its political behaviour during the 1980s. For all Mubarak was relieved at the Brothers' absence from the Assembly, their decision to boycott the elections marked the first formal dispute between them and the regime. One of the Brothers' unpublished internal documents admitted that in addition to their position to the Gulf War and their opposition to Mubarak's third term presidency in 1993, the movement's decision to boycott the elections constituted a further explanation of the regime's anger and a reason for it to revoke its tolerant policies.[11] 'Esam Al-'Aryan, a Brother and former deputy in the 1987 Assembly, criticised the movement's decision to boycott the elections, believing that the regime's decision to confront the movement was encouraged by their absence from parliament.[12] His views reflected those of many younger Brothers, who thought they could continue to build on their successful performance in syndicates and other civil institutions by planning and establishing a political party.

The tendency to translate social legitimacy into legal legitimacy, and the mobilisation involved in the process, was manifested in unsuccessful efforts to establish *Al-Amal* and *Al-Wasat* parties. The idea of the *Amal* (or Hope) Party, initiated and carried out by Mohammad Al-Samman, a Brother from the engineers' syndicate, emerged in the 1990s as a result of the regime's repressive policies against the Islamists in syndicates (exemplified in Law No. 100 for 1993). It represented a frustrated effort to try and end the repression by formalising their existence in a political party. Al-Samman claims that the idea of the Party was an individual endeavour that was not formally sanctioned by the *tanzim*, but was supported by many syndicate members and artisan workers in factories and elsewhere (who constituted 50 per cent of the Party membership in compliance with the Parties' Law). Al-Samman admits that if the Party had been approved by the Parties' Committee, he was prepared to bring it under the control and management of the Brothers. Initially, however, he presented the Party as representing the artisan workers (*al-'umal al-hirafiyyin*) and denied any connections with the Muslim Brothers:

> When my application was looked at by the Parties' Committee, I made sure I distanced myself from the Brothers and kept a low profile with the media. In my statements and interviews to the press, I emphasised that the Party had nothing to do with the Ikhwan. I even made sure that the founders and immediate supporters of the Party were not affiliated with the Brotherhood.[13]

Al-Amal's manifesto was far simpler and less politically controversial than the manifestos of *Al-Islah* and *Al-Shura*. It focused on five issues: terrorism, drugs, tourism, economic reform, and the role of religion and morals in human development. On terrorism, it stressed the need to widen public participation and the opportunity for all political trends to express themselves and fulfil their role in assisting and developing society.[14] With regard to economic reform, priority should be given to economic development through increased exports, improved tourism, improvement of the performance of the Suez Canal, and a focus on industry and agriculture as important revenue sources.[15] The manifesto was immediately rejected by the Parties' Committee, apparently on technical grounds, and, on appeal, by the court in 1998. Al-Samman maintains that the *Amal* was obviously rejected on the basis of the regime's assumption that it was a front for the Brotherhood.

The *Wasat* (or Centre) Party, which emerged in 1996, was a more visible front for the Brothers than *Al-Amal*, and was also rejected by both the Parties' Committee and the court. *Al-Wasat* too was founded by a group of engineers, led by Abu Al-'Ila Madi and Salah Abdul Karim.[16] Both were of the same generation as Al-Samman, and were quite popular and powerful in their syndicate. However, *Al-Wasat*'s manifesto differed from that of *Al-Amal*, combining a more developed version of the *Islah* Party's manifesto (see Chapter Five),[17] with the modifications that represented the *tanzim*'s new vision with regard to religion, *hizbiyya*, women and non-Muslims, and the possibility of accommodating them into the membership of the Party.[18]

Both the *Amal* and the *Wasat*, spearheaded by syndicate activists rather than by professional politicians, in the Egyptian sense, confirmed to the regime that the presence of Islamists in these social spaces was not an 'innocent' endeavour, but was being exploited to further their political aspirations and compete with the state for power. With the absence of formal political platforms for the Brothers to express their views and demands, their activism in syndicates and on campuses became more political, as the state increased its repression.

The Politicisation of Legitimacy

An important reason for the increased politicisation of syndicates and campuses was the lack of an alternative and effective platform for the Brothers who, while tacitly tolerated, continued to be denied legal existence. And what caused the process of politicisation to have such an impact on the regime was that it followed a period of impressive performance in the field of welfare services, supported by a powerful *tanzim*. In other words, politicisation would not have been so powerful had there not been a social base of beneficiaries to support the movement, and a powerful *tanzim* to carry its achievements beyond its own limited scope.

During their five years of absence from the Assembly (1990 to 1995), the Ikhwan focused more on the syndicates and on the political opportunities they provided. In 1992, they secured an unexpected success in the elections to the board of council of the lawyers' syndicates. According to Nabil Abdul Fatah, this was one of

Egypt's most significant political events since the assassination of
Sadat in 1981,[19] since the success of the Brothers in the lawyers'
syndicate was perceived differently by the regime. This was because
the lawyers' syndicates, in contrast to the medical or engineers'
syndicates, comprised an already politicised constituency and were
therefore more susceptible to mobilisation.[20] An informant with
contacts in the Gulf told me that when Mubarak visited the United
Arab Emirates following the Ikhwan's unexpected success in the
lawyers' syndicate, he remarked to Shaikh Zayd Al-Nihyan: "Can
you believe that the Ikhwan won the elections in the lawyers'
syndicate? I think if they competed against me in a presidential
election, they would win that as well!" This may of course be
apocryphal, and Mubarak's comment might have been an
exaggeration, but it does illustrate the extent of the influence
wielded by the Brothers during the 1990s.[21]

The Brothers in other syndicates continued to increase the
services provided to their constituents, before the regime intervened
and brought all activities to a halt. In the engineers' syndicate, which
included over 230,000 members, the number of beneficiaries of the
health scheme had increased by 36 per cent since 1989, while the
beneficiaries from the social solidarity scheme, which provided
interest free loans or assistance, was 57 per cent higher in 1993 than
when it was first launched in 1991.[22] The same was true of the
medical syndicate where the beneficiaries of the health scheme rose
by 54 per cent in 1993 compared to 1988, and where the number of
beneficiaries of the social solidarity scheme doubled from 3,500 to
7,000, over a period of only six months in 1993.[23]

Furthermore, attitudes to the performance of the Islamists in
syndicates could be seen in the rise in voter turnout in the
syndicate elections. In the medical syndicate elections in 1990,
there were 22,000 voters, compared with previous years when,
according to an Islamist source, 17,000 voted for the Brothers.[24]
With an enhanced social legitimacy, and a powerful *tanzim*, and
prompted by two main episodes (the 1991 Gulf War and the 1992
earthquake), the Brothers' politicisation efforts became increasingly confident.

The Gulf War

The Ikhwan were quick to condemn Iraq's invasion of Kuwait on
2 August 1990. Their request to Saddam Hussein, the former Iraqi

president, to withdraw his forces from Kuwait, was essentially in accordance with the position taken by the Egyptian regime.[25] However, Western intervention in the crisis soon created a break between Mubarak and the Brothers, who condemned such involvement and protested against the bombing of Iraq.[26] Although absent from parliament, the Brothers used their control over syndicates and campuses to express their views against the regime's policies in support of the war.[27] In mobilising the masses against the populist legitimacy of the President, who had sanctioned the Egyptian army's participation with the Western Alliance against a neighbouring Arab country, the Islamists were seen as exploiting the spaces tolerated by the state.[28] Moreover, the resources of the *tanzim* were somehow merged with the resources of the syndicates to orchestrate a more powerful and effective campaign against the regime.

Prompted by the invasion of Kuwait and the threats of war, syndicates under the control of the Brothers began to form coalitions to co-ordinate their actions, and for the first time in the syndicates' history since 1952, a Committee for Co-ordinating the Action of Syndicates (*lagnat tanseeq al-'amal al-niqabi*) was established in 1990. The idea behind the Committee was not new, having been thought of by the Brothers syndicates in the late 1980s,[29] However it was also realised in the 1990s as a response to the state's efforts to create a Union for Professional Syndicates, similar to trade unions, in which it could exert greater control and offset the growing hegemony of Islamists. The formation of the Committee was therefore seen as an institutionalised effort to undermine the corporatist controls of the regime and to deprive it of its long assumed privileges. In what was considered a provocative statement, the Committee condemned the Western presence in the Gulf and held the government responsible for the safety of Egyptians working in Kuwait and in Iraq.[30]

Infuriated by the tone of this statement, the regime forced the *naqibs* of the syndicates that were not under the Brothers' control to withdraw from the coalition of the Committee and to comply with the regime's official policy. This certainly weakened the Committee but not to the extent of ending its political campaign against the regime. In a second statement, signed in the name of fewer syndicates, the Committee harshly condemned Egyptian involvement in the war, and called for the immediate return of the army.[31] 'Esam Al-'Aryan, former General Secretary of the medical syndicate, contributed to the wording of the statement and believes that it marked a turning point in the relations between Mubarak and the Muslim Brothers: According to Al-'Aryan:

> I see it as the straw that broke the camel's back. When we met in the medical syndicate to write the statement, we did so in a very provocative manner. Only then do I assume that the regime said to itself: 'that is enough. The syndicates have overstepped the line', where the lines comprised the state's foreign policy and the army.[32]

The signatories of the statement soon became victims of a state-sponsored smear campaign, articulated by the media and by powerful officials, such as Yusuf Wali and Kamal Al-Shadhili, who accused Islamists of "disloyalty" and "treason" and of receiving funds from Saddam.[33] The syndicates became the new focus for the attention and intervention of the security services, and dozens of members, most of whom were also members of the movement, were harassed and arrested.

On the other hand, even though the regime was quite brutal with the Brothers, the movement was still able in its own way to influence the religious discourse of the state. In response to the Ikhwan's criticisms of Egypt's support for the Americans in the Gulf War, and the religious significance this had for the regime's populist legitimacy, Mubarak's NDP was forced to declare that "Egypt was not a secular state but an Islamic one", and to put itself forward as the representative of the correct understanding of the Islamic religion.[34]

The Earthquake

The earthquake was another event that demonstrated to the state not only the extent of the organised power of the Brothers, but also its political implications. Once again, the Brothers employed their resources in the syndicates, as well as the resources of the *tanzim*, to rescue the victims of the earthquake. In the process they publicised their political ambitions. The presence of the *tanzim* in urban and rural areas and the presence of the Brothers in the syndicates, ensured a rapid and efficient transfer of resources towards rescuing the victims. This was done in a manner that outstripped the performance of the state. According to one Brother who was responsible for delivering aid from the medical syndicates to the afflicted areas, it would have been more or less impossible to do this without the connections of the *tanzim*:

> How else could we have reached the victims, if it had not been for our members who lived in that particular locality and reported to us the extent of the damage? It was through such contacts that we were able to distribute our financial and material aid properly, as we otherwise have had no clue as to who needed what.[35]

The performance of the Brothers during the earthquake was noted at home, and more critically, as far as the regime was concerned, abroad. The Western media noted the contrast between the Islamists' success and the state's failure in rescuing the victims and used this to infer a possible Islamist takeover of Egypt. This, combined with news of contacts and dialogue between American officials and the leadership of the Muslim Brothers, exacerbated the regime's fears. Mubarak had been in China when the earthquake happened, but returned immediately to Egypt not only to co-ordinate the state's efforts, but also because he was worried about his image abroad.

Mubarak's fears were exacerbated not only by the CNN and BBC news reports, which highlighted the achievements of the Islamists and their growing influence over Egyptian society, but also by what he saw as political exploitation by the Brothers during the earthquake. In the midst of its relief efforts, the Brothers displayed banners on tents and in front of relief headquarters that carried slogans, such as "Islam is the Solution", that had been used during the movement's political campaign in the 1987 elections. Abu Al-'Ila Madi, founder of the *Wasat* Party, and now an independent Islamist, criticised the use of such slogans since they confirmed the sceptics' view that the Brothers were exploiting tragedies to make inappropriate political statements.[36] Indeed, Al-'Aryan believes that the regime might even have appreciated the Brothers' efforts if their contribution had been silent and a-political. As evidence for this, Al-'Aryan, who played an active role in the relief efforts during the earthquake, notes a conversation between himself and the head of Cairo security:

> The head of security assured me that the government was happy with what we were doing, and encouraged me to

continue to give the people blankets and shelter. However he was unhappy with our political banners and slogans. The medical syndicate accepted his orders to remove these banners, but unfortunately other Brothers, from outside the syndicate, would come and put them up again.[37]

The medical syndicate's response to the security order might have been the exception to the rule, which, in the words of one journalist, was that the Brothers in syndicates acted as a "shadow government",[38] or, as Ahmad Al-Nahas, a Brother and Treasurer of the engineers' syndicate in Alexandria, remarked, "as political spokesmen" for the Muslim Brothers, not just during an earthquake or a Gulf War, but on other general issues as well:

> Syndicates provided us with a political platform, with legal power and with a media organisation. Through them we could publish as many newspapers and magazines as we wished, without the complications of having otherwise to have a license. It was facilities and privileges such as these that made the syndicates act as our political spokesmen for at least eighty per cent of the time.[39]

The Brothers activated the political role of the syndicates to compensate for the ineffectiveness of the National Assembly, and used the means and resources to hand to eliminate the political apathy that was endemic among the lower middle classes. Following its decision to boycott the 1990 elections, the Brothers used the syndicates to convene meetings and conferences on political reform, in which representatives of political parties and of the *tanzim* were invited to participate. The medical syndicate, some of whose active members had run as candidates for the Brothers in previous parliamentary elections and in the 1995 elections, distributed questionnaires similar in nature and purpose to those distributed by the Brothers on campuses, asking members to comment on the 1990 elections.[40] A large number of the questions used the elections as pretext to raise broader political issues related to the Muslim Brotherhood and to the matter of their political and legal rights to exist.[41] Had it not been for the syndicates, which were recognised by the state, the Brothers, as an outlawed organisation, would obviously not have been permitted to hold such conferences and distribute such questionnaires.

The political role of syndicates was recognised by the syndicate laws, and had existed in the past before the Brothers gained control of them. We have seen, for instance, how the lawyers' syndicate, when it was controlled by nationalists in the 1980s, played an active role in opposing Egypt's peace with Israel. The nationalists used the syndicates as a platform to organise meetings and conferences on the issue. 'Esam Hashish, a leading Brother in the engineers' syndicate, rejected the notion that the movement politicised the syndicates; rather, the Brothers used their constitutional rights to raise and discuss political issues, as had been done in the past.[42] The difference, however, was that the Brothers had become an outlawed organisation. Not only did this create further tension between the movement and the state, but it also influenced its political discourse. Their political views were not necessarily those of the people whom they represented, but were in most if not all cases, those of the *tanzim*.

Furthermore, this organisational connection between the Brothers in syndicates and the membership in the *tanzim* led to confusion as to the exact role and purpose of the syndicates. An internal unpublished study written by a known Brother and directed to the leadership of the movement, admitted to the mix-up in the minds of many Brothers, and cited certain examples as proof of this.[43] According to the study: (a) most of the employees in syndicates belonged to the Brothers; (b) syndicates were used by the *tanzim* as venues to hold private meetings; (c) Ikhwan company owners made profits from the sale of consumer durables that were organised by syndicates; (d) guest speakers invited to give talks to the syndicate, regardless of their suitability for the subject discussed, were often from the *tanzim*.

Although he had not seen this study, Mahmoud Abdul Maqsud, a Brother and the General Secretary of the pharmacist' syndicate, agreed with its findings. However, unlike Hashish, he admitted that the *tanzim* played a role in politicising syndicates in accordance with its own agenda, and that this was one of the principal reasons for Mubarak's anger.[44]

Amani Qandil has revealed that following the political role played by the Brothers during the Gulf War and in the earthquake, and the sudden loss of the lawyers' syndicate to the *tanzim* in 1992, a highly-placed political and security official in the Egyptian government asked her to write a confidential report on the Muslim Brothers and on their strategies for influencing syndicates:

Obviously the regime still did not have a clue about what was going on in the syndicates, but was troubled and puzzled by the ability of the Islamists to secure a majority in their elections. In my report to the regime, I tried to identify the mechanisms of the Brothers' influence and to explain why they had become a legitimate force in syndicates.[45]

Although Qandil did not wish to disclose the detailed contents of the report, but was prepared to discuss her findings. First, the Brothers were astute in utilising syndicates as an effective platform, and as an alternative to a weak and unfair political system which denied them existence. Second, a major reason for the Ikhwan's success in syndicates was that they were able to address the concerns of the lower middle classes. Third, they did this in a highly professional and organised manner.[46]

A year after this report was written, the government issued Law No. 100 for 1993, which allegedly aimed to guarantee democracy in the syndicate elections and to prevent an 'organised minority' (or al-'aqlia al-munazma) from winning over others. The law specified that for the elections to be valid there must be at least a 50 per cent attendance and if the turnout was lower, the elections could be re-run twice, in which case a turnout of 33 per cent guaranteed their validity.[47] However, if the 33 per cent turnout was not attained in the second rerun, the syndicate would fall under the administration of officials appointed by the government until new elections were held.[48] In all cases, the elections were to be supervised by the judiciary. The law was an obvious response to the Ikhwan's unexpected rise to authority in the lawyers' syndicate in 1992,[49] and after they had taken control of 19 branches of the syndicate in other provinces.[50]

The State vs. the Islamists

The 1990s had already become a troubled period for Mubarak. Difficult economic conditions coincided with a further increase in the threat of Islamist violence, which began to harm revenues coming from tourism and more dangerously to target officials as high as the President himself. According to Hala Mustafa, an expert on Islamism in Egypt, Islamist militancy constituted the greatest challenge to the political and social stability of the country.[51] Table 6.1 illustrates the extent of this threat and contrasts the rise in violence and various kinds of protests in the early 1990s with the previous decade.

Table 6.1. Religious violence and social disturbances, 1980s-early 1990s.[52]

Year	mass protest		Vandalism	assassination	attempted assassinassions
	demonstrations	strikes			
81	1		2	1	
82					
83					
84	8	1	1		
85	7	1			
86	14	9	8		3
87	16	4	3		1
88	33	1	6		
89	42	16	4		
90	30	13	9		
91	31	20	20		
92	33	28	50		
93	40	40	45	1	3

According to a semi-official report, in 1990 alone there were as many as 51 confrontations between the Islamists and the security apparatus, in which over 115 people died. In 1992 the assassination by Islamists of Faraj Fuda, an outspoken critic of religious extremism, coincided with the rise of the Islamist threat in Algeria, and the assassination of Muhammad Boudiaf, the Algerian president. The incident was a personal shock that by his own admission left Mubarak "shattered".[53] The following year, Egypt saw two failed assassination attempts against two senior officials, Safwat Al-Sharif, the Minister of Information, and Hasan Al-Alfi, the Minister of Interior, who had succeeded Zaki Badr.

There has been speculation as to why the 1990s witnessed this exceptional rise in violence. Some semi-official newspapers, such as *Al-Jumhuriyya*, attributed it to the dismissal in 1990 of Zaki Badr, Minister of Interior, who was said to have been able to contain the Islamists, although certain individuals, like Hassan Al-Sayyid, attributed the rise of violence to the decline in the legitimacy of the regime. Al-Sayyid argued that social and religious violence represented an extreme indication of the wider public disappointment and frustration with the performance of the regime, which had failed to satisfy people's needs.[54] Increased violence against the state and its officials prompted

THE POLITICISATION OF LEGITIMACY

a radical response, which reflected on society and on the attitude of
the state towards the Islamists in general.

Repression of Campuses

University campuses, like syndicates, were also used as political
platforms for the Brothers' *tanzim* to voice its criticisms of the
regime. During the Gulf Crisis, campuses joined forces with
syndicates and university teachers' clubs in organising demonstrations to campaign against the war on Iraq and the participation
of the Egyptian forces in the alliance. Questionnaires were distributed to students at Alexandria University asking for their comments on the Egyptian government's decision to send its forces to
the Gulf, the reasons behind the presence of the United States in
the Gulf, and how they perceived Israel and the American presence
in the region.[55]

Questionnaires were also used on other political issues. During
the *Intifadah* in 1987 and the years that followed, students had been
mobilised to challenge Egyptian efforts to establish peace in the
region and campuses were used to raise interest in the Palestinian
case. A questionnaire on Palestine distributed at Cairo University
stated that it was an attempt to survey the opinions of university
students "regarding an issue that has engaged the mind of the
world for many years. It . . . will reflect the opinions of students who
represent the educated generation and the future of our beloved
country."[56] Again, students were asked to comment on questions
like: "Do you care about the Palestinian question?"; "How did the
Intifadah change your views with respect to the Palestinian issue?";
"How do you see the role of the Egyptian media in covering the
events of the *Intifadah*?"; and "What is the role of the Egyptian
citizen with regard to the Palestinian issue as well as the *Intifadah*?".

In addition, the *tanzim* used campuses to mobilise students who
were eligible to vote for its candidates in parliament. Students at
Cairo University received questionnaires asking them to tick from
a list that included the Islamic Alliance and *Al-Tajammu'* the name
of the party for which they would vote in the 1987 elections: in this
instance 60 per cent of two thousands students ticked the Islamic
Alliance as their preferred choice. Hilmi Al-Jazzar, former President
of the Student Union at Cairo University, admitted that the results
of this, and similar questionnaires distributed on campuses elsewhere were communicated to the political section within the

tanzim,[57] which confirms what was mentioned earlier on the scope and powers of the *tanzim*.

Increasingly, these and other manifestations of activism attracted the attention of, and further interventions by the security services with regard to matters on campuses. The use of tear gas became a frequent tactic to deter student demonstrators during the 1990s. Student activities were closely monitored and, according to Jamal Mohammad, an Ikhwan student leader at Cairo University until 1995, functions that were considered political in nature (e.g. a conference, an exhibition, or posters) were banned.[58]

University administrations also took part in the regime's campaign to restrict Ikhwan activism, and began to apply new policies that were intended to undermine the autonomy of the student unions and their freedom to organise functions and activities. This was achieved through various means, one of which was the introduction of what was called Student Leadership (*al-riadah al-tulabiyya*). This required the student union to seek formal written permission from the administration before holding a function. In addition, a member of staff was entitled to supervise and in extreme cases to block a particular function.[59] In conjunction with the Ministry of Youth and Sports, universities also helped promote a rival student organisation called *Horras* (the name of an ancient pharaonic god) to counter the appeal of the Ikhwan.[60] Students belonging to this organisation were supplied with substantial funds to hold social functions that would attract students. However, *Horras* failed to create a powerful impact since it was unable to provide proper welfare services and because it tended to focus instead on entertainment activities like concerts that did not appeal to all students. It was also discredited for being an obvious agent of the state, and it was widely rumoured that it mishandled its budget. From the mid-1990s the organisation became even weaker as a result of internal disputes and the departure of its main patron, Abdul Mun'em 'Umara, the Minister of Youth and Sport.[61]

The security apparatus also began to step up its intervention in election campaigns and results, in a heightened attempt to obstruct the Brothers' electoral gains.[62] Where they had removed the names of the Islamist candidates in the 1980s, in the 1990s the names of all the candidates began to be removed, except for those who were approved by the university administration as being loyal to the regime. As if this was not sufficient, candidates continued to be harassed and arrested. This had been happening occasionally at Cairo University since 1992, but after 1995 became a regular practice.

Potential candidates and voters were also deterred from taking part in election campaigns through the use of verbal and physical threats, to the extent that security personnel would go to candidates' homes before the elections and threaten their parents. They would be told that if their sons intended to run for the elections they would be suspended from the university. Candidates who were not deterred by such threats were arrested at the beginning of the academic year and released only few days before their mid-year exams. If they then failed the exams, they were expected to repeat the entire year. Another coercive tactic was to pronounce a holiday on the day of the election, whereupon the university would close its doors, and students would stay at home. In cases where the student turnout was lower than the quorum stipulated by the Student Charter, the university chancellor had the right to appoint the members of the student union.

Repression of Teachers' Faculty Clubs

The security services' attitude to the Brothers in the teachers' faculty clubs was not very different from their approach to student unions. At Asyut, Alexandria and Zaqaziq, the elected councils of the university teachers' clubs were disbanded and other more compliant groups were appointed. Where this was found to be difficult, as was the case at Mansura and the Suez Canal, state-sponsored and informal staff bodies were established to compete with those that had been formally elected. Elections would frequently be delayed, with the outcome being the appointment of a new board that was loyal to the government. Furthermore, the clubs' privileges in electing the deans of faculties were undermined, when deans were instead appointed by the higher ranks of the administration within the university.

Economic Reform

During the 1990s, the Egyptian regime embarked more seriously on economic reform (or al-'islah al-'iqtisadi). This was in contrast to the stabilisation that had characterised the period of the 1980s, although some analysts, such as Lofgren and Harik, are correct in arguing that various types of reform had existed since the mid-1980s.[63]

When examining the performance of the regime during the 1990s, one should distinguish between its efforts and achievements on the macroeconomic level, and those concerned with the microeconomic level. The regime's agreements in 1991 with the IMF and with the World Bank were expected to reduce budgetary and external imbalances, being concerned with issues related to subsidies, interest rates, the exchange rate, treasury bonds and general sales tax. On this front, the regime did make some progress. During the seven years following the start of the reforms agreed in 1991, inflation decreased from 20 per cent to 4 per cent, the Egyptian pound appreciated in value, foreign exchange reserves increased from US$6 billion to US$20 billion, and the budgetary deficit decreased from 15 per cent to about 1.3 per cent of GDP.[64] Such progress enabled Egypt to benefit from the various instalments of the loan offered by the IMF and from the gradual forgiving of its external debts. Part of this progress was also facilitated by the lucrative rewards received as a result of Egypt's backing for the Gulf War, although the gains were soon overshadowed by the decline in remittances following the return of large numbers of Egyptians who had been working in the Gulf and Iraq.[65]

Even so, the regime was unable to translate this progress into success on the microeconomic level, which was related more to the living conditions of average Egyptians, particularly those who relied on the public sector, and were therefore victims of its erosion. According to a study funded by the United States Agency for International Development (USAID), the percentage of the poor in urban and rural areas in Egypt increased from 20.7 per cent in 1990/91 to 44.3 per cent in 1995/96. This meant that over the first half of the 1990s, a much larger percentage of the population fell below the poverty line.[66] As Table 6.1 indicates, the number of strikes rose from 13 in 1990 to 40 in 1993, and demonstrations from 30 to 40 over the same period. This, together with the rise of Islamist extremism and other forms of social disturbances, indicates that the regime's legitimacy was open to question,[67] and that this legitimacy, at least in the short term, was not being rescued by improvements on the macroeconomic level.[68]

The regime was aware of the link between its legitimacy, and its ability to maintain its social contrast with society, especially the lower middle classes and the poor, contrary to some views that tended to assume that the regime did not care about them.[69] Khalid Munir is an Egyptian journalist with connections to official circles and to the opposition. When we met in his office at *Al-Hayat* newspaper in Cairo he stressed that government officials were "terrified" of the *harafeesh*, who were usually extremely poor, unemployed, and homeless and lived in the cemeteries. He also believed that the regime would not have conceded to pressures from the IMF, if this had threatened its stability:

> In Egypt, the state might abandon you and me but it would not abandon its own existence. It might concede to pressures on international issues, but not on local ones that would lead it into a state of confrontation with Egyptians. The regime conceded to the IMF only when it believed that if it did so it would not be destabilised.[70]

This view is confirmed by Denis Sullivan, who argues that the state's fear of social upheaval is one reason why the political stability of the status quo takes precedence over economic objectives.[71] Economic reform in the 1990s was neither dramatic nor radical, despite the regime's rhetoric to international organisations and investors. In 1992 the Mubarak government announced that over the five years between 1992 and 1997 it would sell the assets or government shares of 74 companies. However, as far as the Egyptian public were concerned, and as Figure 6.1 indicates, no serious privatisation occurred in practice until after 1995.[72]

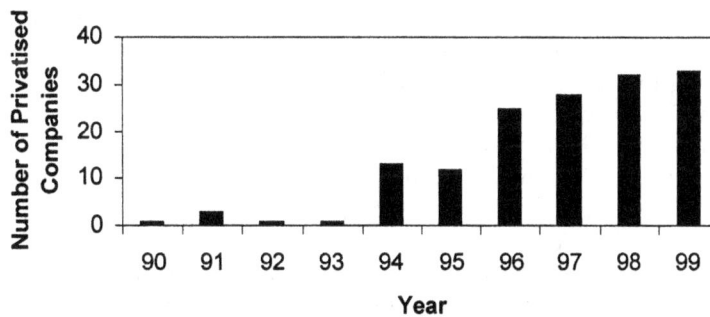

FIGURE 6.1. Privatised companies in Egypt, 1990–1999.

It is important to realise that the increase in privatisation did not mean the withdrawal of the state, which ironically grew more authoritarian. According to Marat Terterov, who kindly provided me with numbers of privatised companies adopted in Figure 6.1, while the private sector was encouraged to partake in the management and development of the public sector, ownership continued to belong largely to the state.[73] However, it can also be argued that privatisation of the public sector did weaken the role of the state in the provision of welfare benefits,[74] which had already weakened since the mid-1980s because of the oil crisis and poor management of the public sector.[75]

During the 1990s, the regime made sure that the social effects of the austerity measures necessitated by the process of reform were balanced by strong palliative measures.

Palliative Measures

Through its political discourse the regime confirmed that economic reform was not contrary to the social role of the state, which would continue to support the impoverished, the unemployed graduates, and those dependent on the public sector. Alongside some of its economic austerity measures, and with the help of the IMF and international creditors, the government introduced a series of social fund programmes, aimed at helping young graduates into employment and providing them with new skills and training. The schemes included the Social Fund Programme with a budget of US$600 million, the Social Fund for Development (SFD), with a budget of US$613 million that mainly provided funds to help create new employment opportunities for young graduates, and the Social Fund for Public Works, which aimed to provide funds for small factories in rural areas and short-term employment.[76] Young graduates were encouraged to take soft loans to establish their own small enterprises, or to acquire up to 5 acres each of land in new development areas that could be reclaimed with government support.[77] Part of the Social Fund's budget covered the expenses of essential public services in rural communities (e.g. the supply of water, sewerage, electricity), which had been neglected by the state during the 1980s. The poor were also given assistance by the Ministry of Social Insurance and Social Affairs. They were provided with free education and literacy programmes by the Ministry of Education, given free health care in local surgeries and public hospitals by the Ministry of Health, received subsidies for bread, wheat flour, sugar and edible oils from the Ministry of Trade and Supply, and were eligible for aid related to the development of rural lands through the Ministry of Agriculture and Land Reclamation.[78]

These social funds were intended to offset the impact of the reforms, but they did not do much to bolster the image of the regime. Living conditions continued to deteriorate, unemployment increased from 8.6 per cent in 1990 to at least 11.3 per cent in 1995, and salaries remained fixed, despite cuts in subsidies and rising prices. Despite state-sponsored projects related to the development of agricultural and rural lands, the government continued to favour expenditure on the modernisation of urban cities like Cairo and Alexandria, in order to attract foreign investors and tourists.

The Confiscation of Islamist Finances

Wherever they were allowed to function, the Brothers tapped into the failures of the regime and utilised the partial withdrawal imposed on the state by the reforms to further their welfare role.[79] In addition to their achievements in syndicates, the significance of the Islamists could also be sensed through the increasing number of charity organisations controlled by the Islamists, which rose from 35 per cent in the mid-1980s to 43 per cent in 1991.[80] The regime did not mind the expansion of these organisations, provided they refrained from politics and were prepared to assist the state in sorting out the consequences of its withdrawal. However, the Brothers were not prepared to do this.

As far as reform was concerned, the Brothers continued to voice their criticisms of the reform and to cast doubts on plans to sell the public sector to foreign investors. The former *murshid*, Ma'mun Al-Hudaybi, insisted that if the government allowed foreigners to purchase Egyptian companies, it must reveal their names and identities to the public as a way of assuring them of their national independence.[81] 'Esam Al-'Aryan also questioned the integrity and independence the IMF and the World Bank, which he believed were dominated by the United States and by its desire to integrate Egypt into the global market, irrespective of the particularities of domestic culture and economy.[82] In his book on the privatisation of the public sector, Shihab Al-Din, an Ikhwan journalist, warned of the consequences for both the state and the society of privatising the health, housing and education sectors.[83]

As far as political activities were concerned, the Ikhwan did not believe that the social, economic and political spheres and activities were separate from each other. This affected not only informal organisations but also private businesses that were owned and run by members of the Brotherhood. In February 1992, the security services raided the Salsabil Computer Company and arrested its owners, Hasan 'Izz Al-Din Malek and Khairat Al-Shatir (the latter was a senior member of the *tanzim* and a former member of the board of directors of the Islamic International Bank of Investment). The two were charged with belonging to a secret group and holding private meetings within the company to plan for the overthrow of the government.[84]

The security services also claimed to have discovered disks containing a detailed plan to take over the country and establish an Islamic state. The plan on the seized disks was called the Consolidation Plan (*khutat al-tamkin*) and outlined the ways in which the movement could further its control over the state and society, and how it should continue to penetrate state institutions and syndicates. There were also guidelines related to their attitude to 'others', including the regime, the Copts, political parties, pressure groups, Islamic movements, the Jews and the United States. Apart from the plan, the fears of the regime were exacerbated when it later discovered that the Salsabil Company had sold many computers to the army and to the intelligence services. The Salsabil case later became an excuse for the regime to launch a more organised campaign against economic ventures by Islamists which, according to its propaganda, were no more than fronts for militant activities against the state.

The government then terminated its partnership with Khalid 'Auda, the entrepreneur from Asyut whose workers were involved in a clothes-manufacturing scheme for government employees (*kisa' al-'amilin bi al-dawla*). This resulted not only in bankruptcy and closure of the factory, but also in loss of employment for the workers. When 'Auda complained personally to the President about what had happened, he was told that the scheme had been suspended as a result of the economic reform, since the state was no longer responsible for providing subsidised clothing for the public sector.[85]

'Auda accused Mubarak of having lied to the Egyptians in the 1980s when he promised that he would not sell profit-making public sector enterprises, yet had terminated the clothing scheme which 'Auda believed was generating income for the public sector. In addition to the fact of his belonging to the *tanzim* and the effect this had on his business, 'Auda thinks that his businesses were also harmed by the reforms and by the mismanagement of the economy. During the 1980s, and with the blessing of the regime, 'Auda's factories flourished, but they deteriorated in the 1990s, largely because the workforce contracted, either through fear of harassment by the security services, or because of the recession. In the *Al-Buniyyan Al-Marsos* brick factory, the number of employees declined from 100 in 1988 to 25 in 1991, and over the same period numbers employee numbers diminished from 120 to 50 in *Al-Fath* wood factory. 'Auda's *Al-Ribat* clothing factory, which had employed 100 workers in 1988, was closed in 1991 when the state-subsidised scheme *kisa' al-'amilin bi al-dawla* was terminated.

'Auda's employees were exposed to further harassment from the police when he decided to run for the parliamentary elections in 2000 as a candidate for the Asyut district. When I met him in Cairo, he talked about his experiences with the security forces in Asyut during the election campaign:

> The security services arrested 26 of the workers in one of my factories and put them in prison until the day after the elections, because they had been assisting me in the campaign. Others who were putting posters on the walls and distributing pamphlets were also arrested and jailed. Of course most of the workers were terrified. Not only did they give up helping me with my campaigning but some of them even left the factory.[86]

After that, 'Auda was targeted by the security services who set out to block his attempts to expand his businesses. One of the ways through which this was achieved with 'Auda as well as with other Ikhwan businessmen was by denying them the licences or commercial registration (al-sigil al-tigari) that they needed to establish a business.

Conclusion

This chapter aimed to show the extent to which the confrontation between Mubarak and the Muslim Brothers in the 1990s was related to their mutual quest for eudaemonic legitimacy. This search occurred in the context of national and international developments that exacerbated the move towards confrontation. The 1990s emphasised the regime's need to refocus on its weakened eudae-monic legitimacy in response to increased social grievances and Islamic militancy. This led to the emergence of a new approach to legitimacy, alliances and tendencies. The regime bargained for part of its eudaemonic legitimacy to be rescued through a long-term process of economic reform that would not be obstructed or challenged by political criticisms and practices. It started to abandon its conciliatory efforts, alienate the political opposition, and affirm its alliances with the commercial elites. The outcome of this shift was a weak Assembly in 1990 and an agreement with the IMF in 1991. Meanwhile it tightened its security grip and relied increasingly on coercive measures to confront the Islamic threat, while appealing simultaneously to religious legitimacy and insti-tutions to accommodate religious grievances. At the same time the regime continued to advance precautionary policies and pro-grammes intended to assure the sceptics that reform did not imply abandonment of the state's social role.

The regime's growing dilemma of legitimacy was exacerbated by the crystallisation of the Muslim Brother's social legitimacy in various lower middle-class institutions. By utilising the state's weak social contract the Ikhwan was able to erect its own Islamic contract. This undermined the regime's contract and disturbed its cor-poratist links. This social legitimacy was then exploited in a political form, not only in reaction to major developments such as the Gulf War and the earthquake, but also in reaction to the regime's persistent refusal to recognise the organisation.

The movement then made political use of its organised social legitimacy to mobilise lower middle class beneficiaries against the state's official denial of the Brothers. This organised and political form of social legitimacy challenged the regime's own quest for legitimacy and caused Mubarak to revoke his tolerant policies towards the Ikhwan and confiscate the spaces he had opened up in the 1980s. This move might have deterred the Ikhwan and weakened their legitimacy, but at the same time it undermined the legal legitimacy of Mubarak and exacerbated his legitimacy crisis. This legitimacy crisis was more noticeable in the mid-1990s.

Notes

1 Mahmoud Abdul Hai, *Economic Reform in Egypt (Motives and Orientations)*, Cairo, Institute of National Planning, 1993, p. 11.
2 Eberhard Kienle, *A Grand Delusion*, London, I. B. Tauris, 2001, p. 52.

3   Hassanain Ibrahim, *Al-Ikhwan al-muslimun wal-nizam al-siyasi al-misri* (The Muslim Brothers and the Egyptian Political Regime), Beirut, Dar Al-Tali'a, 1998, pp. 411–417.
4   *Al-Wafd*, 4 October 1990.
5   Mubarak's speech on May Day, 3 May 1990, reported in *Al-Ahram*, 4 May 1990.
6   See article by Ahmad Fu'ad, "Public Demands Political Reform to Confront Our Difficult Problems", in *Al-Wafd*, 25 March 1990. The article is based on interviews with more than 42 young Wafdists.
7   Personal interview with Khalid Munir, Cairo, 4 July 2002.
8   Nabil Abdul Fattah (ed.), *Intikhabat majlis al-sha'b 1990* (The National Assembly Elections, 1990), Cairo, Al-Ahram Centre for Political and Strategic Studies, 1991, p. 113.
9   Hassanain Ibrahim, *Al-Ikhwan, op.cit.*, p. 416.
10 N. El-Mikawy, *The Building of Consensus in Egypt's Transition Process*, Cairo, American University in Cairo Press, 1999, p. 93.
11 *Al-Azma al-muntada: ilaqat al-nizam al-misri bi al-ikhwan al-muslimin, al-mazahir, al-asbab, al-nat'ij*, (The Continuous Crisis: the Egyptian Regime's Relations with the Muslim Brothers: the phenomenon, reasons and results), internal unpublished document, undated, p. 5.
12 Personal interview with 'Esam Al-'Aryan, Cairo, 19 December 2000.
13 Personal interview with Mohammad Al-Samman, Cairo, 10 January 2001.
14 *Barnamij hizb al-Amal* (The Manifesto of Al-Amal Party), Cairo, November 1994, p. 7.
15 *Ibid.* pp. 11–14.
16 Tal'at Rumaih, *Al-Wasat w'al-ikhwan* [Al-Wasat and the Ikhwan], Cairo, Markaz Yafa, 1997.
17 For the manifesto of Hizb Al-Wasat, see Rafiq Habib, *Awraq hizb al-wasat* (The Papers of Hizb Al-Wasat), Cairo, n.p., 1996.
18 J. Stacher, "Post-Islamist Rumblings in Egypt: The Emergence of the Wasat Party", *Middle East Journal*, vol. 56, no, 3, summer 2002, and *Taqrir al-hala al-diniyya fi misr* 1995 (On the Religious Condition in Egypt, 1995), Al-Ahram Centre for Political and Strategic Studies, Cairo, 1997, pp. 217–234.
19 Nabil Abdul-Fattah, *Veiled Violence: Islamic Fundamentalism in Egyptian Politics in 1990s*, Dar Sechat for Studies, Publishing and Distribution, Cairo, 1994, p. 36.
20 The lawyers' syndicate has a long tradition of political activity, having played a central role in Egypt's political history both before and after the 1952 revolution.
21 The Muslim Brothers were also able to win seats in the lawyers' syndicates in part because of their ability to provide constituencies with services. According to one study, the revenues from these services reached £E5 million in 1993. H. Al-Basir, "Jama't al-ikhwan al-muslimin, wa al-tanshi'a al-siyasiyya lil shabab" (The Muslim Brothers and the Political Upbringing of the Youth) in K. Al-Munifi, and H. Ibrahim, *Al-Thaqafa al-siyasiyya fi misr* (Political Culture in Egypt), vol.2, Centre for Research and Political Studies, Cairo University, Egypt, 1994, p. 1181.

22 Ahmad Hassan, *Al-Su'ud al-siyasi al-islami dakhil al-niqabat al-mihaniyya* (The Islamic Political Ascent to Professional Syndicates), Cairo, Dar Al-Thaqafiyya li Al-Nashr, 200, p. 235.

23 Amani Qandil, *Al-Dawr al-siyasi li jama'at al-masalih fi misr,* Cairo, Al-Ahram Centre for Political and Strategic Studies, pp. 451–53.

24 *Liwa' Al-Islam,* 26 May 1990, p. 62.

25 See their first statement in 2 August in 1990.

26 See the Brothers' statements of 11 August 1990, and 2 and 26 March 1991. For a detailed account on the response of the Muslim Brothers to the Gulf War, see also Jihad 'Auda, "An Uncertain Response: The Islamic Movement in Egypt", in James Piscatori (ed.), *Islamic Fundamentalisms and the Gulf Crisis,* Chicago, American Academy of Arts and Sciences, 1991, pp. 109–130.

27 Personal interview with Mohammad Rajab, Cairo, 5 July 2002.

28 Personal interview with Amani Qandil, Cairo, 2 July 2002.

29 See *Liwa' Al-Islam* 15 February 1989, p. 62.

30 The statement was issued in 15 August 1990.

31 The second statement was issued after the war, on 20 January 1991. Its title summarised its content: "No to the Invasion of Kuwait, No to War in the Gulf, No to the Destruction of Iraq".

32 Personal interview with 'Esam Al-'Aryan, 19 December 2000.

33 Amani Qandil, "Al-Niqabat al-mihaniyya fi misr wa azmat al-khalij" (Professional Syndicates in Egypt and the Gulf War), in Mustafa Al-Sayyid (ed.), *Hata al-tanshb harbun arabiyya-arabiyya ukhra* (So that No Other Arab-Arab War Erupts), Centre of Research and Political Studies, Cairo University, Egypt, 1992, p. 308.

34 Jihad 'Auda, "The 'Normalization' of the Islamic Movement in Egypt from 1970s to the Early 1990s", in M. Marty, and S. Appleby (eds.), *Accounting for Fundamentalisms,* Chicago, University of Chicago Press, 1994, p. 394.

35 Personal interview with an Ikhwan member, who asked not to be named.

36 Personal interview with Abu Al-'Ila Madi, Cairo, 7 January 2000.

37 Personal interview with 'Esam Al-'Aryan, Cairo, 19 December 2000.

38 Steve Negus, *Cairo Times,* vol. 1, issue.3, 3 April 1997.

39 Personal interview with Ahamad Al-Nahas, Alexandria, 10 July 2002.

40 Questionnaire entitled: "The Doctors' Opinion Survey: The 1990 Elections", n.d.

41 Such questions included, e.g., "Do you think there are popular forces, yet still unrecognised by the state?"; "Do you think that present parties reflect all political forces in Egypt?"; and "Which of the political forces would have gained public trust if there were fair elections?".

42 Personal interview with 'Esam Hashish, Cairo, 9 January 2001.

43 *Tagrubatuna al-niqabiyya* (1984–95), (Our Experience in Syndicates), no author, no date.

44 Personal interview with Mahmoud Abdul Maqsud, Cairo, 25 December 2001.

45 Personal interview with Amani Qandil, Cairo, 2 July, 2002.

46 Personal interview with Amani Qandil, Cairo, 2 July 2002.

47 Hala Mustafa, "The Islamist Movements Under Mubarak", in Laura Guazzone (ed.), *The Islamist Dilemma*, Reading, Ithaca Press, 1995, p. 182.

48 Eberhard Kienle, "More Than a Response to Islam: The Political Deliberalization of Egypt in the 1990s", *Middle East Journal*, vol.52, no.2, spring 1998, p. 228.

49 *Al-Mujtama'*, 21 December 1993, p. 29.

50 The branches were in Alexandria, Al-Qaliubiyya, Al-Gharbiyya, Kafr Al-Shaik, Al-Sharqiyya, Dimiyat, Al-Daqahliyya, Al-Faium, Bani Suwaif, Asyut, Qina, Al-Minya, Al-Isma'iliyya, Sinai, Suhaj and Aswan. In Al-Daqahliyya, the Brothers were able to secure the position of the naqib.

51 Hala Mustafa, "The Islamist Movements Under Mubarak", in Guazzone, Laura (ed.) *The Islamist Dilemma*, Ithaca Press, Reading, 1995, p. 182.

52 Hassanain Ibrahim, "Zahirat al-'unf al-siyasi fi misr" (The Phenomenon of Political Violence in Egypt) in 'Ali Al-Din Hilal (ed.), *Al-Nizam al-siyasi al-misri bayn al-taghyur wa al-istimrar*, Cairo University, 1988, p. 917–981.

53 A. Ayalon and H. Shaked, (eds.), *Middle East Contemporary Survey*, Boulder, The Moshe Dayan Center for Middle Eastern and African Studies, The Shiloah Institute, Tel Aviv University, Westview Press, 1992.

54 Hasan Al-Sayyid, *Al-Tahawulat al-dimuqratiyya wa shar'iyyat al-nizam al siyasi fi misr 1981–1993* (Democratic Transformation and the Legitimacy of the Political Regime in Egypt 1981–1993), Unpublished MA. Study, Cairo University, Egypt, 1997, p. 199.

55 Questionnaire on the Gulf Crisis, Alexandria University, October 1990.

56 Questionnaire entitled "Welcome with Your Political View: A Questionnaire Regarding the Palestinian Issue". It does not mention the name of the university or the date.

57 Personal interview with Hilmi Al-Jazzar, Cairo, 5 August 2002.

58 Personal interview with Jamal Mohammad, 5 August 2002.

59 The idea of *al-riyyadah al-tulabiyya* was not new having been introduced by Sadat's new Student Charter in 1967. However it was not put into practice until the1990s.

60 *Al-'Arabi*, 27 September 1993.

61 For details on *Horras*, see *Al-'Arabi*, 9 November 1995.

62 For examples of this, see *Al-Sha'b*, 22 October 1993, *Al-Ahali*, 20 October 1993, and *Al-Wafd*, 17 November 1993.

63 See Hans Lofgren, "Economic Policy in Egypt: A Breakdown in Reform Resistance", *International Journal of Middle Eastern Studies*, vol. 25, no. 3, 1993, pp. 407–421; also Iliya Harik, "Subsidization Policies in Egypt: Neither Economic Growth nor Distribution", *International Journal of Middle East Studies*, vol. 24, no. 3 1992, pp. 485–6.

64 Eberhard Kienle, *A Grand Delusion: Democracy and Economic Reform*, London, I. B. Tauris, 2000, p. 148.

65 *In'ikasat azmat al-khalij 1990/1991 'ala al-iqtisad al-misri* (The Effects of the1990/1991 Gulf Crisis on the Egyptian Economy), Cairo, Institute of National Planning, 1992, pp. 168–176.

66 E. Kienle, *A Grand Delusion, op.cit.*, p. 150.

67 Hasan Al-Sayyid, *Al-Tahwulat al-dimuqratiyya wa shar'iyyat al-nizam al-siyasi fi misr, 1981–1993*, (Democratic Transformations and the Legitimacy of the Egyptian Regime 1981–1993), Unpublished MA. Dissertation, Cairo University, Egypt, 1997, p. 199.

68 Although the regime's macroeconomic performance has improved, according to Cassandra, it was the performance at the microeconomic level that shaped the common person's perception of the regime: "While economists are persuaded by data on balance of payments, level of indebtedness, budget deficits, and other macroeconomic indicators, such data mean little to ordinary people concerned about the security of jobs, low wages, high prices, and inadequate profits". See 'Cassandra', "The Impending Crisis in Egypt", *Middle East Journal*, vol. XLIX, no. 1, winter, 1995, p. 11.

69 These views are expressed, for example, by Dirk Vandewalle, "Egypt and Its Western Creditors", *Middle East* Review, no. 20, spring, 1988, p. 27.

70 Personal interview with Khalid Munir, Cairo, 4 July 2002.

71 Sullivan, Denis. "The Political Economy of Reform in Egypt", *International Journal of Middle Eastern Studies*, 22, 1990, p. 317.

72 Matthew Gray, "Economic Reform, Privatisation and Tourism in Egypt", *Middle Eastern Studies*, vol.34, no.2, April 1998, p. 99.

73 Marat Terterov, *Privatisation of the Public Enterprises in Egypt, 1994–2000: A New Strategy for the Management of the a Statist Economy*, Unpublished Ph.D. Study, St. Anthony's College, Oxford University, Michaelmas Term 2001, p. 303.

74 Hassanain Ibrahim, *Al-Dawla wa al-tanmiyya fi misr* (The State and Development in Egypt), Cairo University, Centre for the Study of Developing Countries, 2000, p. 260.

75 Nazih Ayubi, *Overstating The Arab State: Politics and Society in the Middle East*, London, I. B. Tauris, 1995, pp. 339–352.

76 Marsha Posusney, *Labor and the State: Workers, Unions and Economic Restructuring*, New York, Columbia University Press, 1997, p. 213.

77 Magdi Khalifa, *Socioeconomic Aspects of the Economic Reform Policies in Egypt*, Cairo, Institute of National Planning, 1996, p. 17.

78 See R. Assa'd, and M. Rouchdy, *Poverty and Poverty Alleviation Strategies in Egypt*, Cairo Papers in Social Science, vol. 22, no. 1, Cairo, the American University of Cairo, 1999, pp. 46–47.

79 P. Lubeck and B. Britts, "Muslim Civil Society in Urban Spaces: Globalisation, Discursive Shifts and Social Movements", Working Papers Series, Centre for Global, International and Regional Studies (CGIRS), University of California, Santa Cruz, 2001, p. 28; also Ihab Nijm, *Al-Dawr al-siyasi li al-jam'iyyat al-ahliyya al-islamiyya fi misr, 1921–1992*, (The Political Role of the Islamic Informal Associations in Egypt, 1921–1992), Unpublished MA Dissertation, Cairo University, Egypt, 1996, pp. 90–91.

80 See R. Assa'd, and M. Rouchdy, *Poverty and Poverty Alleviation Strategies in Egypt*, Cairo Papers in Social Science, *op.cit.*, p. 80.

81 Personal interview with Ma'mun Al-Hudaybi, Cairo, 18 December 2000.

82 Personal interview with 'Esam Al-'Aryan, Cairo, 19 December 2000.
83 Shihab Al-Din, Fathi, *Bay' al-qita' al-'am* (The Selling of the Public Sector), Tanta, Dar Al-Bashir, 2000, p. 101.
84 Personal interview with Khairat Al-Shatir, Cairo, 30 June 2002.
85 Personal interview with Khalid 'Auda, Cairo, 7 July, 2002.
86 *Ibid.*

7

THE DISMANTLING OF ISLAMIST POWER

The peak of the confrontation between Mubarak and the Muslim Brothers was reached in 1995, when the regime arrested hundreds of Brothers of different ages, areas and disciplines and tried some of them in military courts. Not only did this register as a relapse from the spirit of tolerance that had coloured the state's attitude to moderate Islamists during the 1980s, but it also represented a reappearance of extreme authoritarian methods of dealing with opponents that resembled those that had been used by Nasser in 1965 when he tried members of the movement in military courts and hanged its ideologue, Sayyid Qutb.

The mid-1990s witnessed several events which made the regime nervous and, at times, out of control. First, were the parliamentary elections of 1995, which the Brothers decided to contest, alongside the opposition, with a comparatively large number of 170 candidates running as independents. Despite Law No. 100 for 1993, which was intended to restrict the progress of the Brothers in syndicates, Islamists were still consolidating their rise to the boards of councils. The prospect of a similar success in the legislature was a nightmare for the regime. The regime also continued to be troubled by the continuous rise of Islamist violence, which in the mid-1990s began to develop bases and networks in Sudan, Yemen and Afghanistan, and targeted the life of Mubarak in 1995, when he visited Ethiopia.

Added to these factors was the failure of the business sector to fulfil the regime's expectations that liberal entrepreneurs would help alleviate the social impact of its economic reforms and privatisations, and the consequent increase in public frustration and dissent that had resulted from this failure.

Mubarak and the 1995 Elections

Unlike previous elections, the 1995 elections saw the rise in the number of independent candidates, some of whom came from the business sector.[1] Official estimates indicated that more than 4,000 candidates contested the Assembly's 444 seats, 439 of whom were from the NDP, 181 from the New Wafd, and 107 from the 'Amal, while the rest belonged either to smaller parties and or were independents.[2] As well as the large number of independent and business candidates, the elections lacked the sort of political alliances that had existed in 1984 and 1987. This confirmed the weakness of Egyptian political parties and the emergence of new actors and attitudes.[3]

The NDP was able to secure a comfortable victory and occupied 417 seats, against 6 seats for the New Wafd and 5 seats for the *Tajammu'*. Out of 170 candidates, the Ikhwan secured only one seat,[4] which was subsequently lost on the grounds that the member had belonged to an illegal movement (i.e. to the Ikhwan). Despite the fact that the NDP occupied 94 per cent of the seats (a higher percentage compared with previous elections), its support had in effect shrunk substantially. Initially it secured 317 seats, constituting 71 per cent of the Assembly's seats (compared to 78 per cent in 1987 and 87 per cent in 1984).[5] However, an extra 100 seats were later added when some independents, mostly businessmen, decided to join the NDP to reap whatever benefits they could from doing so. This decline in initial NDP support indicated the public's disappointment with the regime in comparison with the early 1980s.

Furthermore, and unlike in previous elections where the regime aimed to secure dominance in the Assembly through subtle means, the 1995 elections saw the worst and most coercive interference to prevent the opposition from succeeding.[6] Apart from the hundreds who were harassed by the police and the security forces, at least 51 people were killed during the two days of the voting, 28 of them by police fire, and as many as 878 were injured.[7] The level of violence signified the widening of the hostility and distrust between the state and the political opposition that had followed the latter's decision to boycott the elections in 1990. The regime had perceived this as an attempt to compel it to introduce political reforms. The violence was also a response to the Brothers' announcement that they would contest the elections with 170 candidates since, if left to themselves they would almost certainly win, and their impact in the 1995 Assembly would surpass that in 1987.

In addition, the 1995 Assembly was meant to nominate Mubarak for a fourth term presidency in 1999, and the regime feared that if the Brothers controlled more than a third of the seats in the Assembly (round about 140), they could then obstruct the Mubarak's nomination, especially as they had already voted against his third term nomination in 1993. A large number of Islamists, under the leadership of the Islamic Alliance and backed by the New Wafd, would also challenge repressive legislations, such as the Emergency Law, renewed in 1997 and 2000, and the Press Law of 1995, which imposed high penalties on newspapers if they published what the authorities considered to be false information.

Although the elections were supervised by the Ministry of Justice, a development which the opposition had been demanding for years, the Ministry of Interior managed to intervene and failed all but one of the 170 candidates (he, as noted above, was later stripped of his membership of the Assembly on the basis of belonging to an outlawed *tanzim*). Candidates like 'Esam Al-'Aryan and Abdul Mun'em Abu Al-Futuh were arrested as soon as they announced their intentions to run the elections and were tried in military courts on the same grounds. National and international human rights' organisations condemned the military trial of civilians who had nothing but oppose the government on political grounds.[8] Independent figures who had connections with the regime and with the Ikhwan attempted to reconcile the two and to persuade the former to end the military trials if the latter would reduce the number of its candidates. Kamal Abu Al-Majd, a former Brother who was also well connected to the regime was one such figure. I met him several times in his office in Cairo, where he talked about his efforts to persuade Mubarak to end the trials of the Brothers in return for a political deal:

> I suggested to Mubarak that the Brothers were willing to reduce the number of candidates from 170 to as few as 10, and to exclude names like Ma'mun Al-Hudaybi, Mukhtar Nuh and Saif Al-Islam Hasan Al-Banna from the candidacy list, in return for an end to the military trials. However, my efforts were defeated by certain officials, such as Safwat Al-Sharif, the Minister of Information, who leaked news to the press about the idea of the deal before it had even began to develop.[9]

Abu Al-Majd believes that Mubarak viewed the Islamists as threat to his leadership, and feared a scenario (similar to that in Algeria with the FIS) in which a winning Ikhwan could turn Egypt into another Iran. This view was confirmed by Makram Mohammad Ahmad, editor of *Al-Musawwar* magazine, who has close contacts with Mubarak. Makram confirmed the regime's fear of the Ikhwan, and its worries about the implications of their popularity:

> The Ikhwan are very organised and extremely popular, and if they contested the elections, they could easily win against the NDP. A trend within the regime thinks that the Ikhwan constitute the greatest political threat to Mubarak, and fears that what happened in Algeria could happen in Egypt.[10]

Banning the Islamists From Parliament

In addition to the 170 candidates who were intending to contest the elections as independents, the Brothers also had candidates who contested the elections in alliance with the Wafd. This confirmed official fears that the Islamists were aiming to maximise their impact on the Assembly.[11] Similarly to syndicates and student unions, the Brothers' parliamentary candidates enjoyed a stronger base of support in their respective constituencies, where their popularity stemmed from their active engagement with the local community as councillors, preachers, social workers and lecturers at university or school. Candidates were also popular because of the services they provided to their neighbourhoods through the private health clinics, schools, factories, and supermarkets which the Ikhwan managed to reconstruct as 'avenues of participation' and mobilisation.[12] Moreover, regular attendance at the local mosque, and participation with members of the community on occasions that were both happy and sad, added considerably to the candidates' popularity. Khalid Munir, an *Al-Hayat* journalist, believes that much of the support enjoyed by the Ikhwan candidates was because "people could find them whenever they needed them and whenever they expected to see them, not just during election campaigns." He noted that:

> In Egypt we have what we call 'nuwab al-khadmat' [deputies of services]. These are members of parliament who do not necessarily win the elections because they are good politicians

– in fact some know nothing about politics – but because they
provide services to the constituencies and share the concerns
of their community. This makes them popular and people
vote for them, regardless of whether they have run as party
members or independents.[13]

In other constituencies, and where Islamists had a stronger foothold
at the grassroots level, people supported the Brothers' candidates on
the basis of their membership of the *tanzim*, rather than on their
individual qualities alone, because of the reputation of the former, and
because it was through its networks that services could be achieved.
This was an important reason why harassments and arrests were not
targeted necessarily at the election candidates, but figures that were
perceived to be a major source of the *tanzim*'s power. The 95
individuals who were arrested and turned over to the military courts
in 1995 included Brothers like 'Esam Al-'Aryan, former General
Secretary for the medical syndicate; Mohammad Habib, President of
the Teachers' Faculty Club at Asyut University; Khairat Al-Shatir, owner
of the Salsabil Computer Company; Abdul Mun'em Abu Al-Futuh,
former General Secretary for the Arab Medical Union; Mahmoud
'Izat, a former university professor; and Abdul Wahab Sharaf Al-Din, a
businessman. In addition to their public posts, most of these figures
occupied senior positions in the *tanzim* and were in charge of its bases
and networks. Al-'Aryan was a member of *maktab al-irshad* or the
Guidance Bureau, and had in the past been a member of *maktab al-
tulab* (the students' section) and *maktab al-mihaniyyin* (the
professionals' section). Habib was a member of *maktab al-irshad* and
was also in charge of the section of the teachers' university clubs, while
Al-Shatir was a member of *maktab al-irshad* and in charge of the section
concerned with planning (*qism al-takhtit*).

The Impact of the Military Trials

The military trials dealt a major blow to the *tanzim*. Constituting the
pinnacle of perhaps the most important confrontation with the
Egyptian regime since the period of Nasser, they also influenced the
beliefs and attitudes of the Brothers during the 1990s, and may
perhaps affect them for decades to come. In the initial phase of the
arrests and trials in 1995, most Brothers presumed that Mubarak
would not go all the way and thus risk his public image inside Egypt
and abroad, but that he would intervene and pardon the defend-

ants once the elections had ended. However, the Brothers soon realised their mistake. Most of those tried in the military court were convicted and imprisoned for a period of three to five years with hard labour, and this confirmed the perception that the intentions of the regime were in fact broader than simply preventing the Brothers from contesting the elections.

Following the military sentences, the political section (*al-maktab al-siyasi*) was instructed by the *tanzim* to brief it with what they thought were the reasons for the regime's changed attitude towards the movement, and what the options might be to enable the Brothers to continue to survive under the authoritarian conditions of the 1990s.

During my visit to Egypt in 2001, I managed to meet the late Abdul Mun'em Sileem Jabara, a member of *maktab al-irshad* who was also in charge of *al-maktab al-siyasi*. At the flat in Giza where members of the *maktab al-siyasi* met and ran their activities, Jabara showed me the weekly reports and commentaries on current political affairs that were prepared and distributed by the *maktab* to the members of the *tanzim*. Many of these reports reflected the attitude of the Brothers to current developments, though these views were not always declared in their public discourse. Jabara also agreed to show me some of the studies that had been written by the *maktab* in relation to the confrontation with the regime, and the briefs that had been presented to the leadership of the *tanzim*. He informed me that the more serious documents and studies had been confiscated by the security services during the campaign of arrests and searches for information on the *tanzim*. He therefore saw no harm in some of the studies being published for the purposes of the present book, as long as the names of people in the *tanzim*, and other similarly sensitive details were omitted.

The section below examines some of the documents, which were certainly not initially written for publication, and assesses the reasons for the confrontation with the regime as perceived by the *maktab*, and the options available to the movement to maintain its survival. The four documents examined in this book are concerned with Mubarak's regime and his relations with the Ikhwan, and therefore offer students of state-society relations in the Arab world some useful insights into Islamist thinking. Such views are not generally expressed in the public arena, nor, under the current authoritarian constraints of the state, are they as openly and critically articulated. The documents also discuss the role of the

West and Israel in the confrontation between Mubarak and the Brothers. Written in Arabic, they have been translated into English.[14]

Strictly speaking, the ideas and statements in the documents do not necessarily reflect the formal views of the *tanzim*, but reveal the observations and opinions of the individuals in *al-maktab al-siyasi* who wrote them. Although circulated to the senior members of the *tanzim*, including the leadership, they have also influenced and formed the perceptions and biases of the broader movement.

When Islamists Dare to Speak

The confrontation between Mubarak and the Brothers was the inevitable consequence of an authoritarian regime's inability to tolerate as powerful, organised and popular a rival as the Ikhwan. According to the documents, Mubarak's regime was no more than "an extension to the two regimes of Abdul Nasser and Sadat", which, although it might appear dressed in a civilian uniform, continued to be a military regime.

In essence, the Egyptian regime was a monarchy, rather than a republic, in which leadership was inherited only by those who belonged to the military institution. Further, the regime approved secularism as a base for its rule and relied on secularism as its ideology. It tries to keep religion away from influencing its authority and even the society through a gradual plan that depends on mass media, education and control over the legislative apparatus. The regime's total reliance on its coercive resources was a sign of its internal weakness and decline, while Mubarak was regarded as "hesitant and indecisive", preferring to deal with problems in stages rather than all at once. He was also seen to be supported by an international and regional environment that perceived Islam as the "next threat" and therefore applauded the regime's coercion of the Islamists. By repressing the Brothers, Mubarak proved to the United States that his regime remained in control of its internal affairs, and that American interests in Egypt and elsewhere in the region were not vulnerable.

However, despite the authoritarian features of the regime and the backing it received from abroad, according to the documents the Brothers also retained certain powers that would make them a strong opponent to the state: (i) the structure of the *tanzim*, which remained difficult to uncover or infiltrate; (ii) a broader social base of connections and contacts that served as a shield against the state; and (iii) an ability to mobilise.

The documents identified the developments that had created the context of the confrontation between the regime and the Ikhwan. These included the Brothers' decision to boycott the elections in 1990; their attitude to the Gulf War in 1991; their taking control of the lawyers' syndicate in 1992; and their refusal to support the nomination of Mubarak for a third term in 1993. But the main reason that impelled the regime to confront the Brothers was their preoccupation with legitimacy, and their insistence on competing with the regime on its political terrain, despite the risks of an authoritarian response:

> Most events prove that the regime, in what remains of its tenure, would not grant legitimacy to the Ikhwan that would enable them to consolidate their control over social institutions (syndicates, unions, and teaching staff clubs). However, one result of their insistence on formal political participation, intended to prove their existence, is that they centralize their weight where the power of the regime lies and this leads to political friction and oppression.[15]

As well as the contest with the regime over its own political territory, i.e. the Assembly, and the public statements by the Brothers to the effect that they constituted the main political power in Egypt, the documents revealed that the Brothers tended to politicise the areas they controlled, including the syndicates and campuses. This politicisation was driven by a perception, which they shared with the regime, that the battle between the two was based on a zero sum game, where one's loss was the other's gain, and that defeat should not be accepted.

Strategies for the Future

At the outset, there seemed to be two options for the Brothers in their dealings with the regime: the movement either resorted to violence and risked the public credibility that distinguished it from the extremists, or it exercised self restraint and pursued a tranquil path until the "violent storm" had passed. The latter option was the recommended one, but, the document cautioned, this did not imply full passivity. The Brothers were advised in the first instance to avoid competing with the regime in the territories which the regime believed were its own. Instead they should focus on the areas where the regime was less present, such as in society and in informal groupings and associations (e.g. businessmen's associations, specialised clubs, youth hostels, scouts, women organisations, craftsmen, labourers, farmers. . .etc.). Secondly, they should maintain their current position of control over syndicates through focusing more on professional services and less on politics, even on issues of national concern. Thirdly, they should engage in a serious and critical review of matters related to political, economic, social, and organisational reform.

The documents noted above discussed various issues relating to the national, regional and international factors that contributed to the confrontation between the regime and the Brothers. What was remarkable was the response to state violence. Analysts and students of Islamism in the Arab world tend to assume that state violence against the Islamists usually provoked counter violence. In the case of Egypt this did not occur. Surprisingly, attempts to establish political parties such as *Al-Amal* and *Al-Wasat*, were evident during the 1990s, at the height of state repression. The Brothers were careful not to be dragged into violence since the regime possessed powerful coercive means, and this would harm their public reputation as a non-violent movement. The Ikhwan veterans, such as the late *murshid* Mustafa Mashhur who was a member of the militant Special Apparatus or *al-nizam al-khass*, had suffered in the past from the consequences of involvement in violent activities, and they were not prepared to allow this to happen again, particularly as Mubarak's regime, although authoritarian, could not be compared to the totalitarianism of Nasser.

A few months before his death, I visited Mashhur at his Cairo flat. He confirmed that the Ikhwan were against the use of violence, and cited an instance during the election campaign in 2000 when a young Brother was severely rebuked for carrying a gun with which he was about to shoot a policeman who had assaulted him.[16] This incident showed how dangerously a situation could escalate when the state exceeded its limits in coercion, but also illustrated the role of the Ikhwan leadership in deterring unfavourable responses. One of the documents confirmed that the security agencies were quite sure that the Ikhwan had no weapons and did not purposely infiltrate sensitive installations. This explains why violence was not used against the leaders of the Ikhwan when they were arrested and/or interrogated.

Mashhur flatly contradicted official accusations that the Ikhwan had connections with extremist groups like *Al-Jihad* and *Al-Jama'a Al-Islamiyya*. Remarkably, this lack of association between the Ikhwan and violent Islamists was also confirmed at this point at a confidential meeting with a man who had been a Minister of the Interior in the 1990s. He had previously had connections with senior Brothers when he was a governor, and admitted that during his posting as Minister of Interior, and although the press had accused the Ikhwan of terrorism, interrogations showed no evidence of any link to terrorist groups. The former Minister added:

> The thing with the Brothers is that they are an Islamist move-ment that is not just religious but is also political. The Ikhwan are very organised and are politically active. This is something that the regime does not tolerate. Do not forget, we live in an authoritarian state and not in a real democracy.

What was also remarkable in the documents was their attitude to the future politicisation of professional organisations, which I will look at in more detail when I examine the social situation of Egypt in the mid-1990s.

The State Confronts Society

The mid-1990s saw a further deterioration in state-society relations, evident in the coercive attitude of the regime to civil society and the freedom of the press. In 1995, the NDP-controlled Assembly issued Law No. 93; this placed high penalties and a severe punishment (up to five years in prison plus a fine of £E20, 000) on any newspaper that printed inaccurate news or fallacious information that harmed the public interest.[17] This law angered and enraged the opposition and journalists; those who worked in the state-owned press nicknamed it the 'law to assassinate the press' (*qanun ightial al-sahafa*), and Mubarak was forced to abolish it a year later.

Islamist violence continued to target the state and its highest officials both inside Egypt and abroad. According to the independent Egyptian Organisation of Human Rights (EOHR), during the first 10 months of 1995 no fewer than 333 people were killed in acts of political violence in Upper Egypt, especially in the provinces of Minya, Asyut and Qina.[18] In June 1995, there was an assassination attempt on Mubarak in Addis Ababa, responsibility for which was claimed by *Manazamat talai' al-fath al-islami* (Islamic Conquest Vanguards Organisation – the military wing of *Al-Jihad*). In November, the Egyptian Embassy in Islamabad was attacked, and at least 15 were killed and 70 wounded. According to Nabil Abdul Fatah, a political analyst at the Al-Ahram Centre for Political and Strategic Studies, and an expert on Islamism, these events increased the resentment of the regime, which from this period onwards made no distinction between 'radical' and 'moderate' Islamists.[19]

Contrary to the situation in the 1980s, Mubarak now began to stress the similarity between the Muslim Brothers and *Al-Jihad*,[20] and spoke of a 'division of labour' between the Brothers and the extremists.[21] The regime escalated its campaign against the Ikhwan on campuses and even more so against those in professional syndicates. In February 1995, the regime introduced new amendments to Law No. 100 for 1993. This had given extra powers to the judges to supervise syndicate elections, as well as the right to disqualify candidates, after the law preventing the Ikhwan from winning had failed. When the amendments also failed to do their intended job, the Interior Ministry, which had been assigned to enforce the powers of the judges, intervened and halted the elections, on the basis that the Islamist candidates belonged to an outlawed movement. This happened to 'Esam Al-'Aryan in the medical syndicate in 1995, and to Sayf Al-Islam Hasan Al-Banna in the lawyers' syndicate in 1996.[22]

Professional Syndicates or Political Platforms?

In addition to the arrests of Ikhwan in the medical and lawyers' syndicates, and following a court case to do with financial irregularities, the engineers' syndicate was also placed under the supervision of judges until another date had been set for the elections. The Brothers, who saw the timing of the case as an orchestrated campaign to stop them from winning seats in the elections, refused to comply with the court's ruling. When the security forces broke into the syndicate to enforce the ruling and suspended the board of council, the council, which was dominated by the Brothers, filed a court case against the person of Mubarak for the suspension.[23] The arrests and trials of members of the medical, lawyers and engineers' syndicates confirmed that the confrontation with the regime was not related simply to the 1995 parliamentary elections but to the broader impact of the Ikhwan on politics and society.

Furthermore, what occurred in the engineers' syndicate showed that the Brothers would not easily relinquish what they had gained during the regime's period of tolerance. This agreed with a suggestion in one of the documents that the movement "should not give up its positions of influence, unless it is sure that the losses incurred owing to such positions will be larger than the gains". It should also aim "to regain the sites we have lost, but with a new spirit and methods and with ways of action that are different from those of the past". This reflected the broader spirit within the movement' leadership, which emphasised that the Ikhwan should not be deterred from their progress in influencing politics and society, but instead try to expand that influence even further. In one unpublished internal document, the former *murshid*, Mustafa Mashhur, blessed the Brothers' social legitimacy and emphasised the importance of maintaining it. In Mashhur's words:

> Our activities have become known because of the increase in our public activism and because we are becoming open to sectors of society through effective fronts like syndicates, unions, associations, people's assemblies and local councils. Society has become aware of this activism and of our sincere intentions of seeking to please God by benefiting people. These activities have enabled us to achieve <u>great expansion</u> and have led to the appearance of [public] <u>symbols</u> *and* <u>figures</u> by which people can identify us. The activities also resulted in our acquisition of a <u>political legitimacy</u> that no one can doubt. This legitimacy must be preserved and deepened by social legitimacy. This can be achieved by integrating further with vital sectors of society.[24]

While the above quotation shows the extent of the Brothers commitment to maintaining their achievements, it also shows the effect of the trials, particularly with regard to the attitude towards syndicates. In Chapter Six, I referred briefly to an unpublished internal document, which assessed the performance of the Ikhwan in syndicates and admitted that they had confused their respon-sibilities in the *tanzim* and their duties to the wider constituency of the syndicates.[25] The study was given to me by its author, who was also a member of *maktab al-mihaniyyin* (the professionals' section). It had been presented to the leadership of the movement, who wanted to examine the Brothers' attitude in syndicates and the extent to which these attitudes had contributed to the crisis with the regime. The major findings of this document with regard to the issue of politicisation did not differ much from those discussed above, except that it appeared to be more critical of the Ikhwan's role in syndicates and more subservient to the powers of the state.

First, the document criticised the use of syndicates to mobilise in support of the movement and against the regime, being unaware that this harmed the syndicates and the interests of its professional members, which the movement had promised to serve. The Ikhwan in syndicates functioned as if they were *mu'aridun hizbiyyun*, or an opposition party, to the government. They ignored the fact that syndicates in Egypt were essentially part of *jihaz al-dawla*, or the apparatus of the state.[26] Furthermore, the Brothers became pre-occupied with developing *shar'iyya igtima'iyya*, (social legitimacy), through the provision of services such as health care and housing, and did not realise that these services would not be facilitated without the co-operation of the bureaucrats and the Ministries of Health and Housing, which the movement opposed.[27] It would be impossible under these circumstances for the Ikhwan to continue to serve their professional constituencies, while they were simultaneously engaged in a process of politicisation that provoked the wrath of the regime.

The internal study did not object to syndicates assuming a political role, provided this reflected the interests and concerns of the broader constituencies and not the interests and concerns of the *tanzim*. It differentiated between the lower and higher forms of politics and argued that the Ikhwan served the interests of the constituencies if they focused more on the lower form of politics and functioned as a "pressure group" by lobbying for reforms in housing, industry, and education.[28] Involvement in the higher form of politics should not be abandoned, but had to represent the collective outlook of the constituencies and not just the views of the *tanzim*. The Ikhwan should initially engage themselves in raising the level of political awareness among their constituencies, and this should be done with the co-operation of other political powers. Meanwhile, the Brothers should recognise that their attempts to create change from outside the state apparatuses were doomed to fail, since the state remained in control over the major institutions and organisations of society and could intervene at any time.[29] It concluded that confrontation with the state occurred whenever the Brothers alienated the state, behaved as if they were independent, or relied on their informal legitimacy as their source of power.

Privatisation

The deterioration in state-society relations in Egypt was also seen in the economic sphere, which imposed further restrictive procedures on the regime in the hope that economic reform and privatisation would deliver favourable results. As was mentioned in Chapter Six, from the 1990s onwards, the regime seemed to depend less on legal reform and on what a relatively pluralistic Assembly demanded in terms of conciliation with political parties and powerful forces in society, and relied more on the business community that would facilitate economic liberalisation and support the state in its pursuit of legitimacy. Mubarak hoped that in the long run, economic liberalisation would lessen the grievances generated out of the regime's worn-out social contract and support the role of private sector, whose proponents had began to assume a remarkable presence in the political as well as in the economic spheres. So whereas the regime accommodated the political opposition in the 1980s in order to bolster its legitimacy, the growth of economic difficulties and of socio-religious disturbances in the 1990s prompted it to focus more on the agents of economic liberalisation.

Alliance with the Business Community

The emergence of the business sector began with Sadat's *infitah* policy in the mid-1970s and grew in the 1980s with Mubarak's efforts to stabilise the economy through encouraging exports and the inflow of remittances from Egyptians working abroad.[30] During the 1990s, businessmen utilised the shift towards structural re-adjustment to further their economic gains and used the 1990 electoral law, based on individual candidacy, to increase their political influence and to run for the 1990 elections that had been boycotted by most political parties. Their presence in the Assembly became even more remarkable in 1995, when they occupied 71 seats, compared with 31 and 14 seats in the 1990 and 1987 Assemblies respectively.[31]

According to El-Mikawy, during the 1990s the Egyptian business community either accepted the status quo and sought the support of the regime, or were critical and demanded political as well as economic liberalisation.[32] In another study the business community was divided into a nationalist or conservative trend that was usually centred in the Egyptian Chamber of Commerce, and a more liberal trend that was dispersed throughout the American Chamber of Commerce (i.e. tied to the American Embassy in Cairo), along with the Society of Egyptian Businessmen, the Society of Egyptian-American Businessmen, and the Society of Egyptian-French Businessmen.[33] Regardless of the divisions, the regime sought to appease whichever trend it perceived as more acquiescent and willing to facilitate its political and economic objectives.

As far as political objectives were concerned, the business community supported the regime's efforts to bring about peace in the region, and participated in diplomatic missions to warn against the implications of Israel's behaviour for regional prosperity. In 1995 a group of Egyptian businessmen met the Israeli ambassador to explain how difficult it was for them to launch private businesses in Tel Aviv while Israelis continued to arrest and kill Palestinians.[34] A year earlier, a delegation from the Union of Israeli Industries, representing 14 different industries inside Israel, had visited their counterparts in Egypt to discuss future prospects for economic co-operation, and some months later, a delegate from the Union of Egyptian industries had also visited Israel to discuss the Arab-Israeli stalemate and its impact on regional investment.

As for the economic objectives, the regime relied on the strong presence of the business sector in parliament to help in drawing up new laws on investment and taxes that would facilitate privatisation. At the same time the government facilitated loans for businessmen; these were taken from public sector banks, occasionally without guarantees. The regime also employed senior Egyptian business-men who had contacts with Western organisations and financial groups as intermediaries between the state and foreign invest-ment,[35] hoping that foreign revenues would compensate for the erosion of the public sector and help unemployed graduates find jobs elsewhere. Thus, a certain social role emerged, which involved assisting the state in its efforts to redefine its social contract, without risking its legitimacy.[36] The regime expected the business com-munity to perform this new role in addition to its customary economic and political roles.

However, the public image of businessmen was that many were corrupt and were not concerned either with the problems of society or with their social responsibilities. Stories of businessmen engaged in suspicious deals including some involving weapons and drugs, were extensively reported in the opposition press, and negative perceptions of the business community were confirmed when four businessmen were stripped of their membership in the 1995 Assembly, because they had been prosecuted in corruption cases. According to Amani Qandil, who has also written about the role of businessmen in Egyptian politics:

> There is strong public opinion against businessmen in Egypt, where they are widely perceived as no more than corrupt parasites who feed on government support and privileges. They did nothing for the benefit of the country, or for the benefit of the government, and eventually the regime began to realise that they were not going to provide it with anything useful.[37]

The regime initially facilitated a large amount of financial support for the Egyptian business community in terms of large loans without guarantees, which were seized on by some businessmen (such as Rami Lakah, the notorious member of parliament) who promptly fled the country. The theft of billions of Egyptian pounds and American dollars from public sector banks enraged and frustrated many ordinary Egyptians, especially when this corruption was protected by senior government officials,[38] including the President's sons who insinuated themselves into business deals merely to collect huge commissions.[39] As stories of corrupt businessmen began to fill the pages of the opposition press, one informed source, with connections to business circles, revealed that Mubarak had held a private meeting with senior businessmen in the mid nineties at which he expressed considerable anger at what he had heard and read, and warned them of the social implications. According to the source:

> Mubarak was very angry. He warned a group of influential businessmen about the angry mob. He told them: 'one day the public will express its wrath against you and against the wealth you have accumulated. They will vandalise your expensive black Mercedes cars that are parked outside if you are not careful, and you might not even be able to afford bicycles to ride'.[40]

Qandil believes that the alliance between the regime and the business community was a failure as far as the social objectives were concerned. By the beginning of the new millennium it had started to weaken as the regime became aware that businessmen were unable to deliver what was expected of them.[41]

The End of Islamist of Finances?

While the regime was facilitating and supporting its business allies, it continued to escalate its confrontation with the Muslim Brothers and to target their financial resources. Of the four military cases against the Brothers, one was filed against Abdul Wahab Sharaf Al-Din, who was accused by the regime of having contacts with extremist Islamist groups inside Egypt and abroad, and sentenced to three years imprisonment. Sharaf Al-Din was an Ikhwan business-man who owned a large import-export company based in Suez and other private enterprises located in Cairo. He was the only member of the Brothers to be tried alongside two members of *Al-Jihad* group as a way of confirming his link to terrorism. The trial was, in fact, part of the scheme to discourage Islamist entrepreneurs and to weaken their financial resources, which the regime believed were being used to fund the election campaigns of the movement's candidates.

There was no targeting of Islamist businessmen during the 1995 parliamentary elections, but it was apparent in the elections of 2000, when the movement managed to get 17 of its candidates into the Assembly. According to Khairat Al-Shatir, owner of the Salsabil Computing Company, the security services identified about 900 companies which were thought to belong to the Brothers and that were suspected of providing funds to candidates during the 2000 election campaigns.[42] The owners of these companies were often harassed, and threatened with the confiscation of their wealth if they continued to provide financial support to political campaigns, which had become 'commercialised' and costly in the 1990s.

However, and for various reasons, not all ventures were nega-tively influenced by the regime's confrontation with the Brothers. First, according to Al-Shatir's rough estimate, the assets of the Islamists' business enterprises were less than £E300 million in total during the 1990s. Their political impact was therefore seen to be limited, in comparison with the combined assets of the Islamic investment companies in the 1980s, which amounted to billions of pounds. Secondly, if the regime was to confiscate the Islamists' business ventures, whatever the justifications, this would ultimately discourage foreigners from investing in a country which they perceived as unstable or hostile to parts of the private sector. Thirdly, in the prevailing circumstances of privatisation and dismantling of the public sector, the Islamists' ventures helped by employing hundreds of Egyptians who would otherwise be jobless and alienated.

Only in the case of the syndicates did the regime seemed prepared to alienate the professional constituencies, who were affected by the expulsion of the Brothers and the ultimate impact this had on the syndicates revenues and services. Following the removal of the Ikhwan from the boards of councils, many of the services were ended, or deteriorated as a result of the gradual decline in revenues that had subsidised the services. For example, the subsidies for the health care scheme in the engineers' syndicate came primarily from the subscriptions of the constituencies and from the profits from other popular projects such as the sales of consumer durables. However, the sales lacked the networks that had made them successful, and thus became less profitable and more costly to organise. According to Al-Shatir, who had been an active member of the engineers' syndicate as well as involved in organising sales, the average profits from the sale of consumer durables used to be as high as £E100 million a year. When the regime had intervened and imposed its cronies on the board of council, the sales did not make more than £E5 million in profit.[43]

Although Al-Shatir's account might have been biased, the negative impact of the Brothers' departure on revenues was confirmed by Ahmad Hasan, an independent researcher whose examination of the role of Islamists in syndicates was focused particularly on the engineers' syndicate. Hasan asserts that a few years after the Ikhwan had been absent from the engineers' syndicate, revenues began to dry up and some of the services that had previously been provided to the constituencies ceased to exist. This was the case with the hardship fund scheme, which was used to provide financial help and interest-free loans for engineers. The scheme was extremely popular during the period of the Islamists, and its beneficiaries had increased from 1068 in 1988, when it was first launched, to 4000 in 1994. When the syndicate was placed under judicial supervision in 1996, applicants for the scheme were rejected on the basis that sufficient funds were no longer available.[44]

In addition to the effects of confrontation on the Brothers'
private ventures, the financial capacities of the *tanzim* as a whole
and not just of the movement's individual members were badly
affected. As well as meeting the expenses of lawyers, fines, bail costs,
and so on, the *tanzim* was expected to take financial responsibility
for the dozens of dependants of those who were tried in the courts.
Salah Abdul Al-Maqsud, who was closely connected to this process
of aid, confirmed that the *tanzim* was responsible for the financial
needs of the families of the defendants for as long as they were
imprisoned:

> The families of the arrested Ikhwan needed social and health
> care, and regular financial help. A large amount of this was
> provided by the *tanzim* and it was a regular procedure for the
> *tanzim* whenever its members suffered at the hands of the
> regime or went to prison. During the absence of the father,
> the *tanzim* became the new supporter of his family. However
> the 1995 trials were a special case, because the numbers
> arrested and jailed were significant. This certainly put extra
> financial strain on the *tanzim* which, at the end of the day, had
> to depend on limited resources.[45]

Within these limited resources were the regular subscriptions or
ishtirakat that were paid by the thousands of members of the *tanzim*,
and the donations from abroad. Because of its ignorance of the
tanzim and the number of members who belonged to the Muslim
Brotherhood, the regime could not obstruct the *ishtirakat*, but it
could somehow hamper the donations coming from abroad.

The regime utilised its role during the Gulf War in 1991 to exert
pressure on most of the Gulf countries to halt their donations to
the Ikhwan in Egypt. The United Arab Emirates' government
imposed tight controls on Islamic organisations that were known to
have affiliations and affinities with the Brotherhood. In Kuwait, the
process was rather easier, since the Kuwaiti government and the
local Islamic organisations disapproved of the position taken by the
Ikhwan in Egypt during the war, and wealthy Islamists were already
prepared to distance themselves from the movement.

A year after the war, and as a result of the politicised performance of the Ikhwan during the earthquake, the regime also stopped
donations going through the syndicates to the victims, which was
bad news for the Ikhwan as far as syndicate revenues were con-

cerned. Egyptians were obliged to deposit their donations into government accounts, which many were reluctant to do. Donations to the syndicates from abroad were also hampered by the government's restrictions, and one informant in the medical syndicate told me that his donations from the Gulf had to be received through indirect means of transfer. Egyptian pressure on the Gulf States escalated following the trials of 1995, and the regime certainly gained regional and international back-up following the terrorist events of 11 September 2001.

Conclusion

The period from 1995 to 2000 witnessed the regime's heavier dependence on coercion, and this was reflected in its attitude to politics and society. The elections in 1995 saw larger scales of violence and confrontation with the security apparatuses, compared to the elections of 1984, 1987 and 1990. One reason for this was that the 1995 Assembly was expected to nominate Mubarak for a third term presidency in 1999, and the regime, which had alienated the opposition in 1990, wanted to secure an easy nomination.

The shift to repression was the regime's response to the increased threat from Islamist extremists, which targeted the life of Mubarak on his visit to Ethiopia in 1995. Following the failed attempt, the regime's attitude to Islamists became brutal and indiscriminate, as it arrested and tried leading members of the Muslim Brotherhood who were now seen as being linked to extremism and seeking to destabilise the government. Most of those who were tried decided to contest the 1995 elections, but found themselves obstructed.

The repressive policies of the regime were a response to the growing political and social impact of the Brothers. The Brothers had accumulated a social legitimacy in syndicates and on campuses and had begun to make political use of it, as was seen in their attempt to form a political party in 1996. The trials of the Ikhwan in military court had a significant impact on their ability to expand in society, and also affected their views of the regime and their strategies for the future. Some of these views were expressed in the unpublished internal documents that were discussed above. The documents held negative opinions of the regime, but warned that these should not draw the movement into violence. The documents also underlined the importance of continuing to provide various constituencies with social services, but without politicising the movement's performance.

The regime's reliance on coercion did not imply that legitimacy had become trivial, and Mubarak was still concerned with how Egyptians viewed his rule. However, his approach to legitimacy was modified. He ceased to count on legitimacy emerging from political pluralism and the accommodation of the opposition, but saw it as coming from the promises of economic reform. Mubarak hoped that, in the end, such reform could redress the grievances generated by the regime's worn-out social contract. The regime relied on the commercial sector to boost its damaged legitimacy, but the alliance between the state and the business sector failed to rid the regime of its crisis with society. Privatisation might have partly succeeded in improving Egypt's macroeconomics, but it certainly failed to improve the living standards of most Egyptians.

Notes

1 A. Minysi, "Rigal al-a'mal fi intikhabat 1995" (Businessmen in the 1995 Elections), in H. Mustafa (ed.), *Al-Intikhabat al-barlamaniyya fi misr 1995*, Cairo, Al-Ahram Center for Political and Strategic Studies, pp. 83–87.
2 *Al-Hayat*, 29 November 1995.
3 A. Al-Shubki, "Al-Ma'raka al-intikhabiyya: zawahir jadida" (The Election Contest: New Phenomena), in H. Mustafa (ed.), *Al-Intikhabat . . ., op.cit.*, p. 57.
4 The Nasserist Party and other independent candidates occupied the rest of the seats. See *Al-Taqrir al-istratiji al-'arabi*, 1996 (The Arabic Strategic Report, 1996) Cairo, Al-Ahram Centre for Political and Strategic Studies, 1995, p. 386.
5 Hala Mustafa (ed.), *Al-Intikhabat al-barlamaniyya fi misr 1995*, (Parliamentary Elections in Egypt 1995), Cairo, Al-Ahram Centre for Political and Strategic Studies, 1997, p. 45.
6 Eberhard Kienle, "More Than a Response to Islam: The Political Deliberalization of Egypt in the 1990s", *Middle East Journal*, Vol.52, No.2, spring 1998, p. 234.
7 *Ruz Al-Yusuf*, 11 December 1995.
8 Centre for Human Rights Legal Aid, *Military Courts in Egypt: Courts Without Safeguards, Judges Without Immunity, Defendants Without Rights*, Cairo, CHRLA, n.d, p. 2.
9 Personal interview with Kamal Abu Al-Majd, Cairo, 5 December 2000.
10 Personal interview with Makram Mohammad Ahmad, Cairo, 17 July 2002.
11 *Al-Nida' Al-Jadid*, 10 January 1996, p. 10.
12 The term 'avenues of participation' is taken from Diane Singerman, *Avenues of Participation: Family, Politics and Networks in Urban Quarters of Cairo*, Princeton NJ, Princeton University Press, 1995.

13 Personal interview with Khalid Munir, Cairo, 4 July 2002.

14 The first two are entitled *Al-Ikhwan al-muslimun wa al-nizam al-misri: mu'adlat al-sira' wa al-bahs an masar* (The Muslim Brothers and the Egyptian Regime: the Formulae of the Struggle and the Search for a Path), 1996; and *Al-Azma al-mumtada: 'ilaqat al-nizam al-misri bi al-ikhwan al-muslimin, al-mazahir, al-asbab, al-nata'ij* (The Extended Crisis: Relations of the Egyptian Regime with the Muslim Brotherhood: Aspects, Reasons, Results). The third document is untitled, and the fourth document is *Al-Synariuhat al-mustaqbaliyya al-badila: muhawla li al-bahs an masar Jadid fi daw' mu'adlat al-azma bayn al-nizam al-misri wa al-ikhwan al-muslimin* (Alternative Future Scenarios: an Attempt to Explore a New Path in Light of the 'Formulae' of the Crisis between the Egyptian Regime and the Muslim Brotherhood). Only one of the documents is dated.

15 See Document 1.

16 Personal interview with Mustafa Mashhur, Cairo, 15 December 2001.

17 *Al-Mujtama'*, 6 June 1995, p. 21.

18 Quoted by AFP, 7 November 1995.

19 Personal interview with Nabil Abdul Fatah, Cairo, 5 August 2002.

20 Mubarak's interview in *Le Monde*, 17 November 1995; and in *Al-Hayat*, 18 November 1995.

21 The President's statement is quoted by AFP, 1 May 1995.

22 Personal interview with 'Esam Al-'Aryan, Cairo, 19 December 2000.

23 Reinoud Leenders, *The Struggle of State and Civil Society in Egypt: Professional Organisations and Egypt's Careful Steps Towards Democracy*, Amsterdam, Middle East Research Associates, Occasional Papers, no.26, April 1996, pp. 25–26.

24 Mustafa Mashhur, *Wuduh al-ru'iyya*, (A Clear Vision), undated, p. 2. [Underlining in the original Arabic text]. I am indebted to Muhsin Al-Sharkawi who supplied me with this internal and unpublished document.

25 *Tagribatuna al-niqabiyya 1984–1995: durus wa ibar lil-mustaqbal* (Our Experience in Syndicates: Lessons for the Future), n.d., 21pp.

26 According to the law, syndicates are expected to provide professional consultation to the government, ministers are responsible for their respective syndicates, and the government's professional employers must belong to a syndicate.

27 *Taqrubatina al-niqabiyya*, p. 14.

28 *Ibid.* p. 18.

29 *Ibid.* p. 11.

30 M. Al-Jamal, *Al-Nukhba al-siyasiyya fi misr* (The Political Elite in Egypt), Beirut, Markaz Dirasat Al-Wihda Al-'Arabiyya, 1993, pp. 131–132.

31 N. El-Mikawy, and H. Handoussa (eds.), *Institutional Reform and Economic Development in Egypt*, Cairo, American University in Cairo Press, 2002, p. 55; also A. Minysi, "Rigal al-a'mal fi intikhabat 1995" (Businessmen in the 1995 Elections), in H. Mustafa (ed.), *Al-Intikhabat al-barlamaniyya fi misr 1995*, (The Parliamentary Elections in Egypt in 1995), Cairo, Al-Ahram Centre for Political and Strategic Studies, pp. 83–87.

32 N. El-Mikawy and H. Handoussa, (eds.), *Institutional Reform*, p. 51.

33 Mahdi Al-Dijani, *Dawr al-fi'a al-mustaghriba min rigal al 'amal*, (The Role of the Westernised Sector of Businessmen), Cairo, unpublished paper, pp. 4–6.

34 *Ibid.* p. 28.

35 Amani Qandil, "Jama'at al-masalih wa al-siyasa al-kharijiyya: dirasa li dawr rigal al-'amal fi misr" (Interest Groups and Foreign Policy: A Study on the Role of Businessmen in Egypt), *Al-Mustaqbal Al-'Arabi*, Issue 128, October 1989, pp. 95–82.

36 Moheb Zaki, *Egyptian Business Elites: Their Vision and Investment Behaviour*, Cairo, Arab Centre for Development and Future Research, 1999, p. 118.

37 Personal interview with Amani Qandil, Cairo, 2 July 2002. See also Najwa Samak, *Al-Qita' al-ahli wa al-tanmiyya al-iqtisadiyya fi misr*, (The Informal Sector and Economic Development in Egypt), Cairo University, Centre for the Study of Developing Countries, 1999, p. 97.

38 Ninette Fahmy, *The Relationship Between State and Society in Contemporary Egypt*, Unpublished PhD thesis, University of Exeter, UK, 1999, p. 243.

39 C. Murphy, "The Business of Political Change in Egypt", *Current History*, vol. 94, no. 588, January, 1995, p. 19.

40 Personal informer, who requested anonymity, Cairo, 6 July 2001.

41 Personal interview with Amani Qandil, Cairo, 2 July 2002.

42 Personal interview with Khairat Al-Shatir, Cairo, 30 June 2002. Al-Shatir was tried in the military courts in 1995 and imprisoned for five years with labour, then arrested for shorter periods during 2002.

43 Personal interview with Khairat Al-Shatir, Cairo, 30 June 2002.

44 Ahmad Hasan, *Al-Su'ud al-siyasi al-islami dakhil al-niqabat al-mihaniyya* (the Islamic Political Ascent to Professional Syndicates), Cairo, Dar Al-Thaqafiyya li Al-Nashr, 2000, p. 239.

45 Personal interview with Salah Abdul Maqsud, Cairo, 2 July 2002.

8

LEGALISED EXCLUSION OF THE ISLAMISTS

During the period from 2000 until Mubarak's fall in 2011, several crucial events transformed the conflict between the Brothers and the Egyptian regime. The 11 September 2001 attacks marked the beginning of a new strategy in the region. Now, security took priority over political reform. This reprioritisation caused a worsening of relations between the authoritarian regimes and Islamists. In the case of Egypt, the surprising rise of the Brothers, in parallel with similar successes by Islamists in other Arab and Islamic countries (such as the Palestinian Territories and Turkey), and their taking control of 20 per cent of the seats in the People's Assembly in the 2005 elections, aroused an unprecedented level of fear in the regime that pushed it to follow a strategy that one analyst described as 'legalised exclusion'.[1]

While increasingly afraid that the Brothers' strong showing could lead to events like those in Algeria in 1991 or Palestine in 2006, the regime was also going through other changes, related to the president himself, in first years of the twenty-first century. With Hosni Mubarak turning 80 in 2008 and both foreign observers and ordinary Egyptians increasingly raising questions about his health, power brokers, including the armed forces and the NDP, began bracing for a transitional period led by Mubarak's son Jamal and his inner circle. At the time, of course, no one imagined that Mubarak's rule would end in a popular revolt benefiting his traditional rivals, the Islamists. Although it had been trying to impede the Brothers without completely cracking down on them since the 1990s (as seen in Chapter Six), the regime started, in 2007, to legalise its conflict with the Brothers and put rules in place for their political, economic and social exclusion. This legalisation would prove to be the final stage of the conflict between the Brothers and the Mubarak regime before the regime's collapse in 2011. This chapter will address the political, economic and social developments that occurred during the period starting with the elections in 2000 and ending in 2007.

The 2000 Elections

The People's Assembly elections in 2000 took place under complete judicial supervision, a development without precedent since the beginning of the multi-party experiment in 1976.[2] This unprecedented action had the benefit of allowing for elections that were largely unmarred by the irregularities seen in previous polls.[3] Consequently, the Assembly provided a more accurate picture of Egypt's political topography and demonstrated clearly the declining popularity of both the ruling NDP and the opposition parties in contrast to the Islamists and independents, both of whom gained ground.[4]

Only 172 of the NDP's 443 candidates won seats, compared to 317 in the 1995 elections, meaning that the party lost 145 seats in the People's Assembly in the year 2000.[5] The other opposition parties fared no better, with the New Wafd party winning seven seats and Tajammu' six seats; negligible numbers compared to the number of deputies in the Assembly (444) and the number of nominees both parties put forward (270 for the New Wafd and 57 for Tajammu').[6] Independent deputies took the largest number of Assembly seats, suggesting both that the political parties in Egypt were on the decline and that a culture of individual political action was resurgent. Prior to some of the independents joining ranks with the NDP after election results were announced, as was typical during this era, independents had held 232 seats, a narrow majority.[7] Among the independents, the Muslim Brothers had 75 candidates, 17 of whom were victorious (compared to a single deputy in 1995), allowing the Brothers to claim third place behind the independents and the NDP in what were relatively transparent elections.

Although the NDP retained control over the People's Assembly, the results still unnerved the regime. An unexpectedly large number of veteran NDP leaders were unseated in districts they had long controlled, which strengthened the impression that there was a growing popular desire for change. Ironically, the voters' desire for change was directed not only against members of the ruling NDP, but also against the opposition parties.

The Brothers in the 2000 Elections

The Muslim Brothers entered the elections as independents, and were not allied with any party as they had previously been with the New Wafd Party in 1984 and the Labour Party in 1987. Although the electoral system opened the door for a banned movement to take part in the elections, it was far from perfect. The Brothers responded to the opportunity with prudent caution, so as not to give the authorities an excuse to void the elections. The Brothers fielded only 75 candidates, down from 170 in 1995, to avoid crossing paths with the government. They also avoided overly ideological slogans such as 'Islam is the Solution', which would label their candidates as members of an underground organisation and could lead to their arrest. Instead of the central Brothers organisation assuming election campaign management, individual candidates were allowed to choose their own slogans and electoral platforms according to their own preferences and their constituencies' concerns.

Despite the judicial oversight and a blind eye being turned towards the Brothers' participation in the democratic game as independents, the 2000 elections, like previous ones, witnessed violence by security forces against the Brothers' candidates and supporters in an effort to obstruct the Brothers from reaching polling places. Election violence has been a regular feature of Egyptian politics, with the opposition at large a target, especially when the Brothers have been the toughest challenger.[8] In the face of the state's violence, the Brotherhood was able to win 17 seats in the People's Assembly – thus, as its largest block, claiming the mantle of the opposition. The Brothers' former Supreme Guide (*murshid*), Ma'mun Al-Hudaybi, called the electoral wins "an unprecedented achievement for the group, rivalled only by the Brothers' winning 36 seats in the 1987 elections". An internal memo attributed their strong showing to the judicial oversight, the Brothers' organisational performance, their members' popularity from social work and the opportunities afforded by modern technology, such as the internet and mobile phones, to chip away at the state's control over campaign advertising.[9]

The Brothers' 17 members in parliament were highly active, using the oversight tools at their disposal. Although some of the deputies had been nominated due to their popularity or family ties in their constituencies, and did not necessarily have any political experience, the Brothers' political bureau held courses for its deputies on current political topics and how to raise parliamentary interest in a given topic, while acting within the confines of the law and professional standards.[10] The political bureau was able to offer this training thanks to the experience accumulated by incumbent deputies in previous sessions of parliament.

According to a report commissioned by the People's Assembly on its deputies' performance, the 2000 parliament saw a high number of parliamentary question asked (53), 11 of which were initiated by Brothers (compared to four by the New Wafd and six by Tajammu'). The Brothers' questions covered a range of issues from public debt to corruption in a variety of arenas including banking, food subsidies, private sector companies with monopolies over public utilities (such as mobile phones), and government bodies (such as the Ministry of Agriculture). Questions were also asked about reports of torture taking place in police stations, and on everyday matters such as inflation and shoddy public services.[11] In foreign policy, the deputies jumped on the issue of bloodshed in the Holy Land after the outbreak of the Second Intifada in order to pressure the government to cut ties with Israel. Similarly, when the US occupied Iraq, the Brotherhood called for Egypt to freeze relations with America.[12]

The 2005 Elections

Egyptians went to vote in the 2005 parliamentary elections during a time of political activism resulting from the presidential elections earlier that year, when the movement against President Mubarak nominating himself for a fourth term gained steam.[13] This also coincided with growing American pressure on the regime to demonstrate a higher level of political fairness in dealing with the opposition, including the Brothers. Although the election results guaranteed the ruling NDP's continued control over the People's Assembly with a comfortable majority, the fairness of the elections, particularly in the first and second rounds, resulted in an unexpectedly strong showing for the Brothers, who surged from 17 seats in the 2000 elections to 88 seats in 2005. The rest of the opposition parties, meanwhile, combined for a mere 9 seats (including six for the New Wafd and 2 for Tajammu' and 1 for Al-Gad). The Brothers became the new face of the opposition, a development that coincided regionally with Hamas's victory in the Palestinian elections. The increased presence of the Brotherhood also ushered in a new phase of conflict between the state and the Brothers that manifested itself first in the Brothers' financial and political leadership being put on military trial and then again in 2007 with the passing of a constitutional amendment that was designed to prevent a repeat of the 2005 elections.

In these elections, the NDP was hardly at its best. Despite a push for party reform led by the president's son Jamal Mubarak, a number of external factors undermined his efforts and NDP's electoral performance, including Egyptians' desire for change, an internal power struggle between the old guard and the youth and increasing defections. The NDP's grip over the People's Assembly slipped, as only 141 of its candidates won seats in 2005, compared to 172 in 2000. Analysts attributed the NDP's weakness to its poor organisational structure, its lack of standards in selecting candidates, its poor management of the election campaigns and its association with the state.[14]

Popular discontent with the NDP's inability to distinguish itself from the state was not only limited to the regime's failure to meet people's principal needs in terms of jobs, education, health care and economic and political reform, but also stemmed from the regime's violence against voters in the elections – with heavy-handed security force intervention on the NDP's side. These tactics of using ex-convicts to harass voters, referred to in Egypt as 'thuggery' (al-baltajiya), and the tight security cordon around polling centres which prevented many from casting their votes, fed popular dissatisfaction with the government which culminated in the 2011 revolution. Consequently, the NDP's disappointing results in 2005, in addition to reducing the state's legitimacy based on its accomplishments, also revealed escalating state-sanctioned violence against its own citizens. Both of those factors fed straight into a growing hatred of the ruling party.

The Brotherhood in the 2005 Elections

Although it is all too common in Egypt, election violence did not reach its peak until the third round of the 2005 parliamentary elections when the conflict between the state and the Brothers took centre stage. "[M]ore like a war between the security forces and the Egyptian population",[15] the unprecedented violence was a direct result of the regime's shock at the unexpected victory being claimed by the Muslim Brothers. The Brothers fielded

161 candidates, twice as many as in 2000, and 88 of them were victorious. The elections took place in three rounds in the various districts, with the Brotherhood winning 34 seats in the first round (half as many as the NDP's 68), 42 seats in the second round (compared to 40 for the NDP) and 12 seats in the third round (with 37 for the NDP). The final results were widely perceived as a victory for the Brothers as they made huge gains at the expense of both the other opposition parties (12 seats) and the NDP. This came as a surprise to everyone, including the Brothers themselves. As former Deputy of the Supreme Guide Mohammad Habib said:

> We were not expecting this mass turnout in the elections, and we were not expecting the judges to courageously defend the ballot boxes, with some judges even having broken arms, with others humiliated and cursed. We were not expecting all this. When they were asking me on the satellite channels about the number of candidates that would win, I had been saying roughly 50 or 60 at most. This number was based on our previous experience in dealing with the regime, and the extent of the vote-rigging that would take place. For example, if 90 per cent of the votes were rigged, I would have 10 winning candidates, and if 80 per cent of the votes were rigged, I would have 15 winning members, and so on.[16]

The election results confirmed that the Brothers' practical legitimacy was solidified, as the Brothers "exploited their presence in offering goods and services to citizens at reduced prices, which poised them to gain thousands of votes as soon as free, fair elections were held".[17] Two other factors enhanced the Brothers' legitimacy. First, the Brothers were able to offer alternative services to the regime's at a time when the regime's legitimacy was quickly being eroded by its declining economic and social performance. Secondly, the group's well-run organisation allowed it to offer its services efficiently. This is not to deny the importance of other factors such as the Brothers' appealing religious rhetoric, or the tribal or family ties of some Brotherhood deputies in the countryside that could influence voting. However, given the declining economic situation and citizens' unmet basic needs, the efficient provision of services remains the most important dynamic in explaining the Brothers' popularity in Egypt.

The Constitutional Amendments

The Brothers' surprise ascendency to the People's Assembly with 88 deputies coincided with local, regional and international developments that pushed the regime to adopt a strategy of 'legalising' exclusion of the Brothers from politics. The regime achieved this through constitutional amendments proposed by President Mubarak and approved by the People's Assembly in March 2007.[18] Locally, the regime began paving the way for a post-Mubarak era, as the president was 79 years old in 2007. This proved to be a complex transitional period in which the president, his son Jamal Mubarak and his coterie, the armed forces, and the NDP were all jockeying for position.[19] Regionally, the 76 of 132 seats that Hamas won in the Palestinian legislative council elections heightened the regime's fears that, should the Brothers' sway in the People's Assembly expand even further in the following elections, a similar scenario to the one in Palestine could play out in Egypt.[20] On the international stage, the US abandoned its Middle Eastern political reform agenda in 2006, in large part due to the ascendancy of Islamist parties, and decided instead to renew alliances with authoritarian regimes in order to confront terrorism more effectively.

According to political scientist Amr Hamzawy, the regime hoped that the constitutional amendments would narrow the space for political participation available for the Brothers, prevent the opposition from creating a united front incorporating Islamists and secularists and create constitutional tools guaranteeing its control over the results in presidential, parliamentary, and local elections. Even though the constitutional amendments would close doors to the Brothers politically, the group was confident that the amendments would not detract from its deeper legitimacy in Egyptian society.[21]

The Party's Political Platform

Confronted with the regime's attempt to exclude the Brothers from the political game, and under the siege imposed by the constitutional amendments, former Supreme Guide (*murshid*) Mahdi 'Akif announced that the Brothers would be forming a political party. The party released its first draft platform to the media in September 2007, without it being officially submitted to the government Party Affairs Committee. Of course, the Brothers' intention to form a political party was nothing new. The desire can be traced back to the 1980s when, inspired by the Supreme Guide (*murshid*) at the time, Umar Tilmesani, the Brothers reversed their historical negative stance towards political parties and successfully took part in the 1984 and 1987 elections. The Brothers' 2007 discussion about creating a clearly outlined party platform was also not without precedent since the group had previously experimented with the founding of political parties at least four times: Al-Shura (Consultation Party) in 1987, Islah in 1991, 'Amal in 1994, and Al-Wasat (Centre Party) in 1996.[22] It would not be possible to understand the dimensions of the Brothers' proposed political party without examining the contexts surrounding their previous attempts. With the exception of Al-Shura, all of the others came into existence during the 1990s as the Brothers began to run up against the Mubarak regime and were looking for spaces in which their existence would be legal. The 'Amal Party, for instance, was formed "because of the regime's crackdown on the Brothers-dominated professional syndicates",[23] while the Wasat Party was in response to the military tribunals of 1995.[24] Similarly, 'Akif's announcement in April 2007 came shortly after the Al-Azhar students' incident in December 2006 and was motivated by a desire to "alleviate the security forces' pressure against the Brothers",[25] and "to break the political impasse with the state".[26] The Brothers' initiative clearly came as part of their attempt to lift the government's siege and to obtain legal recognition, but not necessarily by obtaining a licence directly from the Party Affairs Committee. The Brothers' leadership was convinced that the Mubarak regime would not recognise the group, whether or not it formed a party, but felt that floating the idea of a political party could help the Brothers in a way that obtaining a Party Affairs Committee permit could not. For example, the Brothers believed that the suggestion of a party was a good way of testing the political waters and encouraging the public's acceptance of a politically active Brotherhood in the post-Mubarak era. This latter belief explains why the group decided to publicise its political party aspirations in 2007, whereas it had not done so in its previous experiments.

The Brothers' experiments at founding a party in the 1980s and 1990s must be understood in two contexts. Firstly, it was the reaction of a generation of professional syndicate members seeking to reconcile their expansion within society with their affiliation with an organisation eager to reassure society that its plans were peaceful and political. Secondly, it was the vision of the group's political leadership, which believed that going too far into politics would trigger another government crackdown. These early attempts since 1986 at forming a party had all been formulated under the leadership of the late Ma'mun Al-Hudaybi.[27] Al-Hudaybi believed that the political circumstances, with the rising violence in Egypt in the early 1990s, would make the state unwilling to allow the Brothers to create a political party, and if an application were submitted to the Party Affairs Council it would be rejected, shutting the door to political legitimacy for the movement.[28] However, the generation that joined the Brothers in the 1970s, a group that had contacts with a broader segment of society and had been successful in expanding the movement within Egyptian civil society, saw things differently. Some of them believed that it would be possible to dupe the regime and apply for a party that seemed to be independent; should this party be granted a permit, then the Brothers could join it, which was the logic behind the 'Amal Party. Others were optimistic that an application could be submitted to the Party Affairs Committee without permission from the Brothers' leadership, even if this meant they would be expelled from the organisation, as happened with the Wasat Party. Whereas this 1970s generation thought that announcing a political party would prompt the government to relax its restrictions on the Brothers, as the regime's argument that the Brothers were a secret, underground organisation rejecting political participation would be invalidated, Al-Hudaybi believed that the timing was not right for this step, and that the government would respond by intensifying its crackdown.

The political circumstances shifted with the passing of Ma'mun Al-Hudaybi in 2004, his replacement by Mahdi 'Akif, the Brothers' electoral success the following year, the emergence of a stronger popular opposition to Mubarak after he nominated himself for a fourth term also in 2005, and then later the constitutional amendments of 2007. 'Akif differed from Al-Hudaybi in his handling of political affairs. The most important change 'Akif instituted had to do with the Brotherhood's voice. No longer would there be a single person in charge who was the group's official spokesperson, as with Al-Hudaybi, who had monopolised this position himself.

Ma'mun Al-Hudaybi as a counsellor and judge made very precise calculations, and was overly cautious. He had had the political file since the days of Hamed Abu al-Nasr, and did not let anyone other than him talk. For that reason, the Brothers barely had speakers, because he was the speaker. I'm not like that, from the first day I said: 'All of the Brothers have the right to speak for the Brothers, on the satellite channels and elsewhere. When someone makes a mistake, we'll correct him. The Brothers have multiplied and grown, and there cannot be just one person speaking for them.'[29]

While Al-Hudaybi had been ready to postpone starting a political party until a post-Mubarak Egypt, 'Akif and those in his circle like Mohammad Habib, Abdul Al-Mun'em Abu Al-Futuh and 'Esam Al-'Aryan argued that the rationale for postponement no longer held given the group's spreading influence in the street before an aging regime. Al-Hudaybi, with his legal background and conservative outlook, was concerned primarily with avoiding a confrontation that would set off a crackdown. In contrast, the more spontaneous and occasionally defiant 'Akif believed the opposite: established political vitality could thwart attempts to stifle the Brothers.

Beyond 'Akif and Al-Hudaybi's differences in personality, and more important, were the political circumstances in Egypt and the region, which emboldened the Brothers in the 2000s to venture beyond what Al-Hudaybi had seen as a red line in the 1980s and 1990s. American pressure on the Arab regimes to democratise, oppositional challenges to the ossified regimes by demonstrating in the street (such as the *Kifaya* movement), Islamist victories in Palestine (Hamas), Egypt (the Brothers), Yemen and Kuwait, and the greater openness created by satellite channels and the internet were all transformations not conducive to a culture of risk avoidance. According to 'Akif:

> The global atmosphere today does not allow us to accept from [the regime], what used to happen to us in the 1980s and 1990s. At that time, there were not any satellite channels, and in the days of Mustafa Mashhur we put up with a lot. Nobody knew what was happening to us, so we just said we'll have to put up with it. The reality of the world has changed now, the global atmosphere is open. We see demonstrations against Bush in America, Blair in London, and every country is in a situation different than what was the case in the 1990s.[30]

Locally, the Brothers winning 88 seats in the 2005 elections transformed the rhetoric of Egyptian opposition leaders, Islamist and secularist alike, as the Brothers' vision of political reform became an important component. The Brothers' draft political platform was not directly aimed at obtaining a permit from the Party Affairs Committee, which, particularly after the constitutional amendments, the organisation believed was next to impossible, but rather was designed to address the public's concerns and uncertainty about the Brothers' views on political, economic, and social issues. According to al-Aryan, outlining their political platform had become necessary for several reasons:

> The party for us does not mean simply a permit, but rather means clarifying our vision, and means inter-party relations. The issue of the Brothers' political party is on the table for the elites and the parties, which is 'Why don't the Brothers have a party?' There are also questions for the Brothers from the international community: 'What will you do about so-and-so, what is your stance on so-and-so?' The last reason is that proposing a party now breaks a political impasse, and a breakthrough could come at any time, there could be a democratic breakthrough, so shouldn't we be ready from the beginning instead of waiting and being outpaced by events and then thinking of what to do?[31]

Rather than target the Party Affairs Committee, the Brothers, with the draft political platform, were aiming at the elite of society as well as the opposition front which, due to regime policies, had been both growing in size in recent years and seeking to build on the Brothers' popularity in the street. The Brothers were hoping to amass public opinion, as expressed by the elites, in favour of pressuring the government to recognise their movement should a democratic breakthrough occur after the end of the Mubarak regime.

Inter-party Relations and the Organisation

The draft party platform prompted questions about the nature of the relationship between the party and the Brothers as an organisation. The debate within the movement is still unresolved as to how to run two organisations which are different in their structural nature: an openly announced party and a covert religious organisation, each with their own members, roles and audiences. There is a small minority within the Brothers, which could perhaps be said to represent, that believes that "the Muslim Brothers organisation in Egypt is transforming into the Muslim Brothers party, the Muslim Brothers' supreme guide is becoming the head of this party, the guidance bureau is the political bureau of this party, and the Muslim Brothers' local offices are this party's branches".[32] The majority, like 'Esam Al-'Aryan, are of the view that there should be a system for coordination between the party and the organisation, similar to that in Jordan between the Muslim Brothers and the Islamic Action Front.[33] Meanwhile, the independents believe that "it is not only important that the party and the broader organisation have separate identities, but also full (and not merely formal) autonomy".[34] (There is more on the relationship between the party and the organisation in Chapter Seven.)

The Party Platform

The Brothers distributed their party platform to a select group of Egyptian intellectuals,[35] a move that came under fire from those who had been expecting the movement to openly announce its platform in a press conference, as had happened in the 2004 reform initiative. This move would also have given more substance to the Brothers' labelling of the Egyptian people as the source of authority and having the inherent right to choose their ruler and deputies. However, the most controversial item for a broad segment of society in the draft platform was the Brothers' limiting the presidency to Muslims.[36] When I met with Al-'Aryan in April 2007, five months before the first draft was circulated, I asked him whether the platform would stipulate that the head of state had to be a Muslim. He replied: "We have not yet determined this, and it is a controversial issue within the group. That the president would be a Muslim is a fait accompli, so why should we even stipulate it and provoke controversy?"[37] In the Postscript, I shall address the evolution of the Brothers' partisan ideology after the fall of Mubarak and the group founded the Freedom and Justice Party.

The Syndicates

From 2000 on, the professional syndicates began to lose the reputation they had held from the mid-1980s through the 1990s as Brotherhood strongholds, even though the Brothers continued to dominate the Doctors' Syndicate, the Lawyers' Syndicate and the Scientists' Syndicate.[38] The cancellation of syndicate elections after 1990 checked the Brothers' sway within the syndicates, and the syndicates are now relatively inactive because most of their board members have been in position for a very long time.[39] According to Mohammed Fouda, a Brothers leader and member of the Dentists' Syndicate board:

> The last time I was elected was 1990, and I've remained a member of the board until now, which is 17 continuous years, besides the previous terms. Of course lethargy has set in amongst those in the syndicates, because the people have not changed, there is no new blood, and there are very few effective people in the syndicate, because people's concerns change. My own concerns in the syndicate board will not necessary stay the same through the length of my presence in the syndicate. The lack of elections has definitely caused the syndicates' work to stagnate.[40]

This stagnancy was reflected in the syndicates' reduced role in Egypt's political developments, and they played no role in either the elections of 2005 or the 2007 constitutional amendment. The Doctors' Syndicate no longer had active leaders such as those who pushed it to quickly mobilise after the 1992 earthquake, "because some had died, some had travelled abroad, and others had aged and were unable to contribute".[41] According to Abu Al-Futuh, the regime did not expel the Brothers from the syndicates; rather, it obstructed them from being effective by abolishing the elections. Even though the group's charitable activities did not stop, it was no longer able to take the initiative as it could in the 1980s. In some syndicates, such as the Doctors' Syndicate, the Brothers sought to file a lawsuit against the government to force it to allow syndicate elections. Abu Al-Futuh says that the courts did rule in favour of holding the elections, but that the government refused to enforce the ruling.[42]

Mohammad Habib disagrees with any generalisation about all of the syndicates, arguing that each was going through its own unique circumstances, and that there were impediments other than the regime crackdown or the inactive syndicate boards. In the Scientists' Syndicate, which had a heavy Brothers presence, for instance, the syndicate is unable to offer attractive benefits to its members such as health care, insurance, and pensions, due to "the low syndicate budget and the low financial resources from memberships".[43]

The movement believed that it lost an important civil society space as the syndicates' role faded, but remained confident that it still maintained its legitimacy among the middle and lower classes due to its active presence in other spaces where the state is unable to eradicate it, such as in charitable organisations, schools and neighbourhood medical clinics.[44] By offering neighbourhood social and charitable activities, and through other spaces out of the state's realm such as mosques, the Brothers accumulate 'real legitimacy' which at least partially compensates for their loss of legitimacy from syndicate activism. This can be seen clearly in the parliamentary elections, with votes cast for the Brothers' candidate as a result of service/charity-related motivations, tribal/family ties (as in Upper Egypt), or out of spite for the ruling NDP.

The Student Movement

Inside the universities, the Brothers continued to enjoy a freedom of movement not available to them in other social spaces, even as tensions with the government escalated. This was reflected in student political and community activism, particularly from 2004 to 2007, when such activism was at its height, which enhanced the group's legitimacy on the Egyptian street. The community services offered were focused on student-specific needs, such as printing study guides, offering revision sessions, and holding book, clothing, and lab equipment exhibits with subsidised prices. Over time, the services offered became more professional, targeting a broader range of the student body regardless of ideological affiliation, including Copts.[45] At schools such as Alexandria University and Minya University, the organisation sought to offer discounted charter buses for students commuting from outlying areas, but the security agencies intervened to put an end to this.[46]

The services offered were tailored to meet student needs, with the grassroots student leaders themselves determining what type of services were needed, rather than the central student leadership within the organisation (as Al-Jama'at Al-Islamiyya had done in the 1970s). The Brothers kept abreast of student needs through regular opinion surveys, which, since 2000, have also evolved to become more strictly focused on student issues and less politicised. The Brothers formed what they named the Student Service Committee to plan ahead for the services they would offer over the course of the academic year, which were recently amended to include psychological and social counselling for students.

It could be said that what most distinguished the Brothers' services in the universities is that they were social rather than religious in an ideological sense. This allowed the Brothers to improve outreach to students religiously or politically unaffiliated with the Brothers, including Copts. Furthermore, the services were carefully tailored to student needs rather than to the organisation's religious and political line, and the organisation leadership following a decentralised, grassroots model well suited to the university atmosphere and the greater level of freedom afforded on campus.

Suspending Student Elections

The cancellation of the professional syndicate elections may have checked the Muslim Brothers' influence within these institutions, but it did not block other avenues to reach a group just as important as middle-class professionals, namely university students. While the Brothers' ascent in the syndicates during the 1980s (see Chapter Three) justifiably drew heavy attention from scholars examining the movement, from the year 2000 on, the Brothers' rising fortunes in the universities has arguably been one of the most important developments, along with of course the Brothers' greatly expanded influence in Parliament. The Al-Azhar University students' incident in 2006 was but one of the indicators of the emergence of university campuses, taking the place of the syndicates which had been so prominent in the 1980s, as an arena of conflict between the Brothers and the state.

Whereas cancelling the syndicate elections had deflated the Brothers' syndicate-based activism, the security forces' moves to exclude the Brothers from taking part in student body elections backfired. Rather than paralyse the group's student movement, the security forces' move actually reinvigorated it and encouraged it to play the active role it had failed to play in the 1980s. The difference between the two can be attributed to the fact that universities in Egypt are by nature very different from syndicates. Egyptian syndicates at the end of the day are government or semi-governmental institutions, reliant on state resources from their respective ministries to offer their services to members. Most syndicate members, or at least a key segment of them, work in public sector institutions,

and consequently have limits on their freedom to mobilise politically or to offer services, and can be constrained by laws which
overall affect the syndicates' performance. Universities, meanwhile,
are also governmental institutions, but by their nature are more
detached from the state, and there is a greater degree of freedom
on a university campus than elsewhere, as long as any activities
remain on campus and do not spill out into other social spaces.

Furthermore, the student demographic is inherently different
from the professionals, since the former, being younger (17
to 20 years), tend to be more active and therefore less affected
by whether or not there are regular elections, unlike with the
syndicates. The fact that students only spend typically four years in
university also serves to constantly renew this demographic group's
vitality with the passage of time.

Students' need for belonging and the group dynamics of the
friendships they form also tend to encourage active participation in
a shared organisation, which gives them a sense of identity and vision
for dealing with the complex environment in which they live. These
are all elements encouraging campus activism which are not present
in the syndicates. Due to these differences between the university
and the syndicate as institutions, as well as between students and
professionals as demographic groups, it is unsurprising that the
state's attempt to suppress the Brothers met with different results
on the university campus, and even backfired and provoked more
Brothers activism, as was the case in the Al-Azhar University student
incident.

By 2000, free and fair student body elections were a thing of the
past in Egyptian universities, and the election setup was skewed
towards student groups loyal to the NDP, with Brothers students
denied a chance to compete. Although these practices were present
in the 1990s, they did not fully undermine student body elections
until 1998. It was at that point that the elections lost all value, with
the results preordained. Even though the Brothers continued to
dominate the most prestigious colleges within the top Egyptian
universities with their numerical advantage, such as the College of
Medicine and the College of Engineering, they were nevertheless
successfully excluded by the security forces from the student union
leaderships representing these colleges. The exclusion was so
extensive that that the Brothers lost control of the student union
leaderships that they had held since the mid-1980s and early 1990s
in Alexandria, Minya, Asyut and Zaqaziq.

At the beginning of the year 2000, university administrations, in close cooperation with the security forces that maintained a heavy and constant presence on campus, began to intensify efforts to hinder the Brothers' participation in student body elections. In the 1990s, nominations had been conducted openly, and the university administration was reliant on the security forces to use violence and student thugs against the Brothers' members and supporters to prevent them from reaching the ballot box. When this proved insufficient in the face of the Brothers' determination to take part – some Brothers even won elections – the university administration used a new method. University administrations stopped announcing that nominations had begun and held elections secretly or with little advance notice. In the end, the administrations' manoeuvres worked in the favour of pro-government student groups such as Horras, with the administration sponsoring candidates under the pretext that there were no competing nominees.[47] As a result, by 2002, the Brothers had been pushed out of the student unions: an unprecedented development.

It appears that the regime believed that by shutting the Brothers out of the student unions, it had paralysed the organisation's campus activism, as had happened in the syndicates. However, the inherent differences mentioned above between the student demographic and the syndicate professionals, even though both belonged to the same overarching organisation, stymied the government.

Faced with a policy of exclusion, the student Brothers took two countermeasures. Firstly, instead of working under the label of 'the Islamic Current', as they had previously, the students announced their affiliation to the officially banned Muslim Brothers movement and continued their campus activism under this name. Secondly, the Brothers announced elections for a shadow student government they called 'the Free Union', working in parallel to the student union controlled by the university administration and State Security (*amn al-dawla*). By 2000, the regime was so concerned that student groups were openly operating under the Muslim Brothers name that it moved to expel or suspend some students as well as remove any fliers they posted.

The Al-Azhar University Students Incident

The formation of the Free Union and the Free General Union for Egypt's Universities resulted in more suspensions of students who had taken part in the parallel elections, regardless of their affiliation. Specifically, a large number of Brothers students at Al-Azhar University, where the organisation has long been powerful, were suspended.[48] The suspended students then started a sit-in preceded by a parade resembling the parades occasionally put on in support of the Palestinian Intifada in an effort to draw media attention to their cause. Mahmoud was one of the journalists whom the Al-Azhar students invited to attend the parade:

> They called me and told me that they were going to have an athletic parade before the sit-in against the suspension policy. I didn't understand what they meant by an 'athletic parade', so I asked the person who had invited him, whose name is Abdel-Rahman, 'Why an athletic parade?' He told me 'So we can get as many cameras as possible'. The only media that attended the sit-in was a single newspaper, *Al-Masry Al-Yaum*, which depicted the event as being paramilitary militias, not an athletic parade, even though the editor of the news item, and the person who photographed the event, did not say that. Without a doubt the students' idea to express their anger was abnormal, and we as Brothers were saying that their idea was abnormal, but it was the political context through which the country was passing that made the regime follow a policy of jumping on the mistakes to escalate the pressure against the group.[49]

Under pressure from the students' bureau in the Brothers organisation, of which Mahmoud was a member, the Al-Azhar students issued a statement apologising for the means to which they resorted to express their anger, explaining: "what pushed us to conduct this parade was our feeling that no one was listening to us or moving to demand our freedom within the university".[50] The pro-regime newspapers did not publish this statement, while the security forces launched an armed night raid in the Abraj Al-Safa dorms where Al-Azhar students who were Brothers live, arresting 180 students.[51] Diaa Rashwan, an expert on Islamist movements, attributed the heavy-handed response by security to the inflammatory language used by the pro-NDP press, such as *Ruz Al-Yusuf* and *Nahdat Misr*.[52] The arrests not only included Al-Azhar students, but were broadened by the government to target the Brothers' leaders, including the deputy Supreme Guide, Khairat al-Shatir. All of those arrested were put on military trial for the events at Al-Azhar.[53]

Student Political Activism

In 2004, Egypt witnessed an unprecedented surge in political activism that began as a popular reaction against President Mubarak's move to take a fourth presidential term and grew in size during both the 2005 elections and the 2007 constitutional amendments. The political action could be seen clearly in the intellectual elite, which founded the *Kifaya* ('Enough') movement as a means by which to spearhead the peaceful anti-Mubarak protest movement. Interestingly as well, the *Kifaya* movement was also visible on university campuses.[54] In 2005, Brothers students began the Together for Reform campaign jointly with socialists and independent student groups. The campaign was launched at Cairo University under the Brothers' name with a march by the movement's students from several universities.[55] 'Together for Reform' focused on student concerns, most importantly to undo the restrictions on student activities imposed by Sadat in 1979. Offering a modernised model for student rules and regulations instead, the group declared that student elections should be free and fair and that the General Union of Egyptian students should return.[56] The students also addressed corruption in education, arguing that "the university lecture halls are ancient and decrepit, the laboratories are not equipped with equipment that would allow us to practically apply what we are learning, and the overall atmosphere is corrupt, so we cannot make progress in our studies as long as we lack freedom".[57]

The Brothers exploited the relative freedom on campus to mobilise students for political participation in support of the organisation in the parliamentary elections of 2000 and 2005 (as in previous elections).[58] The students used the walls encircling Egyptian campuses as a space to put up posters of Brothers candidates, distribute their electoral platform, and encourage students to vote for them, hoping to increase support for the Brothers' candidates from students ideologically unaffiliated with them based on the services the organisation offered on campus. The Brothers also benefited from the NDP's declining popularity, even among Copts: "we have Christian classmates who told us that they cast their votes for the Brothers to spite the corrupt [National Democratic] Party".[59]

The group's student voter turnout efforts extended off campus as well, and they distributed their candidates' platforms in the dorms, urging those of voting age (18 years, usually in their second year of university) to do what they needed to in order to vote. Actions required to vote ranged from going to the police station to obtain a voter registration card, to going to a polling place in their area of residence on election day. The student campaigns included the 'We Refuse' campaign against the 2007 constitutional amendments, which involved the distribution of literature on campus: an action the Brothers were unable to do outside of the university setting.[60] The campaign emphatically rejected the principles of reduced freedoms, the exclusion of the judges from the electoral process and the separation of religion and state.[61]

By studying the performance of the student movement from 2000 until the 2007 constitutional amendments, a number of conclusions can be made. Firstly, the student demographic was inherently active, and able to resist the stagnancy that overcame the syndicates, due to both age and the nature of the university space. Secondly, the Brothers' rhetoric had evolved within the university to incorporate more outreach to non-members, including Copts, whether in the services offered to students or in political mobilisation. Thirdly, moving away from the name 'the Islamic Current' and openly embracing 'the Muslim Brothers', which came as the Egyptian political scene stirred to life in 2004, signalled the organisation's determination to establish its presence in the face of the state's refusal to recognise its legitimacy.

Money in the Regime–Brothers Conflict

The wave of arrests in December 2006 primarily targeted the Brothers' financiers. Those arrested were charged with money laundering and sent to military tribunals in April of the next year, a move that drew attention to the financial dimension of the struggle between the Brothers and the regime.[62] Whereas referring the Brothers' leaders to military tribunals in 1995 is understandable given that those leaders comprised the heart of the movement within the syndicates and parliament, the motivation for targeting financiers 12 years later is debatable, even considering that the arrests occurred in an advanced stage of the conflict. In general, the movement's rising influence in politics and on the street, Islamists gaining power in some neighbouring countries (specifically Hamas in Palestine), Islamists' electoral successes in Egypt, Kuwait, Bahrain and Morocco and the American alliance with authoritarian regimes in the War on Terror were all factors working in parallel to encourage the regime to move against the Brothers. However, this does not answer the question of why the Brothers' financing was in the crosshairs this time.

Diaa Rashwan maintains that the Brothers' financing was targeted so that the security services could "try out a new method of reducing the movement's influence" after its previous methods, including arrests, trials and smearing the group in the media, had failed. Rashwan says the new security strategy has also failed, arguing that the Brothers' strength lies not in their financial resources but rather in their strong organisational structure and their members' commitment to the group's objectives.[63] He goes on to suggest that the organisation's financial resources are not as extensive as portrayed by Egyptian government media, and that the costs of their activities are covered by efforts from individual members.

The movement's leadership links the arrest and military trial of their financiers to the Brothers' surprise victory in 88 parliamentary districts in the 2005 elections, claiming that the Mubarak regime was trying to "dry up the sources of financial support" for their electoral campaigns. To understand the relationship between financing and the Brothers' growing political strength, we should know where the group obtains its funding. The funds come primarily from (1) businessmen within Egypt, (2) Egyptian businessmen abroad, and (3) individual membership fees and election campaign contributions.

Businessmen such as the contractor Abdel Rahman Saudi, the corporate titan Hassan Malek and his partner Khairat al-Shatir offer vital financial backing to the Brothers during the election campaigns.[64] The fees which members regularly contribute to the Brothers are substantial, a set percentage of 10 per cent of their annual income.[65] Brothers who work abroad in the Gulf and Libya pay regular monthly membership fees, which increase during the election season. Finally, although the number of Brothers members in Egypt is not public information, it is in the hundreds of thousands, and they pay membership fees supporting the group's activities.[66]

While there was nothing new in businessmen backing the Brothers, they had provoked the government's wrath in 2007 by playing a larger role in the 2005 elections than in the 1995 and 2000 elections. The 2005 elections were characterised by heavy spending on advertising, with one study concluding that five billion Egyptian pounds had been spent on the 2005 elections by candidates, four times the amount spent in 2000.[67] The study further concluded that the average candidate in 2000 spent 375,000 pounds, and that the cost of a single seat in the People's Assembly was 12 million pounds.[68] Based on these estimates, the domestic intelligence agencies concluded that the Brothers spent over 300 million pounds to back their 161 candidates, and that businessmen were the primary source of funding; and thus the reason they drew the attention of the security services.

In parallel with the counter-arguments, such as al-Aryan's, that financial donations to election campaigns do not justify arresting businessmen so long as they are financing peaceful activities,[69] a number of Brother and independent sources also question the validity of the 300 million pound figure. They point out that the number was calculated based on the expenditures of NDP candidates, which would suggest that the Brothers were able to compete financially with the regime. According to former Brothers leader Abdul Al-Mun'em Abu Al-Futuh:

> I met one of the security officials in the Interior Ministry, and he told me 'You spent more than 300 million pounds in the People's Assembly elections, and this bothered us.' I told him 'I know where you got that figure. You asked one of the NDP members who ran in the 2005 elections how much he spent in his race, and he told you 2 million pounds on advertising, so you said that the Brotherhood had 161 candidates, and 161 times 2 million equals 322 million pounds.' This is a huge figure, and he asked me 'Where did you get the money?'[70]

Abu Al-Futuh estimates that the Brothers spent no more than 10 million pounds on the 2005 races, because "90 per cent of the effort exerted by candidates in their districts was built on volunteering by other organisation members in the district to support the campaign".[71]

The Brothers' Financial Structure

To understand the repercussions of the arrest of the organisation's businessmen, and whether their arrest could have decided the conflict in favour of the regime, we should examine the Brothers' financial structure. More specifically, we should investigate the financiers' influence relative to the organisational structure and the movement's dynamics within Egyptian society. Firstly, there is a dividing line between the organisation's budget and its members' private capital, and no analysis should confuse the two. Secondly, since the Brotherhood was dissolved and its holdings confiscated in 1954, the group has been careful to not directly own any enterprises, and to rely on member fees to fund its activities, as well as contributions from non-members in society at large due to its social legitimacy.[72] Thirdly, the group manages its overall activities, including campaign advertising during elections, through two types of spending: centralised spending from the organisation's fund in Cairo and decentralised spending through the organisation branches' funds in the other areas and provinces. While the arrest of the financiers could hurt the group's centralised funding, it certainly could not have had an impact on its decentralised spending.[73]

The centralised spending in the Brothers organisation covers two basic activities, which is the annual Ramadan *iftar*, as well as the election advertising campaigns in some of the larger provinces like Cairo and Alexandria. Diaa Rashwan, who studied both activities, reports that the role of businessmen in them is important, but not as vital as the state security services believe:

> The Brothers have only two centralised activities: the first activity is the annual *iftar* which the Brothers do, which according to the security services' estimates for this year [2007] and according to the receipts was 225,000 pounds, by someone fairly well-off, by which I mean a small businessman. The second activity is the elections, and elections do not happen every day, but rather every five years, and not all of the districts spend as much as each other. In the cities like Cairo and Alexandria, costs are high, but in the countryside the expenditures could be one per cent of those in Cairo.[74]

As for the other Brothers activities in various areas, their costs are covered by the funds of one or more of the branches, which comprise the total membership fees of the branch members, the social institutions controlled by the Brothers, or the donations from members of society who benefit from the Brothers' services. Once again, Rashwan explains the nature of the decentralised spending:

> The Brothers in any branch office have more than one way to take action. Firstly, they have the organisation's expenditures from the branch or family membership fees, and then the Brothers also are active through NGOs. They have hun-

dreds or thousands of NGOs, whether they own them or are
partners in their boards, and they are all legal NGOs. With
regard to the election campaign advertising in the countryside, in Upper Egypt, and in the provinces, you don't spend
as much on them as you do in the large cities like Cairo and
Alexandria, because the matter is related to voluntary contributions by your relatives and the people in your district, and
it is socially shameful to take money. Consequently, what is
being said – that the Brothers spent half a billion pounds on
the elections – is nonsense.[75]

Businessmen's Influence

The decentralism in the organisation's actions, the Brothers'
reliance on membership fees, its members' volunteerism, and the
mobilisation of the NGOs which it controls all limit the influence
of businessmen over the group's dynamics. Consequently it has to
be said that the impact of their arrest was limited with respect to
the Brothers' struggle against the regime. Furthermore, the size
of the businessmen's capital is still unclear, as is the percentage of
this which is given to the Brothers as an organisation. There are
contradictory figures on the wealth of the Brothers' financiers, and
confusion between the value of the capital in their enterprises, as
opposed to the actual profits from these enterprises.

According to newspaper reports which cited the investigation
records of the detainees, the Brothers' total investments added up
to between 7 and 20 billion Egyptian pounds.[76] For instance, the
size of the investments of Abdel Rahman Saudi, one of the Brothers
businessmen and owner of the Urban Development Company,
Giza Medical, and the chain of 'Saudi' stores, was 300 million
pounds, while Hassan Malek's investments were worth more than
250 million pounds.[77] However, Brothers sources believe that the
media campaign waged by the government to sully the Brothers'
image exaggerated the businessmen's influence in order to justify
their arrest and military trial, arguing that the businessmen's actual
investments were more modest in size, and that their financial
contributions to the organisation were also limited. According to
Badr Mohammed Badr, "in my experience of over 30 years inside
the Brothers, I have not found that any of the businessmen's
companies have backed the Brothers' work as some assume, due to
the poor economic conditions in Egypt, the meagre liquidity and

the heavy taxes and corruption".[78] Badr cites the example of Abdel Rahman Saudi:

> [With] a company like Abdel Rahman Saudi's company, which is a contractor ... I personally arbitrated with the company's financial director to have it pay money that was over nine months overdue to one of the engineers working there, because these companies work with the state here and there,[79] and sometimes these payments are late, and these companies suffer from accumulating debts, including interest. You can barely find a company that says it has a surplus. This is a general economic situation with which every Egyptian is familiar, and I am certain of what I have said due to my closeness to them.[80]

Whereas the Brothers businessmen's wealth is estimated to be in the hundreds of millions, it is unclear whether these figures are referring to assets such as land and buildings that have been frozen or to liquid profits, or both together.[81] Given the deteriorating economic situation in Egypt, the poor environment for foreign investment, and the limited purchasing power of Egyptian consumers, it seems farfetched that the pro-Brothers businessmen would have had the kind of liquidity which the government media claimed. The decentralised structure of the Brothers' financing makes the organisation's dynamic in the provinces self-reliant and independent from businessmen's funds.[82]

The direct impact of the businessmen's arrest on the national economy was difficult to ascertain, taking into consideration the modest profits of their companies. However, the indirect impact will be negative in two respects. Firstly, the arrest of the businessmen, some of whom deal with foreign companies, creates a climate that is not conducive to attracting the foreign capital badly needed by the state to burnish its economic credentials. A study by the Egyptian Capital Market Authority found that the targeting of businessmen sent a negative message to businesses abroad about the investment climate in Egypt. According to Hassan Malek, a well-known Brothers businessman, "before I was arrested, I had contracted with a leading foreign [Turkish] company to invest in Egypt, and agreed with it to set up a huge factory to produce furniture for export abroad. After all of the approvals had been finished and the necessary land for the factory was set aside, I was arrested, and the company broke off the contract and left Egypt."[83] The

Capital Market Authority added that the escalation by the security services could mean a setback for the Egyptian stock market, after word spread of traders pulling out of the stock market, taking with them some 21 billion Egyptian pounds (about US$3.3 billion).

Secondly, the arrest of the Brothers' financiers directly resulted in the loss of jobs for hundreds of employees in their factories, compounding the growing problem of unemployment in Egypt.[84] This came as Egypt went through a phase of growing labour discontent about wages and the privatisation of the public sector,[85] presenting a quandary for the Mubarak regime. At the same time that it was taking aim at the Brothers' bankrolling by wiping out their members' investments and thereby exacerbating unemployment and worker frustration, the regime was also trying to improve the poor economic situation within the country. When I met with Khairat al-Shatir in 2002, he dismissed as remote the chance that the regime would strike the Brothers' economic entities due to their useful social role in alleviating unemployment.[86]

However, that the regime did in fact take aim at businessmen who were members of the Brothers shows that the regime had reached a stage where it was willing to trade off some social legitimacy for political survival, at least until 2011. This is the subject of the Postscript to this book.

Notes

1 Personal interview with Diaa Rashwan, Cairo, 8 April 2007.
2 The Supreme Constitutional Court issued a ruling on 8 July 2000 that judicial oversight was to be for all stages of the elections, from voting to announcing the results. Furthermore, instead of being limited to only the vote tallying centres, as had previously been the case, judges would also be present at the local polling places.
3 This hardly means that the 2000 elections were completely free and fair as the judicial oversight was, in practice, incomplete due to interventions by security. Likewise, some districts were supervised by bodies that take orders from the executive not judicial branch, such as the Administrative Prosecution and the State Litigation Authority.
4 Hala Mustafa (ed.). *Intikhabat majlis al-sha'b 2000*. (The 2000 People's Assembly Elections), Center for Political and Strategic Studies, Cairo, 2001, p. 307.
5 The NDP's share increased to 388 seats when some deputies who had run as independents joined the NDP. However, this was still less than the number of NDP representatives in 1995 after the same process took place and it had controlled 417 seats, so this does still indicate the party's declining popularity.

6   *Ibid*, pp. 9–10.

7   Independent candidates are nothing new to Egypt politics, but just as the phenomenon of businessmen entering politics coincided with the state withdrawing from its economic role and choosing a policy of privatisation, so too the rise of the independents in the People's Assembly coincided with the decline of political parties' role in Egyptian politics, and the existence of other, more vibrant and effective channels, both legal and illegal, to win over voters. For an analysis of the rise of independents in this election cycle, see Amr el-Chobaki, "Al-mustaqilun wa al-intikhabat" (Independents and the Elections) in Hala Mustafa (ed.), *Intikhabat majlis al-sha'b 2000* (The 2000 People's Assembly Elections), Center for Political and Strategic Studies, Cairo, 2001, pp. 87–102.

8   Al-Manissi, Ahmed. "Al-'Unf wa al-Intikhabat" (Violence and the Elections) in Hala Mustafa (ed.). *Intikhabat Majlis al-Sha'b 2000.* (The 2000 People's Assembly Elections), Center for Political and Strategic Studies, Cairo, 2001, pp. 211–225.

9   "Al-Ikhwan al-Muslimun wa al-Intikhabat" (The Muslim Brothers and the Elections), unpublished internal paper, no date.

10 Interview with an anonymous member of the Muslim Brothers' political bureau, Cairo, 11 April, 2007.

11 To see the Brothers deputies' record in the 2000 People's Assembly, refer to: "Al-Ikhwan fi Barlaman 2000: Dirasa Tahliliya li-Ada' Nawab al-Ikhwan al-Muslimin fi Barlaman 2000–2005" ("The Brothers in the 2000 Parliament: An Analytical Study of the Muslim Brothers' Deputies' Performance in the 2000–2005 Parliament"), Al-Umma Studies and Development Center, 2005.

12 *Ibid*, pp. 207–226.

13 In February 2005, Mubarak asked the People's Assembly to amend Article 76 of the constitution to replace the presidential referendum with multi-candidate elections. He labelled this a step towards greater democracy, while the opposition argued that it was only window dressing to defuse popular sentiment against Mubarak running for a fourth term.

14 Rabia, Amr Hashim. "Nata'ij al-Intikhabat al-Barlamaniya 2005" (Results of the 2005 Parliamentary Elections) in *Intikhabat Majlis Al-Sha'b 2005 (2005 People's Assembly Elections)*, Center for Political and Strategic Studies, Cairo, 2006, pp. 527–530.

15 Abu Talib, Hassan. "Al-'Unf fi al-Intikhabat: Tafaqum al-Baltajiya wa al-Tadakhulat al-Amniya" (Violence in the Elections: Exacerbated Thuggery and Security Interventions) in *Intikhabat Majlis Al-Sha'b 2005 (2005 People's Assembly Elections)*, Center for Political and Strategic Studies, Cairo, 2006, p. 352.

16 Personal interview with Mohammad Habib, Cairo, April 10, 2007.

17 Rabia, Amr Hashim. "Nata'ij al-Intikhabat al-barlamaniya 2005" (Results of the 2005 Parliamentary Elections) in *Intikhabat Majlis Al-Sha'b 2005 (2005 People's Assembly Elections)*, Center for Political and Strategic Studies, Cairo, 2006, p. 530.

18 The constitutional amendments included Article 179, allowing police to enter houses, conduct surveillance of mail and email, and eavesdrop

on telephone conversations without a warrant, as well as granting the president the power to refer civilians to military tribunals. Article 88 abolished judicial supervision of the elections, while Article 5 forbade political parties founded on a religious basis from taking part in the People's Assembly elections.

19 Personal interview with Diaa Rashwan, April 8, 2007.

20 From 2000 onwards, Islamists recorded successes in parliamentary elections in Kuwait, Yemen, Bahrain, Egypt, Morocco, Jordan, Iraq, and Turkey, and eventually came to power in Turkey, Egypt, and Tunisia.

21 Personal interview with Mohammad Habib, April 10, 2007.

22 See Chapter Three for details on the Shura and Islah parties, and Chapter Five for more about Amal and Wasat.

23 Personal interview with the founder of the 'Amal Party, Mohammed El-Samman, Cairo, January 10, 2001.

24 For details of the military tribunals, see Chapter Six.

25 Personal interview with Badr Mohammed Badr, Cairo, April 9, 2007.

26 Personal interview with 'Esam Al-'Aryan, Cairo, April 11, 2007.

27 Personal interview with Badr Mohammed Badr, Cairo, April 9, 2007.

28 According to Abdul Al-Mun'em Abu Al-Futuh, the Brothers' leadership stopped talking about applying for legal party status with the Party Affairs Committee in 1992, as a result of growing violence between hardline Islamists and the authorities, which made the security forces favour a heavy-handed approach to dealing with the Islamist movements at large. The group's leadership realised that the circumstances were not favourable to bringing up the topic of a political party, which Al-Hudaybi was certain would be flatly rejected. Personal interview with Abdul Al-Mun'em Abu Al-Futuh, Cairo, July 23, 2002.

29 Personal interview with the former Supreme Guide Mahdi 'Akif, Cairo, April 10, 2007.

30 Personal interview with the former Supreme Guide Mahdi 'Akif, Cairo, April 10, 2007.

31 Personal interview with 'Esam Al-'Aryan, Cairo, April 11, 2007.

32 Personal interview with Abdul Al-Mun'em Abu Al-Futuh, Cairo, April 10, 2007.

33 Personal interview with 'Esam Al-'Aryan, Cairo, April 11, 2007. 'Al-'Aryan believes that the party leadership needs to be independent from the organisation leadership, "such that the supreme guide is not the party head", and that the party's policies should be independent from the organisation's policies, "since no political system in the world can accept a party being moved by someone behind the curtain".

34 Amr Hamzawy, Marina Ottowa, and Nathan J. Brown. "What Islamists Need to be Clear About: The Case of the Egyptian Muslim Brotherhood," Carnegie Endowment for International Peace, February 2007, p. 7.

35 There were two drafts of the party platform distributed to intellectuals, the first in August 2007, and the second draft in September of the same year.

36 Party platform, first draft, September 2007.

37 Personal interview with 'Esam Al-'Aryan, Cairo, April 11, 2007.

38 Despite the laws passed by the Mubarak regime to impede the Brothers' control over the Lawyers' Syndicate, Brotherhood members controlled 15 of 24 seats in the syndicate council.

39 The elections were cancelled in most of the key syndicates, which the Brothers could have controlled, except for the Journalists' Syndicate and the Lawyers' Syndicate, which continued to hold regular elections.

40 Personal interview with Dr Mohammed Fouda, Cairo, April 10, 2007.

41 Personal interview with Abdul Al-Mun'em Abu Al-Futuh, Cairo, April 10, 2007. The Doctors' Syndicate had two board members from the Brothers pass away, including Anwar Shehata, whom I had interviewed about the Brothers' track record in the Doctors' Syndicate as they gained influence in the 1980s (see Chapters Three and Five).

42 Personal interview with Abdul Al-Mun'em Abu Al-Futuh, Cairo, April 10, 2007.

43 Personal interview with Mohammad Habib, Cairo, April 10, 2007.

44 The Brothers control at least 23 private hospitals offering low-cost services superior to that of the public hospitals.

45 For instance, the Brothers have discontinued the practice of including religious slogans such as "The hijab is an Islamic obligation" in their study guides, which are noticeably sleeker productions that can appeal to all students, without alienating anyone.

46 Personal interview with Abdul Al-Mun'em Abu Al-Futuh, Cairo, April 11, 2007. I am grateful to Mahmoud, a former student activist at Alexandria University in 1997, who is a former leader in the Muslim Brothers' student bureau, for the information he offered me on the Brothers' student movement within the universities, which was a valuable resources in writing this section.

47 If the Brothers were not able to find out about an upcoming election by chance or through leaks.

48 Students were suspended from the university for periods ranging from two weeks to a year, and were only allowed back on campus to take their end-of-year exams. Some students are forced to repeat the academic year due to incomplete coursework, even if they do well on the final exams. In rare cases a suspension can last longer than a year, as with Helwan University, which suspended a number of students for three years for taking part in the Free Union elections.

49 Personal interview with Abdel Moneim Mahmoud, Cairo, April 11, 2007. Mahmoud left the Muslim Brothers after the January 25, 2011 revolution.

50 Al-Azhar Students Statement of Apology.

51 The Muslim Brothers students in Egyptian universities issued a statement in their name entitled "For whom are the students being slaughtered?" in which they accused the regime of "seeking to suppress voices and discriminate based on ideological belief and political views," going on to state that "the regime using the fist of security is not a solution in facing its permanent bankruptcy."

52 Personal interview with Diaa Rashwan, April 8, 2007. According to Rashwan, the rhetoric in these newspapers was sharply critical of State Security (*amn al-dawla*) for not taking action against what it described

as illegal "military forces" at Al-Azhar, which in turn prompted the security forces to arrest students some five days after the actual event.

53 Although an administrative court ruled to void President Mubarak's decision to put them on military trial, al-Shatir and 15 other Brotherhood financiers remained behind bars.

54 *Kifaya*, or the Egyptian Movement for Change, was founded in the summer of 2004 by a group of intellectuals, lawyers, and university professors opposed to Mubarak taking a fourth term, and gained popularity through peaceful demonstrations in various provinces. Among the prominent intellectuals in Kifaya were the councillor Tarek Al-Bashari, Dr Abdel Wahhab Al-Masiri, Ishaq Rouhi, and Abdel Halim Qandil, who was the movement's spokesperson. The Reform Initiative was announced by the Brothers' Supreme Guide, Mahdi 'Akif, in March 2004 at the journalists' syndicate.

55 Brothers students from 16 different universities in Egypt went to Cairo University to join in a march inaugurating the campaign, with estimates putting the number of students demonstrating from across the ideological spectrum in the thousands.

56 The proposed rules and regulations were written by a select committee of students from the Brothers and other organisations, including socialists, and were reviewed by Dr Atef al-Banna, a professor of constitutional law. During their march, the students submitted the proposal to the minister of education at the time, Dr Ismail Salama, but it did not lead to any tangible result.

57 Personal interview with Abdel Moneim Mahmoud, Cairo, April 11, 2007.

58 See Chapters Three and Four.

59 Personal interview with Abdel Moneim Mahmoud, Cairo, April 11, 2007.

60 The literature is printed and distributed on campus, with the number of pamphlets in the larger universities ranging from 30,000 (Alexandria University) to 60,000 copies (Cairo University). The pamphlets distributed at the various universities with a strong Brothers presence had the same logo, giving a sense of a tightly run, unified student organisation.

61 The "Student Campaign Against the Constitutional Amendments" statement was issued in the name of the Muslim Brothers Students in Egypt's Universities on March 5, 2007.

62 The campaign arrested the deputy supreme guide, Khairat al-Shatir, owner of the now-defunct Salsabil IT firm, Hassan Malek, CEO of Istiqbal Furniture and Sarar Clothing, Medhat al-Hadad, CEO of the Arab Development Company, Abdel Rahman Saudi, CEO of the Urban Development Company, Khaled Auda, son of Abdel Qader Auda and a businessman in Asyut, and others on charges of money laundering, funding the group's secret activities, and bankrolling three satellite TV channels with 20 million dollars to spread the movement's ideology. The ruling in absentia was also against some figures living abroad, including the Brothers' international relations coordinator Yousef Nada, residing in Switzerland, Tawfiq al-Wai in Kuwait, and Ibrahim al-Zayyat in Germany.

63 Personal interview with Diaa Rashwan, Cairo, April 8, 2007.

64 Personal interview with Mohammad Habib, Cairo, April 10, 2007.
65 Some businessmen also pay their annual *zakat* (alms tax) to the organisation.
66 Governmental journalistic sources like *Al-Ahram* estimate the number of members in the Muslim Brothers in Egypt to be around 800,000.
67 A study conducted by Hamdy Abdel Azeem, *Nahdat Misr*, December 18, 2007.
68 *Ibid.*
69 According to 'Esam Al-'Aryan, "What should scare the regime is funding spent for terrorist or military purposes, or suspicious purposes aiming to embarrassing the regime and exposes its faults, not funding for peaceful political purposes." Personal interview with 'Esam Al-'Aryan, Cairo, April 11, 2007.
70 Personal interview with Abdul Al-Mun'em Abu Al-Futuh, Cairo, April 10, 2007.
71 Personal interview with Abdul Al-Mun'em Abu Al-Futuh, Cairo, April 10, 2007. Amr el-Chobaki quoted Ali Bayoumi, an observer with the Egyptian Organisation for Human Rights, as saying that the Brothers managed their election campaigns by gathering small, regular individual donations in the Islamic *takaful* system, which the Brothers have long used. Choubaki quoted Makaram Al-Badiri, a Brother candidate from the Medinat Nasr district as saying that "election campaign funding is through joint donations, that the staff are volunteers and contribute by writing posters, hanging them up, making drawings, and campaign, all without any pay, and the campaign materials at the cost of materials, thanks to some businessmen." See el-Chobaki, Amr *Al-Ikhwan Al-Muslimun fi Intikhabat Majlis Al-Shaab 2005* (The Muslim Brothers in the 2005 People's Assembly Elections), Centre for Political and Strategic Studies, Cairo, 2006, pp. 163–166.
72 See Chapter Two, under the heading "Private Enterprises", p. 70.
73 Personal interview with Mohammad Habib, Cairo, April 10, 2007.
74 Personal interview, Diaa Rashwan, Cairo, April 8, 2007.
75 Personal interview, Diaa Rashwan, Cairo, April 8, 2007.
76 Zaina, Abdu. *"Al-Adhra' al-Maliya lil-Ikhwan: Istihdaf Mumawwili al-Ikhwan fi Misr ... 'Iqab 'Alaa Tabyid Amwal aw Khatwa li-Muhasiritihim qabla al-Ta'dilat al-Dusturiya?"* ("The Brothers' Financial Arm: the Brothers' Financiers are Targeted in Egypt ... Punishment for Money Laundering or a Step to Surround them before the Constitutional Amendments?"), *Al-Sharq Al-Awsat*, February 2, 2007.
77 *Ibid.*
78 Personal interview with Badr Mohammed Badr, Cairo, April 9, 2007.
79 The Urban Development Company owned by Saudi carried out a large number of government projects for the Ministries of Education, Higher Education, and Health.
80 Personal interview with Badr Mohammed Badr, Cairo, April 9, 2007.
81 The investigation record shows that the size of the earnings losses of the Brothers companies reached half a billion pounds, while the capital for these earnings was estimated to be 20 billion pounds. Reported in *Al-Sharq Al-Awsat*, February 2, 2007.

82 As evidence to the fact that the Brothers were not substantially affected
    by the arrest of their financiers is the fact that the organisation has
    been spending on the dependents of the arrested businessmen, whose
    holdings were seized by the state, as well as other detainees, giving
    them monthly aid estimated to be 2,000 Egyptian pounds per family.
    Personal interview with an anonymous Brothers source. According to
    Ikhwan Online, which is run by the Brothers, the businessmen were
    providing for more than 50 families, meaning that the total expendi-
    tures on the families of the detainees is around 100,000 pounds a
    month.

83 According to the official Brothers website, Hassan Malek was one of the
    hardest hit by the government's war on the Muslim Brothers' invest-
    ments, because the state shut down 11 enterprises of his, including
    Malek Commerce and Ready-made Clothing, the Malek Textiles fac-
    tory, and Istiqbal Furniture. According to Malek, the factory which was
    supposed to have been built but was cancelled would have employed
    1,000 workers. Hamad, Hassouna. *"Bil-Arqam: al-Khasa'ir al-Iqtisadiya
    bisabab al-Mahkama al-'Askariya li-Qiyadat al-Ikhwan"* ("In Numbers: the
    Economic Losses due to the Military Trial of the Brothers' Leaders"),
    www.ikhwanonline.com, 17/12/2007.

84 There are no precise statistics available about the total number of
    employees affected by about 25 companies and factories affiliated with
    the Brothers being closed. According to statistics on some of the indi-
    vidual businessmen, the total number of companies owned by Saudi
    included 1,400 employees, and Hassan Malek employed 500 people.

85 A report by the Egyptian Land Center found that in 2007, some
    124,000 workers were fired, and there were 179 sit-ins and 74 worker
    strikes about wages and threatened firings due to privatisation. For
    more details, follow the link for *Al-Ihtijajat al-'Umaliya fi 2007* (Labor
    Protests in 2007) at www.hrinfo.org (accessed on January 31, 2008).

86 Personal interview with Khairat al-Shatir, Cairo, June 30, 2002.

CONCLUSION

The aim of this book was to examine and analyse the dynamics that shaped the relationship of Mubarak with the Muslim Brothers, and that were responsible for the change in the characteristics of that relationship in the period from 1982 to 2011. The relationship went through two distinctive phases, where the first, from 1981 to 1990, was a period of accommodation and tolerance, and the second, from 1990 to 2011, was a period of confrontation and repression, and where the dynamism of the relationship was shaped by a search for legitimacy by both sides. Mubarak and the Muslim Brothers both sought to gain legitimacy to maintain their survival, and only when the legitimacy of the Muslim Brothers had begun to threaten the legitimacy of Mubarak, did the regime's policy against the movement change.

The focus on legitimacy was intended to stress the importance of the concept, even when one analyses the attitude of authoritarian regimes such as that of Mubarak. Despite its reliance on coercion, the Egyptian regime needed a measure of legitimacy to help it maintain stability, and this concern had a significant bearing on its behaviour towards its rivals. The rivals of the regime, if they hoped to exist and function under authoritarian rule, also and probably more so than the regime, needed some form of legitimacy, especially one that was based on the recognition of the state.

Chapter Two underlined the importance of legitimacy for authoritarian regimes like that of Nasser, where reliance on modes of legitimacy, as much as on coercion, was manifested in the arbitrary social contract. The contract, based on an exchange of publicly subsidised services for political acquiescence, was introduced as a way of appeasing the lower middle-classes, who might otherwise have turned into opponents of the state. Sadat

relied on more traditional and rational forms of legitimacy, which
were exploited by the Brothers and which, after a short period of
tacit accommodation, later caused tension between them and the
regime.

When Mubarak came to power in 1981, he was also concerned
with legitimising his political leadership with whatever modes of
legitimacy were available. Chapter Three illustrated how, from 1981
to 1984, Mubarak pursued a series of policies that were intended
to strengthen his populist, legal and eudaemonic legitimacy. His
populist legitimacy came from his foreign policies, which aimed
to court Egyptian and Arab sentiment (e.g., he slowed down the
normalisation with Israel and resumed relations with the Arab
countries); his legal legitimacy came from his emphasis on the rule
of law and the freedom of the press; and his eudaemonic legitimacy, linked to welfare performance, came from his maintenance
of Nasser's social contract and the improvements to Egypt's infrastructure. Mubarak was preoccupied with stabilising the country's
rule following a period of tension within society caused by Sadat,
and was unprepared at that stage to engage in unjustified conflict
with any of his rivals except Islamist extremism, which constituted
an immediate threat.

As an outcome of the conciliatory approach, where Mubarak
assumed that the effect of the movement was controlled if it
remained outlawed, the Muslim Brothers were accommodated but
not officially recognised. The Brothers, who had been banned since
1954, exploited Mubarak's tolerance. They began to rebuild and
to expand the resources of the *tanzim*, and persisted in securing
their official legitimacy. This fact is an essential element in understanding the movement and the incentives behind the development
of its religious, social and political attitudes. Chapter Four aimed
to show the link between legitimacy and the Brothers' decision to
participate in the 1984 elections, to forge political alliances with the
secular New Wafd party, and to modify their sceptical attitude to
political partisanship or *hizbiyya*.

The failure of the Brothers to secure their official legitimacy
through the courts or the national assembly led the younger cadres
to pursue legitimacy through another route that did not rely on
the state to boost its credibility, but rather on the social spaces
which the regime had opened up. Legitimacy in these spaces was
gained as an outcome of the social services that were provided to
lower middle-class constituencies. Social legitimacy was not seen as

an alternative to the recognition of the state, but as an alternative means towards securing this recognition.

Mubarak's accommodation of his political opposition in the parliamentary elections of 1984 and 1987 gained him a measure of legal legitimacy, and his performance with regard to the improvement of the state infrastructure, though modest, was undeniable. But these achievements were not in themselves sufficient, in the view of the lower-middle classes and the poor, most of whom sensed no significant change in their everyday lives. The regime's inability to address the wider public concerns was related to a number of factors including the international oil crisis, which affected the revenues from oil, the Suez Canal, and tourism. This and other crises hampered the regime's ability to provide welfare services and thus weakened its legitimacy, manifest in the increase in public grievances and the re-emergence of socio-religious disturbances.

The Muslim Brothers used the syndicates to build an Islamic version of the state's social contract, and succeeded in gaining a measure of social legitimacy, despite state denial. The impact of the movement was also felt on campuses and in urban neighbourhoods, Islamic investment companies and, to the embarrassment of the regime, in parliament. The movement was equally successful in recruiting new members and expanding the *tanzim*, as seen in the development of the internal structures and offices that dealt with students, syndicates and parliamentarians. The movement later utilised the structures of the *tanzim* to co-ordinate among, and join forces with, the various spaces it occupied, and this disturbed the regime's corporatist links, which Mubarak had utilised to control the boundaries of the spaces. Towards the late 1980s, the regime encountered what I called the dilemma of legitimacy, where the spaces that the regime had opened up to buttress its legitimacy, gradually developed into a source of threat to that legitimacy.

The height of the dilemma was reached in the 1990s when the Brothers began to politicise their organised social legitimacy. This could be seen in their attitude to the Gulf War in 1991, the earthquake in 1992 and their attempt to form political parties (*Al-Amal* in 1992 and *Al-Wasat* in 1996). The movement utilised the professional syndicates to mobilise lower middle-class constituencies and to create pressure on the regime to grant it recognition. Chapter Six showed that the politicisation of legitimacy provoked the regime and prompted it to use coercion against the Muslim Brothers.

The regime's resort to coercion in the 1990s also resulted from other developments, such as increasing Islamist violence and deepening social dissent. Both developments, along with the attempt to assassinate Mubarak in 1995, radicalised the policies of the regime, and increased its dependence on the security services. This, however, did not imply that the regime had ceased to be concerned with its legitimacy, but rather that its approach to legitimacy had changed. During the 1990s Mubarak pursued legitimacy through promises of economic reform and privatisation, rather than through political reform and the accommodation of rivals. He anticipated that economic liberalisation would ultimately strengthen the state's economy, and that this would then alleviate the grievances generated by its fraying social contract.

Chapter Seven showed that while the regime's dramatic shift to privatisation in 1995 might have partly succeeded in improving Egypt's macroeconomics, it did not improve the living standards of most Egyptians. This was partly related to the failure of its alliance with the business community, which did not reflect positively on the Egyptian society as a whole. The resort to coercion in dealing with social movements like the Muslim Brothers also contributed to the weakness of Egypt's civil society, at a time where the state's welfare role was shrinking, and certainly deepened the regime's legitimacy crisis. The model (Diagram 1) is an attempt to summarise the development in the relationship between Mubarak and the Brothers in terms of their pursuit for legitimacy.

The model shows the cyclic relationship between the Muslim Brothers and the regime of Mubarak. Mubarak assumed power in 1981, when the regime suffered a *legitimacy crisis* that was the result of Sadat's later tensions with the Egyptian society. This prompted Mubarak to open up economic, social and political spaces in order to stabilise his regime. The spaces seemed autonomous but were essentially controlled by the state's corporatist links. The Muslim Brothers (MB), failing to secure the recognition of the state, occupied and later controlled these spaces. The aim was to mobilise the alienated constituencies within the spaces to put pressure on the regime to grant the movement recognition. This was achieved by the build-up of an Islamist social contract, which was parallel to that of the state. The organised and political use of the social legitimacy that was gained from this social contract constituted a *legitimacy dilemma* for Mubarak, who had either to continue to maintain these spaces, and risk erosion to his legitimacy, or confiscate them through the use of *coercion*. The use of coercion, while the state failed to pursue alternative means to legitimacy, restarted a legitimacy crisis for the regime, and which led to the revolution of 25 January 2011.

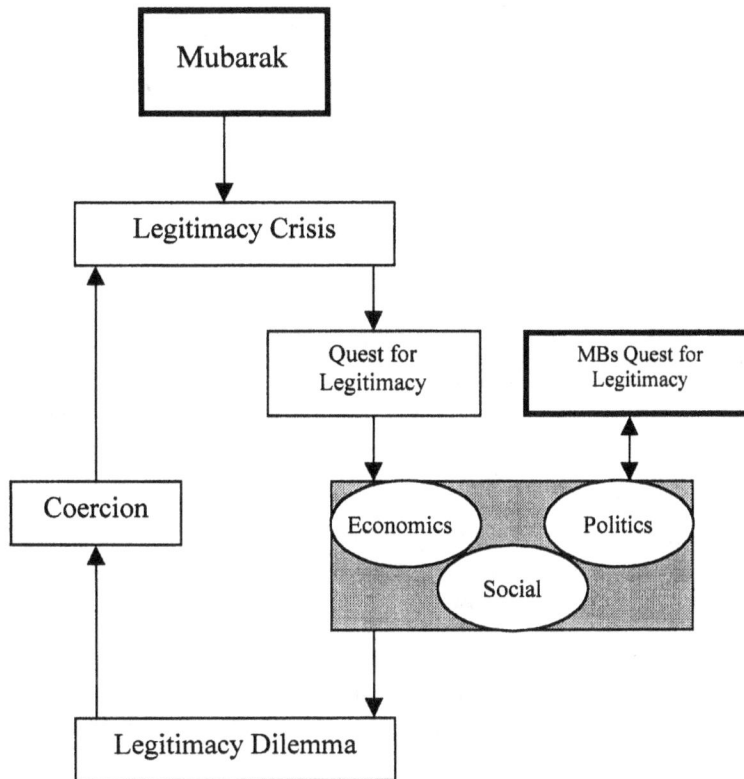

DIAGRAM 1. The Pursuit of Legitimacy.

POSTSCRIPT

The Islamists in Power

No one imagined that the revolution of 25 January 2011 would topple the Mubarak regime in 18 days and then bring the Muslim Brothers into power in Egypt's first free presidential elections in May 2012. Even the Brothers and Mubarak were surprised to see youth-led non-politicised spontaneous demonstrations turn into a popular revolution, forcing the army to deploy in the streets and that chants of Bread, Freedom and Human Dignity on 25 January would soon embrace the Tunisian slogan of 'the people want the overthrow of the regime'. This groundswell of popular protest led to Mubarak stepping down from the presidency on 11 February 2011, after having ruled Egypt for 30 years, with events unfolding so quickly that neither Mubarak nor the Brothers were able to keep up, their reactions being delayed and fitful. Even more remarkable was the ouster by the Egyptian military of Mohammad Morsi, Egypt's first elected president, on 3 July 2013, after only one year in office. Despite Morsi's victory in presidential elections, and forceful disruption of his four-year term by the army, the leading member of the Muslim Brotherhood failed to translate his legal legitimacy to a wider populist legitimacy based on tangible achievements.

During the brief course of the revolution, Mubarak gave speeches on 29 January, 1 February and 10 February 2011, offering superficial, piecemeal reforms, suggesting that he was either being intransigent or was actually unaware of what was happening in the streets. Mubarak formed a new government, appointed the 75-year-old veteran head of intelligence Omar Suleiman as vice-president, and promised not to seek a sixth term in the presidential elections slated for September 2012. In his speeches, the president reminded

Egyptians of his accomplishments and sacrifices, and the role he played in the October 1973 war with Israel, but his emotion-charged rhetoric was unable to placate the angry demonstrators or stop their revolution. he security forces' heavy-handed attempts to break up the protests, particularly with the bloody assault on Tahrir Square by pro-regime thugs on 2 February 2011 (known as the Battle of the Camel, since some thugs charged into the fight against the protestors on horses and camels) backfired by erasing any remaining faith in the government's promises, and strengthening the demands for Mubarak's resignation. Although everyone knew it was a distortion of a complicated reality, Mubarak steadfastly accused the Brothers of being behind the revolution and of responsibility for the deaths of protestors in Tahrir Square.

The Brothers and other political movements had been aware that popular discontent was surging in Egypt, with the emergence of protest movements such as the *Kifaya* ('Enough') movement in 2005, the April 6 movement in 2008, and 'We are All Khaled Said' in 2010. From 2005 until 25 January 2011, some 5,000 demonstrations took place, not only in Cairo and Alexandria, but also throughout Egypt's 27 governorates. Both the rapid growth of these movements and the sheer number of protests were unprecedented. Most of the demonstrations featured young people and were non-politicised, such as the Youth for Change offshoot of the *Kifaya* movement in 2005, which had limited economic and social demands related to higher wages, equal opportunity, social justice, etc.[1] With time, these disparate grassroots movements began to join ranks, and their demands came to focus explicitly on political change.

The Brothers supported some of these protests, although they did not envision the protest movement possibly leading to Mubarak's downfall, and instead hoped at most that the government would undertake more reforms. When the Tunisian revolution got underway on 17 December 2010, the Brothers issued a statement calling on the Egyptian government to avoid similar protests by making reforms, specifically to end emergency law, hold free and fair parliamentary elections, and to amend the more restrictive constitutional items in the constitution (Articles 5, 76, 77, 88, and 179).[2] As the first demonstrations in Cairo took place on 25 January, the Brothers officially refrained from participating, fearing a confrontation with security forces and believing that the results would be limited, although youth members took part on an individual basis.[3] The movement had long since lost hope of any imminent change, and had no clue that the demonstrations would snowball and drastically alter the destinies of both the Mubarak regime and the Brothers.

This chapter will examine the period during the revolution itself, and how the Brothers dealt with its rapid developments until coming to power later in 2012. The main argument is that the organisation benefited from its social legitimacy to fill the vacuum created by the regime's collapse, but that this legitimacy was insufficient to support the Brothers in power, and was eaten away as long as Mohammad Morsi did not create new national accomplishment-based legitimacy. The Brothers were unable to count on Egyptians' sympathy for their rough treatment at the hands of the Mubarak regime lasting indefinitely, because the revolution changed everything, including people's expectations, and spread knowledge of how to punish rulers who fail to meet these expectations: street demonstrations and sit-ins. The other argument is that the Brothers when in power no longer suffered from a lack of legal legitimacy; their main worry was to satisfy the public with their performance in power, which was not nearly as impressive as their performance in opposition.

The Brothers and the Revolution

The 25 January revolution was a spontaneous, non-religious, unpoliticised mass revolt, which the Brothers neither organised nor even participated in initially. The only link between the Brothers and the protests was through the youth who were Brothers and simultaneously part of the independent protest movements which had been growing since 2004, and who took part on an individual basis. The Brothers had distanced themselves from the calls for street protests, fearing that participation by other groups would be merely symbolic and that the Brothers would be the ones targeted by the security services. The increasing government crackdowns since the mid-1990s had led the Brothers to adopt a strategy of 'seeking refuge in society' and avoiding sticking their neck out by leading any protest movements. Rather than stake a claim to lead the protest movements, the Brothers sought to remain indistinguishable from the other opposition groups.

The Brothers dismissed the seemingly remote chance that the calls for demonstrations overlapping with Police Day on

25 January would resonate, and chose to stay on the sidelines as usual. According to Ahmad Rami, a mid-level leader:

> The group believed that the 25 January demonstration would not be a mass event, and that if it participated in full force at the forefront, this would give the demonstration a certain nature, provoke the security forces, and give an excuse to single [the Brothers] out and drag their members through the streets without fearing the West and international opinion, which was already prejudiced against Islamists.[4]

This belief prompted the Brothers to make only a token show of participation, spread out over stages. The Brothers assigned some of their more visible members (parliamentarians, journalists, members of the labor syndicate boards, etc.) to take part, without officially approving or ordering other members to take part. Only days before the revolution, the group had been specifically warned by Mubarak's security forces against joining the demonstration, but chose instead to assert its independence by announcing it would neither require nor forbid its members from demonstrating.[5] When the Brothers realised belatedly that 25 January was unlike any other previous protest movement, both in terms of numbers (an estimated 20,000 in Tahrir Square) and the diversity among the demonstrators, including a large number of women, it decided to go forward with officially endorsing participation in the demonstrations starting on 28 January until Mubarak's resignation on 11 February.[6]

The Muslim Brothers' Youth

There is no youth division within the Brothers organisation, but rather a student division liaising between the central organisation and its university student members. The department is overseen by recent graduates in their late 20s and early 30s, part of a Brothers generation that stands out for its openness towards other ideological currents, stemming from friendly relations with their classmates of varying political affiliations, and which solidified with the anti-regime protest movement starting in 2005. The Brothers youth were influenced by the non-violent means used by the more secularist groups to protest government policies, such as strikes, marches and sit-ins.[7] They saw civil disobedience or non-violent resistance as an effective middle ground between violent confrontation with the state and avoiding any activism for fear of government repression.[8] Some Brothers activists received hands-on training on how to organise civil disobedience campaigns and offered their experience to the group's leadership, which responded unenthusiastically. This did not deter the Brothers' student division from airing its argument before the Guidance Bureau in 2010 that as the presidential elections scheduled for 2011 approached, the movement should launch a sweeping pro-change campaign called 'New Egypt' utilising civil disobedience and mass protests – a proposal which was again vetoed by the central leadership. According to Mohammad Al-Qassas, an activist who helped draft this proposal:

> We offered a clear, written proposal, an integrated plan of action on the national level, mentioning phrases such as civil disobedience, strikes and revolution. We said that change would be in Mubarak's hands, that genuine change would require a direct confrontation with the regime, and that any indirect confrontations would be of no use, but the Guidance Bureau turned down the proposal, and emphasised that we should be concerned with missionary and educational work, not confrontation, because the Egyptian regime was repressive and clashing with it would be useless.[9]

The gap continued to widen between the two generations of Brothers, a younger generation believing that Egypt was witnessing a growing mass anti-government movement which the Brothers should lead or at least play an active role in, and an older, traditionalist, conservative generation resolute in its belief that the regime was still too strong to be shaken by popular discontent and that the Brothers should avoid triggering a government crackdown. The leadership's refusal did little to deter younger Brothers from individually joining youth protest movements and being active in wide-reaching youth networks, whether on the ground or online.[10] The most prominent groups in this network were the Change Youth Coalition which called for the 25 January demonstration, then the Revolutionary Youth Coalition which was formed in Tahrir Square on 25 January, incorporating socialists, liberals and independents.[11]

Thus, the Brothers youth were a step ahead of their leaders, bolder, and more ready for change. It is not known how many Brothers youth participated as individuals in the first three days of

the revolution, but their ranks swelled when the organisation officially endorsed the protests from 28 January onwards. The Brothers
youth played a very prominent role in the 2 February Battle of the
Camel, mounting a courageous defence of the revolutionaries from
the assault launched by pro-regime thugs. Thousands of Brothers
youth also poured into Tahrir Square from other governorates, bol-
stering the morale of the protestors and putting their management
skills to use in organising the protestors. However, this did not heal
the rift between the youth and their leaders.

The disagreements can be divided into two types: one related
to the Brothers' stance towards the 25 January Revolution, and
another, more far-reaching in its implications, related to the
youth's status within the organisation. There was a widespread
impression among young members that the leadership did not
rise to the occasion during the revolution, with overly cautious,
plodding decisions and demands that were far too modest.[12] A
case could be made for its traditional organisational principle of
'compliance and obedience' while living under dictatorial regimes,
but the youth-led revolution set the stage for political openness,
which in the youth's view required reshaping its organisational
model to allow for dialogue between the leadership and the youth.
There was a growing feeling that youth were marginalised within
the movement, and that the leadership, specifically the Guidance
Bureau and the Shura Council, was deaf to their voices, despite the
fact that it had been the youth who brought about political change
in Egypt. "There are no representatives for youth, students, women,
or professionals within the Guidance Bureau or the Shura Council,
and the organisational structure needs to be developed, even if this
means the organisation expanding the number of Shura Council
members so that it includes these marginalised groups."[13] By individual initiative, the Brothers youth held an internal conference
with about 400 members, who demanded that organisational pro-
motions be based on competence, and emphasised the importance
of involving youth and women in the decision-making process.[14] A
second internal conference was held, this time sponsored by the
organisation, in which the youth also called for modernising both
the organisational structure and decision-making process, while
evolving from a secretive into an open organisation.[15] The Brothers
responded with promises to make changes and put Khairat
El-Shatir in charge of instituting reforms, but there have been no
changes since 2011. Subsequent defections from the organisation

by frustrated members have included not only revolutionary youth, but also some upper-level leaders.

Defections

During and shortly after the revolution, several well-known veteran leaders in the Muslim Brothers were either dismissed or stepped down. Defections are hardly a new phenomenon, and have been taking place since the days of its founder Hassan Al-Banna, but carried special significance after the revolution. The rapid unfolding of events in late January and early February 2011 forced the leadership to make difficult choices that were bound to be unpopular with some of its members. With the end of the Mubarak era, which had tended to unify the Brothers' ranks in opposition to the government, and because the organisational leadership had limited conflict management skills and historically relied instead on 'compliance and obedience', there was a series of high-level defections. Shura Council member Ibrahim Al-Za'farani stepped down in April 2011, citing the lack of any meaningful reforms since the revolution, followed by Kamal El-Halbawi in March 2012, to protest the Brothers' decision to field a candidate in the presidential elections, while Abdul Al-Mun'em Abu Al-Futuh, and Mohammad Habib both quit the Guidance Bureau.[16] Regardless of the details, the overriding reason for the resignations was dissatisfaction with the way in which the organisation was being run.

Abu Al-Futuh resigned to protest the Brothers' initial decision to not field a presidential candidate, while announcing his own candidacy as an independent. However, the deeper reasons began more than ten years earlier, when he began to become disillusioned with the group's administration.

> When I left prison in 2000, I found that the group was being run with an exclusionary organisational mentality. Clashes began to take place between myself and the administration which has been in place since that time. I disagreed with the leadership about two key issues: the first was that I wanted the group to legalise itself, which the leadership did not want. Secondly was for the group to separate between its work in party politics and its overall religious missionary work, a need which the leadership rejected.[17]

Abu Al-Futuh had suffered at the hands of the Mubarak regime, having been arrested and imprisoned several times since the 1990s on charges of belonging to an illegal organisation, and believed that the only way for the Brothers to avoid these charges was to seek legal status as a civil society association. The senior leadership argued that inclusion under the Associations Law would belittle the Brothers' weight in society, as they saw the organisation as more comprehensive and larger than a mere association. Abu Al-Futuh also criticised the group's function in party politics and vying for power.

Mohammad Habib, another veteran leader in the Guidance Bureau and former Deputy Supreme Guide who chose to resign in July 2011, did so protesting the lack of consultation in the decision-making process within the organisation, and the tyrannical rule of a small minority. Despite the fact that Habib himself was a prominent member of the Guidance Bureau, he had become marginalised within the decision-making process. Habib was particularly shocked when a powerful faction within the Guidance Bureau determined the next Supreme Guide to succeed Mahdi 'Akif, before the entire Bureau had met to make an official choice, meaning that the internal election process was only a formality. Habib also cited other authoritarian decisions such as the group agreeing to join negotiations with Mubarak's vice-president Omar Suleiman during the revolution, to discuss the constitutional amendments drafted by the army in February 2011.

Undoubtedly, the defections of leaders such as Habib, Aboul Futouh, Al-Za'farani and others had an impact, but the effectiveness of the movement as a whole was not significantly changed. Its strict disciplinary values remained in place, with a spiritual and ideological conviction that the organisation has divine support, and so its destiny is not reliant on individuals, regardless of the celebrity status they enjoy. Instead, the departure of reformist and more liberal leaders worked to consolidate the influence of the group's traditionalist, conservative wing, while the exit of a number of ambitious, intelligent youth will deprive the organisation of the newer generation's abilities to modernise the movement.

The Freedom and Justice Party

The transitional period in which the army was in power after Mubarak's resignation led to amendments to the political parties law, allowing the Brothers to form the Freedom and Justice Party (FJP) in June 2011. The FJP won a plurality of the seats in parliament (216 out of 508) in the People's Assembly elections later that year, qualifying the FJP secretary-general Saad El-Katatni to become speaker of the People's Assembly in an unprecedented development. There are many reasons for the Brothers' sweeping victory, including the fact that the post-revolutionary elections were free and fair compared to those under Mubarak, particularly the 2010 elections which had been boycotted by the opposition. With the NDP out of the picture, the Brothers' high level of organisation allowed them to mobilise more quickly than their rivals, some of whom were hampered by the public mistrust of the traditional political parties, in addition to the fact that the Brothers already enjoyed broad popularity thanks to their social services.[18] The People's Assembly was, however, dissolved by a constitutional court ruling in 2012 voiding the election laws as having been biased towards party candidates over independent candidates.

The FJP's platform kept Sharia as a point of reference, while asserting its belief in democracy, an elected president, and the *umma*, or Islamic community, as the source of authority.[19] The FJP's stated goals are political reform, improving the economy, enhancing security, and Egypt reclaiming its pioneering role. Party membership is open to all Egyptians, including Coptic Christians (such as Rafiq Habib, who became the FJP's vice-president in June 2011). The FJP provided legal cover for the Muslim Brothers, since all members of the latter organisation (men and women) with a membership card in the party could if necessary avoid the traditional charge of 'membership in a banned group'.

The establishment of the FJP, the first time in the Brothers' existence since 1928 that they were allowed to found a political party, set off a heated internal debate. Abdul Al-Mun'em Abu Al-Futuh argued that this betrayed the intentions of founder Hassan Al-Banna, who had refused to mix religious missionary advocacy with party politics: "The freedom to form parties in Egypt was guaranteed in the 1930s, and Al-Banna could have formed a political party for the Brothers, but he did not do so."[20] Abu Al-Futuh questioned the leadership's claims that the Brothers and the FJP were organisationally autonomous, stating his belief that the FJP was no more than a front organisation, and that the Guidance Bureau was calling the shots behind the scenes. Top FJP leader 'Esam Al-'Aryan acknowledged the existence of a joint committee between the

Brothers and the FJP to coordinate decisions related to the state, and that the group's leadership was naming the leadership of the FJP on an interim basis until complete separation between the two entities was a reality.[21] The movement bans its members from joining any party other than the FJP with the threat of expulsion, meaning that any autonomy is incomplete. Some analysts have voiced their doubts as to whether the Brothers' political party experiment will evolve as the Islamist parties in Jordan, Morocco, and Turkey did, such that the party's organisational relationship with the movement which created it is severed.[22]

The Morsi Regime

Instead of dying down with the dismantling of the Mubarak regime, popular discontent continued unabated and even grew through the beginning of Mohammad Morsi's rule, with 2012 alone witnessing some 558 demonstrations, 514 strikes, and 500 sit-ins.[23] Mohammad Morsi won the first free presidential elections over his opponent Ahmed Shafiq, the last prime minister under Hosni Mubarak, by a narrow margin with only 51.7 per cent of the vote, but only a few months after Morsi came to power, disappointed by his performance, the opposition began to call for the army to step in and hold early elections. The Brothers' decision to take part in the 2012 president elections was a surprise, coming after explicit statements that they would not do so.[24] Morsi was not the group's first choice, but was the backup candidate derisively referred to as the 'spare tyre' after Khairat El-Shatir's candidacy was overturned by the Higher Elections Board. Morsi does not possess El-Shatir's charisma, but does have substantial experience accumulated since joining the Brothers in 1978 and its political department in 1992. Morsi served in the People's Assembly in 2000, was in charge of the organisation's political affairs under former Supreme Guide Ma'mun Al-Hudaybi, was a member of both the Guidance Bureau and the Shura Council, and became president of the FJP in 2011. Morsi's electoral victory can be attributed not only to his personal abilities of course, but also to the Brothers' mobilisational competence.

A comprehensive, detailed evaluation of Morsi's performance is difficult as it was short-lived and forcefully interrupted; however, overall it could be rated unsatisfactory, particularly in tackling the challenges of the economy and security. Morsi inherited a struggling economy, but this does not exempt him from responsibility for the continued rise in unemployment and inflation in Egypt. The president relied on securing a US$4.8 billion loan from the World Bank, which would saddle his government with more debts without even sufficing to cover the budget deficit.[25] He needed to generate economic growth benefiting the lower and middle classes (33 per cent of the people), if he wanted to establish genuine popular legitimacy.[26] The deteriorating security situation can be traced to the mutual mistrust between the public and the security services since Mubarak's rule, the lack of political and security coordination, and the existence of militias within the Ministry of Interior loyal to Mubarak-era leaders. The opposition believed that the Brothers' leadership – the supreme guide and the Guidance Bureau – was now in control of the system, and hard at work 'Brotherising the state'.[27] This belief led to demonstrations in March 2013 in front of the Brothers' headquarters in the Muqattam district of Cairo that set off bloody clashes which left ten dead and more than 200 injured.

Morsi was faced by challenges too overwhelming for his limited political experience. Domestically, these include the gaping budget deficit, high unemployment, inflation outpacing wage growth, street children (around 3 million), crime, entrenched holdouts from the Mubarak regime in key institutions such as the Ministry of Interior and the army. Regionally, there was the diminishing of Egypt's traditional clout as non-Arab countries like Iran and Turkey and smaller Gulf countries like Qatar expanded their influence, and the struggle to achieve balanced relations with Israel (Camp David Accords) and the Brothers' ideological ally Hamas. The underlying challenge was for Morsi to achieve political acceptability and a degree of broad popularity, which could not happen as long as the president appeared to be taking orders from superiors in the Brothers' organisational structure (namely, the supreme guide) instead of making independent decisions. According to Mohammad Habib, the former Brothers leader, "Morsi will not be able to disengage from the Brothers, because they are the ones who chose him and brought him into power, so he feels indebted to them."[28] FJP deputy head 'Esam Al-'Aryan gave further support to this idea, saying "Morsi would be wrong if he thinks that he won through his personal effort, because he is fully aware that without the Brothers, he would not have made it to the presidency."[29] However, the pragmatic dynamics of being in power are quite different from the dynamics of opposition, and sharp disagreements emerging between Islamists once in power is not unprecedented – it happened in Sudan in the 1990s and in Tunisia after the Arab Spring.[30] Egypt's domestic and foreign situation imposed constraints on Morsi completely different from those on the Brothers. Diaa Rashwan predicted that the Arab–Israeli conflict would be the topic over which Morsi and the Brothers eventually part ways, since resistance to Israel is a longstanding source of the Brothers' legitimacy, whereas Morsi would have little option but to uphold Camp David under pressure from the US.[31]

The *Tanzim*

In Chapter Three, I discussed the importance of the organisation or the *tanzim* for the Brothers, and in Chapter Five, the role of organisation in enabling their accomplishments, and thus consolidating their popular legitimacy, defining organisation as "the inner structure, dynamics and hierarchies of the movement's organisation". When I visited Egypt after the revolution to write this chapter, I met Mahmoud Ezzat to investigate the developments which had taken place to the Brothers' organisation in the past decade since writing the first edition of this book. Ezzat's official position is the Deputy Supreme Guide, and he is known as the Brothers' organisational theorist. He joined the movement in 1962 as an 18-year-old student in the Faculty of Medicine, and was jailed under both Nasser and Mubarak; he spent ten years in prison after Nasser's mass arrests of Brothers in 1965, and five years after Mubarak's military trials in 1995. I met Ezzat in his office at one of the Brothers' charity hospitals in Cairo to discuss recent developments in the Brothers' organisational structure.

The Brothers' organisation is characterised by a complex hierarchy starting at the lowest level, that of the 'family', and ending at the top with the Guidance Bureau. None of the Brothers likes to speculate on the total number of members, but estimates range from 100,000 to 500,000.[32] The average size of a Brothers 'family' is five people, headed by a captain, who meet on a weekly basis and pay monthly dues calculated as a fixed percentage of a member's income. The 'section' is made up of several families in a certain geographical region within one of Egypt's 27 governorates, and is the smallest administrative unit at the governorate level. The sections elect a Shura Council for each governorate, which consists on average of roughly 30 people but varies according to the governorate size, and represents all of the governorate's members at the national level. Alongside the Shura Councils, in each governorate there are multiple administrative bureaus managing local organisational affairs, such as the offices for students, missionary work, parliament, etc. The governorate's Shura Council elects members to represent their governorate at the national Shura Council, which is the Brothers' legislative body for Egypt. The national Shura Council has about 118 members, representing all of the governments, serving a maximum of two six-year terms. The Shura Council in turn elects 17 of its own members to comprise the Guidance Bureau, which is the most powerful body in the organisation, and is equivalent to its executive branch.[33]

The Guidance Bureau is headed by the supreme guide. The Brothers have had eight supreme guides since the group was founded in 1928, who up through the fourth supreme guide, Hamed Abu Al-Nasr (1986–1996) were elected for life. Under the fifth supreme guide, Mustafa Mashhur (1996–2002) the supreme guide's term became six years, with a 12-year term limit. Mahdi 'Akif (born in 1928) was then the first supreme guide to not even seek a second term.[34] Under Mohammed Badie (2010– present), the Brothers were wracked by controversy after Morsi became president of Egypt, and questions were raised over the nature of the relationship between the Egyptian president and the supreme guide.[35] At the very least, the balance of power between the two remains ambiguous and unresolved.

The relationship between the Guidance Bureau and the Shura Council within the Brothers' organisation is equally opaque. Although the resolutions passed by the Shura Council are theoretically binding for the Guidance Bureau, since the Shura Council is the legislative body, in practice the Guidance Bureau carries much more weight. The supreme guide, who is head of the Guidance Bureau, has enjoyed historical legitimacy since the days of Hassan Al-Banna, and consequently has substantial moral authority over the other organisation members, including the members of the Shura Council. The Brothers' bylaws include clauses consolidating the Guidance Bureau's power, such as by giving it the right to appoint 15 members of the otherwise elected Shura Council, and that all Guidance Bureau members concurrently serve in the Shura Council as full voting members, besides the fact that the supreme guide himself is head of the Shura Council. Even more significantly, the Guidance Bureau alone was setting the organisation's policies for years without the Shura Council's input, when the latter was refraining from meeting due to frequent arrests under President Mubarak. Mohammad Habib, a former Brothers leader, says:

> The last time the group's Shura Council met was in January 1995, and it did not meet again after that until after the revolution, on 10 February 2011, the reason being the security raids and the members of the Shura Council being put on military trials. The Shura Council members no longer met, and its powers practically *de facto* moved to the Guidance Bureau, which damaged the culture of participation and turned the group into a monolith, moving wherever the leadership moved, without discussion.[36]

The dominance of the Guidance Council over the Shura Council accompanied another equally significant development, what is believed to be the greater influence of hardline Qutbists compared to moderates within the Guidance Bureau. The term 'Qutbists' has become common in referring to Brothers leaders heavily influenced by the ideas of Sayyid Qutb, and who tend to be obsessed with maintaining a strictly hierarchical organisational culture and are sticklers for following regulations and upholding the principle of 'compliance and obedience'. The Qutbists are also called 'the 1965 Organisation' after a secret organisation formed by some Brothers based on Qutb's ideas, whether with or without the approval of the supreme guide (*murshid*) at the time, Hassan Al-Hudaibi (1951–1973). The 1965 Organisation was known for shutting itself off from society and the government, while possessing a sense of moral superiority over others, believing themselves to be what Qutb in his groundbreaking *Landmarks* called "the vanguard of believers". The Qutbists carry more weight than the moderates in the Guidance Bureau, particularly after the departure of two leading moderates, Abdul Al-Mun'em Abu Al-Futuh and Mohammad Habib. According to Aboul Fotouh, the 1965 Organisation is now effectively in charge, and impeding the Brothers' evolution:

> Those present now in the Guidance Council are Sayyid Qutb's pupils, and I do not disagree with most of Qutb's ideas, but he had opinions and ideas which represent neither Imam [Hassan] Al-Banna nor the Brothers' school, and so the 1965

Organisation was like a foreign body when it entered the Muslim Brothers' body, becoming tantamount to an organisation within an organisation, impeding the evolution of the group as a whole.

The Qutbists include Supreme Guide (*murshid*) Mohammed Badie, Mohammed Ezzat, and disqualified presidential candidate Khairat El-Shatir.[37] There are several challenges facing the organisation: these include its duelling factions; the question of who is in control of both the decision-making process and decision-making itself; establishing a separation between the Guidance Bureau and the Shura Council as exists in Muslim Brothers' organisations in other Arab countries; for the Guidance Bureau and Shura Council to better represent the range of demographic groups within the Brothers, most importantly youth and women (there being no women on the Guidance Bureau or the Shura Council); and to amend restrictive regulations once necessitated by a banned presence under a dictatorship which no longer exists.[38]

The greatest challenge, however, which will determine how much social legitimacy the movement has after the revolution, is transforming their trademark culture of secrecy, which was justified under Nasser, Sadat and Mubarak when the Brothers were driven underground, into a culture of transparency and openness more appropriate for an Arab Spring generation that no longer trusts in clandestine organisations. The same applies for the international Muslim Brothers organisation with the ascent of the Brothers in Egypt and the Muslim Brothers-inspired Nahda Party in Tunisia, and regional fears of the organisation plotting against the ruling regimes in the Persian Gulf.[39]

Conclusion

After the fall of Mubarak, the Muslim Brothers reclaimed their legal legitimacy, missing since the group was dissolved by Nasser in 1954. In March 2013, the Muslim Brothers officially registered as a civil society association under the Mubarak-era Civil Association Law. The Brothers had previously refused to legalise their status for a number of reasons: they argued that a civil association was too narrow a category for their comprehensive movement involved in politics as well, and under Mubarak they were understandably hesitant about coming out into the open and exposing themselves to a future crackdown, with their funds overseen by the Ministry of Social Affairs made vulnerable to confiscation. But with the Brothers' rise to power, the group realised that its destiny was in its own hands, and legalisation was more of a foregone conclusion than a sudden break in policy or historical achievement. While the Brothers were no longer haunted by their lack of legal legitimacy as in the past, they faced a new worry: their endangered popularity since coming to power.

The debate in Egypt today is not about the Islamists' legal legitimacy (re-denied by the successive military-led regime in December 2013) but about their track record when in power'. While the Brothers' social performance in the 1980s in the trade unions, student unions and neighbourhoods was certainly impressive, generating public enthusiasm for continued Brothers rule was a much more formidable challenge. While spending decades underground under authoritarian (Nasser) and semi-authoritarian (Sadat and Mubarak) regimes, the group did not fully develop democratic mechanisms and practices.[40] While the Mubarak regime may have fallen, the collapse of a semi-authoritarian regime could not be understand to automatically entail a blooming of democracy. The realistic challenge before Morsi, a product of the Sadat and Mubarak generation, was not whether he could achieve full democracy under his short-lived term; instead, it was whether he could put in place the building blocks to create a somewhat democratic system which would continue evolving at the end of his term. The most pressing challenge for Morsi was to re-establish a popular legitimacy by making tangible economic and social achievements, which did not occur. Whether one likes it or not, Egyptians are still in a revolutionary mood, and are impatient to see the change for which they paid such a dear price. Accordingly, they are being very strict in judging their post-Mubarak rulers. And the anti-Morsi demonstrations on 30 June 2013 which led to Morsi's ouster after one year in power, and brought military general, Fattah Sisi, as Egypt's new president in 2014, is a vivid manifestation of the volatile Egyptian mood.

Notes

1 Zahran, Jamal Ali. *"Al-ihtijajat al-manatiqiyya wa 'alaqatuha bil-markaz iban thawra 25 yanayir fi misr"* ("Regional Protests and their Relationship with the Center during the Egyptian 25 January Revolution") in *al-thawra al-misriyya: al-dawafi' wa al-ittijahat wa al-tahaddiyat* (*The Egyptian Revolution: Motives, Orientations, and Challenges*), multiple authors, Arab Center for Research and Policy Studies, Qatar, 2012, pp. 138–150.

2 See the Muslim Brothers: "Statement on Tunisia's Uprising and the Demands of the Egyptian People", 19 January 2011, http://www.ikhwanweb.com/article.php?id=27890.

3 Personal interview with Mohammad Al-Qassas, Cairo, 10 September 2012.

4 Personal interview with Ahmad Rami, Cairo, 9 September 2012.

5 The Muslim Brothers: "Statement on Tunisia's Uprising and the Demands of the Egyptian People", 19 January 2011, http://www.ikhwanweb.com/article.php?id=27890.

6 Various publications have chronicled the revolution, including Rabia, Amr Hashim (editor). *Thawra 25 yanayir: qira'a awaliya wa ru'iya mustaqilla* (*The 25 January Revolution: An Initial Analysis and Independent Vision*), Al-Ahram Centre for Political and Strategic Studies, 2011; Al-Munawi, Abdul-Latif. *Al-ayyam al-akhira li-nidham mubarak, 18 yawm* (*The Final 18 Days of the Mubarak Regime*), the Lebanese-Egyptian Publishing House, Cairo, 2012. For the Brothers' attitude towards the revolution, see Abdul-Latif, Omayma. *"Al-Islamiyuun wa al-thawra"* ("Islamists and the Revolution") in *Al-thawra al-misriyya: al-dawafi' wal-ittijahat wal-tahaddiyat* (*The Egyptian Revolution: Motives, Trends and Challenges*), Arab Center for Research and Policy Studies, Beirut, 2013, pp. 218–256.

7 By the Brothers youth, I am referring to those under the age of 35, who comprise an estimated 35–50 per cent of the organisation, or 210,000–245,000 members based on estimates of the Brothers' overall size as 600,000–700,000. See Martini, Jeffrey. Kaye, Dalia and York, Erin. *The Muslim Brotherhood Youth: Generational Divides and Implications for US Engagement*, RAND, 2012, pp. 9–10.

8 Personal interview with Ahmad Rami, Cairo, 9 September 2012.

9 Personal interview with Mohammad Al-Qassas, Cairo, 10 September 2012.

10 Youth used their familiarity with the internet to create websites and blogs criticising the police state, with the Facebook page 'We are All Khaled Said' becoming very popular and being the first website to call for protests on 25 January 2011. The killing of Khaled Said, 27, by plainclothes police outside an Alexandria internet café set off a furious reaction that began to break down the Egyptians' longstanding fear of the security forces. For more on the role of this Facebook page in the revolution, see Majdi, Amr. *"Kulluna Khalid Sa'id, shahid yarhal wa sha'b yab'ath"* ("We are All Khaled Said: A Martyr Passes Away and a People is Resurrected") in Hussein, Ahmed (editor). *Yawmiyat al-thawra al-misriya yanaayir 2011* (*Diaries of the January 2011 Egyptian Revolution*), Arab Scientific Publishers, Beirut, 2011, pp. 39–61.

11 Badawi, Mohammed. *"25 and 28 yanayir...al-tariq ila al-tahrir"* ("25 and 28 January: The Road to Tahrir") in Hussein, Ahmed (editor). *Yawmiyat al-thawra al-misriya yanaayir 2011* (*Diaries of the January 2011 Egyptian Revolution*), Arab Scientific Publishers, Beirut, 2011, pp. 64–65.

12 While the youth were perfectly clear about their opinion that the revolution should continue until the Mubarak regime fell, the leadership was willing to come to a mutual understanding with the government

to achieve political gains. The senior leadership gave a green light to negotiate with Mubarak's vice-president and intelligence chief Omar Suleiman over withdrawing its youth from the demonstrations in exchange for the state recognising the Brothers' legitimacy, over the indignant protests of the Brothers' youth themselves, who refused any withdrawal from the streets.

13 Personal interview with Mohammad Al-Qassas, Cairo, 10 September 2012.

14 Personal interview with Mohammad Al-Qassas, Cairo, 10 September 2012.

15 Abdul-Latif, Omayma. *"Al-Islamiyuun wa al-thawra"* ("Islamists and the Revolution") in *Al-thawra al-misriyya: al-dawafi' wal-ittijahat wal-tahaddiyat* (*The Egyptian Revolution: Motives, Trends and Challenges*), Arab Center for Research and Policy Studies , Beirut, 2013, pp. 231–232.

16 *"Ashhar al-inshiqaqat fi tarikh jama'at al-ikhwan al-muslimin"* ("The Most Famous Defections in the History of the Muslim Brothers' Organization"), *Al-Misriyuun* newspaper, Cairo, 8 May 2012.

17 Personal interview with Abdul Al-Mun'em Abu Al-Futuh, Cairo, 11 September 2012.

18 Rabia, Amr Hashim (editor). *Intikhabat majlis al-sha'b 2011–2012 (The 2011–2012 People's Assembly Elections)*, Al-Ahram Centre for Political and Strategic Studies, 2012, pp. 379–382.

19 Rabia, Amr Hashim. *Al-ikhwan wa al-barlaman: dirasa fi al-fikr wa al-suluk* (*The Brothers and Parliament: A Study of Ideology and Behavior*), Al-Ahram Centre for Political and Strategic Studies, 2011, pp. 27–28.

20 Personal interview with Abdul Al-Mun'em Abu Al-Futuh, Cairo, 11 September 2012.

21 Personal interview with 'Esam Al-'Aryan, Cairo, 10 September 2012.

22 Personal interview with Diaa Rashwan, Cairo, 12 September 2012.

23 Egyptian Center for Social and Economic Rights, 2012 report, Cairo. This figure is separate from the protests and violence which wracked Port Said that year.

24 The Brothers' statement that they would not field a presidential candidate was on 5 February 2011. The group decided to participate as a result of the existence of what it labeled a threat to the revolution, democraticisation, and the transfer of power to a civilian government, in a reference to their rejection of the military maintaining power. See the Brothers' statement on 31 March 2012.

25 Egypt's foreign debt is roughly US$35 billion, its domestic public debt is another 962.3 billion Egyptian pounds, and the payments to service the foreign and domestic debt are roughly 210.9 billion pounds (110 billion in interest and 100.1 billion to repay the principal). In the first six months of his rule, Morsi borrowed roughly 112 billion pounds, which made analysts speculate that if he continued borrow at this breakneck rate, in his term he would have borrowed more than the Mubarak regime did over 30 years. *Al-Quds Al-Arabi*, 22 March 2013.

26 Among the proposed economic reform measures are tax reform to increase taxes on the wealthy, on bank interest, and on oil and gas companies according to hydrocarbon prices; reforming the sales tax

collection system to reduce tax evading or nonpayment (there is about 63 billion Egyptian pounds due from high-income taxpayers who are late in making the payment). *Al-Quds Al-Arabi*, 22 March 2013.

27 Since coming to power, Morsi has chosen Brothers loyalists to fill the positions of 8 ministers, 5 governors, and 13 advisors to the governors. *Al-Masri Al-Yaum*, 14 February 2013.

28 Personal interview with Mohammad Habib, Cairo, 12 September 2012.

29 Personal interview with 'Esam Al-'Aryan, Cairo, 10 September 2012.

30 In Sudan, the nature of the relationship between the party's secretary-general Hassan Al-Turabi and Omar Al-Bashir was changed when the latter became head of the government, as was the means of managing state policy. In Tunisia, Nahda Party secretary-general Hamad Al-Jibali and Nahda leader Rashed Al-Ghannouchi fell out over how inclusive to be towards the secularist parties and whether to allow them to join the ruling coalition.

31 Personal interview with Diaa Rashwan, Cairo, 12 September 2012.

32 Tammam, Hussam. *Al-ikhwan al-muslimun: sanawat maa qabla al-thawra* (*The Muslim Brothers: The Years before the Revolution*). Dar Al-Shurouq, Cairo, 2012, p. 35.

33 Personal interview with Mahmoud Ezzat, Cairo, 10 September 2012.

34 According to 'Akif: "I made it conditional for the group that I would step down when I turned 80, because a person's performance changes after the age of 80, and I believe that the supreme guide should be not be above the age of 70." Personal interview with Mahdi 'Akif, Cairo, 8 September 2012.

35 When I asked Mahdi 'Akif, the former Supreme Guide (*murshid*) (2004–2010) who was more powerful, Morsi or Badie, he said "Definitely Morsi, because he's the head of state, and the supreme guide is part of the Egyptian state, and this is clear to both Morsi and Badie." Personal interview with Mahdi 'Akif, Cairo, 8 September 2012.

36 Personal interview with Mohammad Habib, Cairo, 12 September 2012.

37 Personal interview with Mohammad Habib, 12 September 2012.

38 Khairat El-Shatir is known to be in charge of structural development, and sweeping changes had been promised in the wake of the revolution, but more than a year after the Brothers came to power, there have been virtually no changes.

39 Pargeter, Alison. *The Muslim Brotherhood: The Burden of Tradition*, Saqi Books, London, 2010, pp. 96–132.

40 See: Brown, Nathan. *When Victory is Not an Option: Islamist Movements in Arab Politics*, Cornell University Press, Ithaca and London, 2012, pp. 1–31.

BIBLIOGRAPHY

Abdul Fattah, Nabil, 1994, *Veiled Violence: Islamic Fundamentalism in Egyptian Politics in 1990s*, Dar Sechat for Studies, Publishing and Distribution, Cairo.

Abdul Hai, Mahmoud, 1993, *Economic Reform in Egypt (Motives and Orientations)*, The Institute of National Planning, Cairo.

Abdul Halim, Abdul 'Ati, 1994, *Al-Harakat al-islamiyya fi misr wa qadiat al-ta'adudiyya al-siyasiyya 1976–1986*, (The Islamic Movements in Egypt and the Issue of Political Pluralism 1976–1986), unpublished PhD thesis, Cairo University, Egypt.

Abdul Khalek, Gouda, 1979, "The Open-Door Economic Policy In Egypt: A Search for Meaning, Interpretation and Implication", in Herbert Thompson (ed.), *Studies in the Egyptian Political Economy*, Cairo Papers in Social Sciences, vol. 2, no. 3, The American University in Cairo, Egypt.

Abdul Khaliq, Amin *et al.*, 2001, *Al-Jam'iyyat al-ahliyya fi misr* (Informal Associations in Egypt), Cairo, Dar Al-Amin.

Abdullah, A, 1985, *The Student Movement and National Politics in Egypt, 1923–1973*, London, Al-Saqi.

Abdul-Latif, Omayma, 2013, "*Al-Islamiyuun wa al-thawra*" ("Islamists and the Revolution") in *Al-thawra al-misriyya: al-dawafi' wal-ittijahat wal-tahaddiyat* (The Egyptian Revolution: Motives, Trends and Challenges), Beirut, Arab Center for Research and Policy Studies.

Abdul Majid, H., 1994, "Al-Haraka al-islamiyya wa al-nuzum al-siyasiyya al-'arabiyya ma'a 'ishira khassa lil al-hala al-misriyya" (The Islamic Movement and the Arab Political Regimes, with Special Reference to the Egyptian Case), in M. Kharbousch (ed.), *Al-Tatawwur al-siysasi fi misr 1982–1992* (Political development in Egypt 1982–1992), Centre for Political Research and Studies, Cairo University, pp. 471–510.

Abdul Mun'im, Ahmad, 1993, *Al-Sulta al-siyasiyya wa al-tanmiyya munzu 1805 hata al-'an* (Political Authority and Development Since 1805 to the Present), *Al-Ahram Al-Iqtisadi*, issue 64, June.

Abed-Kotob, Sana, 1995, "The Accommodationists Speak: Goals and Strategies of the Muslim Brotherhood of Egypt", *International Journal of Middle East Studies*, vol. 27, no.3.

Abu Azza, A, 1986, *Ma'a al-haraka al-islamiyya fi al-duwal al-'arabiyya* (With the Islamic Movement in the Arab Countries), Kuwait, Dar Al-Qalam.

Abu Basha, Hassan, 1990, *Mudhukrat hassan abu basha* (Memoirs of Hassan Abu Basha), Cairo, Dar Al-Hilal.

Abu Al-Is'ad, Mohammad, 1996, *Zahirat al-fasad al-siyasi fi misr al-mu'asira* (The Phenomenon of Political Corruption in Contemporary Egypt), Cairo, n.p.

Abu-Lughod, Laila, 1997, "Dramatic Reversals: Political Islam and Egyptian Television", in Joel Beinin and Jo Stork (eds.), *Political Islam: Essays from Middle East Report*, London, I.B.Tauris.

Aftandilian, Gregory, 1993, *Egypt's Bid for Arab Leadership: Implications for US Policy*, New York, Council on Foreign Relations Press.

Amin, Jum'a, 1998, *Qadiyat al-irhab: al-ru'iya wa al-ilaj*, (The Issue of Terrorism: the Vision and the Solution), Cairo, Dar Al-Tawzi' wa Al-Nashr Al-Islamiyya.

Ansari, Hamied, 1984, "The Islamic Militants in Egyptian Politics", *International Journal of Middle East Studies*, vol.16, no.3.

Aoude, Ibrahim, 1994, "From National Bourgeois Development to Infitah: Egypt 1952–1992", *Arab Studies Quarterly*, vol. 16, no. 1, Winter.

Apter, David, 1965, *The Politics of Modernization*, Chicago, University of Chicago Press.

Assa'd, R. and M. Rouchdy, 1999, *Poverty and Poverty Alleviation Strategies in Egypt*, Cairo Papers in Social Science, vol. 22, no. 1, The American University in Cairo, Egypt.

'Auda, Jihad, 1988, "Istratijiat al-ra'is mubarak fi al-ta'amul ma'a al-mu'arada (The strategy of Mubarak in Dealing with the Opposition), Hilal, Ali (ed.), *Al-Nizam al-siysasi al-misri: al-tagiur wa al-istimrar*, (The Egyptian Political Regime: Continuity and Change), Cairo University, Egypt.

——, 1991, "An Uncertain Response: The Islamic Movement in Egypt", in James Piscatori (ed.), *Islamic Fundamentalisms and the Gulf Crisis*, Chicago, American Academy of Arts and Sciences.

——, 1994, "The 'Normalization' of the Islamic Movement in Egypt from 1970s to the Early 1990s", in M. Marty and S. Appleby (eds.), *Accounting for Fundamentalisms*, Chicago, University of Chicago Press.

Al-Awadi, Hesham, 2013, "Islamists in power: the case of the Muslim Brotherhood in Egypt", *Contemporary Arab Affairs*, vol. 6, issue 4, November.

——, 2009, "A struggle for legitimacy: the Muslim Brotherhood and Mubarak, 1982–2009", *Contemporary Arab Affairs*, vol. 2, issue 2, May.

——, 2009, Sira' 'ala al-shar'iyya: al-ikhwan al-mulsimun wa mubarak 1982–2007, (Struggle for Legitimacy: the Muslim Brothers and Mubarak 1982–2009), Beirut, Centre for Arab Unity Studies.

——, 2008, "Al-nizam al-masry wa al-ikhwan: sira' 'ala shar'iyyat al-bqa" (The Egyptian Regime and the Brothers: Struggle for Survival), *Al-Mustaqbal Al-Arabi*, issue 353, July.

——, 2005, "Mubarak and the Islamists: Why Did the Honeymoon End?", *Middle East Journal*, vol. 59, no. 1, Winter.

Ayalon, A., and Shaked, H., (eds.), 1985, *Middle East Contemporary Survey*, Boulder, The Moshe Dayan Center for Middle Eastern and African Studies, The Shiloah Institute, Tel Aviv University, Westview Press.

——, 1986, *Middle East Contemporary Survey*, Boulder, The Moshe Dayan Center for Middle Eastern and African Studies, The Shiloah Institute, Tel Aviv University, Westview Press.

——, 1992, *Middle East Contemporary Survey*, Boulder, The Moshe Dayan

Center for Middle Eastern and African Studies, The Shiloah Institute, Tel Aviv University, Westview Press.

Ayubi, Nazih, 1989, "Government and the State in Egypt Today" in Charles Tripp and Roger Owen, *Egypt Under Mubarak*, London, Routledge.

——, 1990, "Etatism Versus Privatisation: the Case of the Public Sector in Egypt", *International Review of Administrative Sciences*, vol.56, no. 1, March.

——, 1991, *The State and Public Policies Since Sadat*, Reading, Ithaca Press.

——, 1995, *Over-Stating the Arab State: Politics and Society in the Middle East*, London, I.B.Tauris.

Azzam, Maha, 1989, *Islamic Oriented Protest Groups in Egypt 1971–1981: Theory, Politics and Dogma*, unpublished PhD thesis, Faculty of Social Studies, University of Oxford, UK.

——, 1996, "Egypt: The Islamists and the State Under Mubarak", in Abdel Salam Sidahmed and Anoushiravan Ehteshami (eds.), *Political Fundamentalism*, Boulder CO., Westview Press.

Badr, Muhammad, 1989, *Al-Jama'a al-islamiyya fi jami'at misr*, (The Jama'a Al-Islamiyya in Egyptian Universities), no publisher.

Al-Banna, Hassan, 1977, *Islamuna: risalat al-mu'tamar al-khamis*, (Our Islam: The Fifth Conference), Cairo, Dar Al-Tiba'a wa Al-Nashr Al-Islamiyya.

Bari, Zohurul, 1995, *The Re-emergence of the Muslim Brothers in Egypt*, New Delhi, Lancer Studies.

Al-Basir, H., 1994, "Jama't al-ikhwan al-muslimin, wa al-tanshi'a al-siyasiyya lil shabab" (The Muslim Brothers and the Political Upbringing of the Youth) in K. Al-Munifi and H. Ibrahim (eds.) *Al-Thaqafa Al-siyasiyya fi misr* (Political Culture in Egypt), vol.2, Centre for Research and Political Studies, Cairo University, Egypt.

Bayyumi, Z. , 1979, *Al-Ikhwan al-muslimun*, Cairo, Maktabat Wahba.

Beattie, Kirk, 1994, *Egypt During the Nasser Years: Ideology, Politics and Civil Society*, Boulder CO, Westview Press.

Beshai, A., 1993, "Interpretations and Misinterpretations of the Egyptian Economy", in Charles Tripp (ed.), *Contemporary Egypt Through Egyptian Eyes*, Routledge, London.

Bianchi, R., 1989, *Unruly Corporatism: Associational Life in Twentieth Century Egypt*, Oxford, Oxford University Press.

Bibars, Iman., 2001, *Victims and Heroines: Women, Welfare and the Egyptian State*, London, Zed Press.

Bill, James and Springborg, Robert, 1994, *Politics in The Middle East*, New York, Harper Collins.

Al-Bishri, Tariq, n.d., "Assessment of Pluralism, Democratic Consolidation and Political Participation", unpublished paper.

Al-Bishri, Tariq, 1988, "Asalib al-sira' hawla tawzif al-amwal" (Methods of the Struggle Over the financial Investment), *Al-Ahram Al-Iqtisadi*, 18 July 1988.

Brown, Nathan, 2012, *When Victory is Not an Option: Islamist Movements in Arab Politics*, Ithaca and London, Cornell University Press.

Brumberg, Daniel, 1992, "Survival Strategies Vs. Democratic Bargain: The Politics of Economic Reform in Contemporary Egypt", in Henry Barkey (ed.), *The Politics of Economic Reform in the Middle East*, New York, St. Martin's Press.

'Cassandra', 1995, "The Impending Crisis in Egypt", *Middle East Journal*, vol. 49, no. 1, Winter.

el-Chobaki, Amr, 2005, *Al-Ikhwan Al-Muslimun fi Intikhabat Majlis Al-Shaab 2005* (The Muslim Brothers in the 2005 People's Assembly Elections), Center for Political and Strategic Studies.

Clark, Janine, 1995, "Democratisation and Social Islam: A Case Study of the Islamic Health Clinics in Cairo", in R. Brynen, B. Korany and P. Noble (eds.), *Political Liberalization and Democratisation in the Arab World*, vol. 1, Boulder and London, Lynne Rienner Publishers.

Dahl, Robert, 1956, *A Preface to Democratic Theory*, Chicago, University of Chicago Press.

Dekmejian, Hrair, 1972, *Egypt Under Nasser: A Study of Political Dynamics*, London, University of London Press.

——, 1985, *Islam in Revolution: Fundamentalism in the Arab World*, New York, Syracuse University.

Al-Dijani, Mahdi, n.d., *Dawr al-fi'a al-mustaghriba min rigal al-'amal*, (The Role of the Westernised Sector of Businessmen), Cairo, unpublished paper.

Sharaf Al-Din, N., 1998, *Umara' wa muwatinun* (Princes and Citizens), Cairo, Maktabat Madbuli.

El-Mikawy, Noha, 1999, *The Building of Consensus in Egypt's Transition Process*, Cairo, the American University in Cairo Press.

El-Mikawy, N. and Handoussa, H. (eds.), 2002, *Institutional Reform and Economic Development in Egypt*, Cairo, American University in Cairo Press.

Easton, David, 1965, *A Systems Analysis of Political Life*, New York, Wiley.

Esping-Anderson, Gosta, 1990, *The Three Worlds of Welfare Capitalism*, Cambridge, Polity Press.

Fahmy, Ninette, 1999, *The Relationship Between State and Society in Contemporary Egypt*, unpublished PhD thesis, University of Exeter, UK.

——, 1998, "The Performance of the Muslim Brotherhood in the Egyptian Syndicates: An Alternative Formula For Reform?", *Middle East Journal*, vol. 52, no. 4, Autumn.

Farhud, Ahlam,1998, *Mawqi' al-sulta al-qada'iyya fi al-nizam al-siyasi al-misri* (The Position of the Legal Authority in the Egyptian Political Regime), unpublished PhD thesis, Cairo University, Egypt.

Ferrarotti, Franco, 1987, "Legitimation, Representation and Power", *Current Sociology*, vol. 35, no. 2, Summer.

Flores, Alexander, 1997, "Secularism, Integralism and Political Islam: The Egyptian Debate", in Joel Beinin and Joe Stork, *Political Islam: Essays from Middle East Report*, London, I.B.Tauris.

Fukuyama, Francis, 1993, *The End of History and the Last Man*, Harmondsworth, Penguin.

Gehlen, A., 1963, *Studien zur Anthropologie und Soziologie*, Neuwied.

Ghanim, Ibrahim Biyyumi, 1992, *Al-Fikr al-siyasi li al-imam hassan al-banna* (The Political Thinking of Imam Hassan Al-Banna), Cairo, Dar al Tawzi' wa al Nashr.

Ghannoushi, Rashid, 1993, *Al-Huriyyat al-'amma fi al-dawla al-islamiyya*, Beirut, Centre for Arab Unity Studies.

Ginsburg, N., 1992, *Divisions of Welfare*, London, Sage Publications.

Gray, Matthew, 1998, "Economic Reform, Privatisation and Tourism in Egypt", *Middle Eastern Studies*, vol. 34, no. 2, April.

Habermas, Jurgen, 1975, *Legitimation Crisis*, Boston MA, Beacon Press.

Habib, Rafiq, 1996, *Awraq hizb al-wasat* (The Papers of Hizb Al-Wasat), Cairo, n.p.

Haddad, Y., 1983, "Sayyid Qutb: Ideologue of the Islamic Revival", in J. Esposito (ed.), *Voices of Resurgent Islam*, New York, Oxford University Press.

Haddad, Yvonne, 1996, "Operation Desert Storm and the War of the Fatwas", in Muhammad Masud (eds.), *Islamic Legal Interpretations: Muftis and Their Fatwas*, Boston, Harvard University Press.

Hamad, Hassouna, 2007, *"Bil-Arqam: al-Khasa'ir al-Iqtisadiya bisabab al-Mahkama al-'Askariya li-Qiyadat al-Ikhwan"* ("In Numbers: the Economic Losses due to the Military Trial of the Brothers' Leaders"), www.ikhwanonline.com.

Hamzawy, Amr, Marina Ottowa and Nathan J. Brown, 2007, "What Islamists Need to be Clear About: The Case of the Egyptian Muslim Brotherhood," Carnegie Endowment for International Peace.

Harb, Usama, 1989, "Al-Mutaghiyyr al-khariji ka muhadid li al-shar'iyya" (The external Variable as a Determinant for Legitimacy) in Mustafa Kamil Al-Sayyid (ed.) *Al-Tahwulat al-siyasiyya al-haditha fi al-watan al-'arabi*, (Modern Political Changes in the Arab Land), Cairo, Centre for Political Research and Studies,.

Harik, Iliya, 1992, "Subsidization Policies in Egypt: Neither Economic Growth nor Distribution", *International Journal of Middle East Studies*, vol. 24, no.3.

Harris, Lillian Craig (ed.), 1988, *Egypt: Internal Challenges and Regional Stability*, London, Routledge and Kegan Paul for the Royal Institute of International Affairs.

—— 1988, "Egyptian Foreign Policy Since Camp David" in William B. Quandt (ed.), *The Middle East: Ten Years After Camp David*, Washington DC, Brookings Institution.

Hassan, Ahmad, 2000, *Al-Su'ud al-siyasi al-islami dakhil al-niqabat al-mihaniyya* (the Islamic Political Ascent to Professional Syndicates), Cairo, Al-Dar Al-Thaqafiyya li Al-Nashr.

Hassan, Naf'a, 1986, "Mulahzat hawl intikhabat 1984" (Comments on the Elections of 1984), in Hilal, A., (ed.) *Al-Tatwur al-dimuqrati fi misr: qadaya wa munaqashat*, (Democratic Development in Egypt: Issues and Discussions), Cairo, Nahdat Al-Sharq.

Hatem, Mervat, 1992, "Economic and Political State Liberalisation in Egypt and the Demise of State Feminism", *International Journal of Middle East Studies*, vol. 24, no. 2.

Al-Hawari, Fakhri, 1997, "Dawr rijal al-a'mal fi al-nizam al-siyasi" (The Role of Businessmen in the Political Regime), *Qadaiyya Barlamaniyya*, Issue 4, Al-Ahram Centre for Political and Strategic Studies, July.

Hilal, Ali, (ed.), 1978, *Democracy in Egypt: Quarter of a Century After the July Revolution*, Cairo Papers in Social Sciences, vol. 1, no. 2., The American University in Cairo, Egypt.

——, (ed.), 1986, *Intikhabat majlis al-sha'b: dirasa wa tahlil* (The National Assembly Elections: A Study and an Analysis), Cairo, Al-Ahram Centre for Political and Strategic Studies.

——, 1991, *Intikhabat Majlis al-Sha'b 1990* (The Elections of the National Assembly 1990), Al-Ahram Centre for Political and Strategic Studies, Cairo.

——, 2000, *Tatawur al-nizam al-siyasi fi misr 1803–1999* (The Development of the Political Regime in Egypt 1803–1999), Al-Ahram Centre for Political Research and Studies, Cairo.

Hinnebusch, R., 1985, *Egyptian Politics Under Sadat: The Post-Populist*

Development of an Authoritarian- Modernizing State, Cambridge, Cambridge University Press.

———, 1990, "The Formation of the Contemporary Egyptian State From Nasser and Sadat to Mubarak" in Ibrahim Oweiss (ed.) , *The Political Economy of Egypt*, Washington DC, Georgetown University, Centre for Contemporary Arab Studies.

Hourani, Hani, 2000, *Professional Associations and the Challenges of Democratic Transformation in Jordan*, Proceedings of Workshops, 'Amman, Al-Urdun Al-Jadid Research Centre.

Hudson, Michael, 1977, *Arab Politics: the Search for Legitimacy*, New Haven, Yale University Press.

Huntington, Samuel P., 1968. *Political Order in Changing Societies*, New Haven, Yale University Press.

———, 1997, *The Clash of Civilisations and the Remaking of World Order*, New York, Simon and Schuster.

Hussein, Ahmed (ed), 2011, *Yawmiyat al-thawra al-misriya yanaayir 2011* (Diaries of the January 2011 Egyptian Revolution), Beirut, Arab Scientific Publishers.

Ibn Taiymiya, Taqiy Al-Din, 1983, *Al-Siyasa al-shar'iyya fi islah al-ra'i wa al-ra'iyya*, (Legitimate Politics in the Reform of Ruler and Ruled), Beirut, Dar Al-Afaq Al-Jadida.

Ibrahim, Hassanain, 1985, *Mushkilat al-shar'iyya al-siasiyya fi al-duwal al-namiyya* (The Problem of Political Legitimacy in Developed Countries), unpublished MA dissertation, Cairo University, Egypt.

Ibrahim, Hassanain, 1988, "Zahirat al-'unf al-siyasi fi misr" (The Phenomenon of Political Violence in Egypt) in Hilal, 'Ali Al-Din (ed.), *Al-Nizam al-siyasi al-misri bain al-taghyur wa al-istimrar*, Cairo University, Egypt.

Ibrahim, Hassanain, and Huda 'Awad, 1996, *Al-Ikhwan al-muslimun wa al-siyasa fi misr* (the Muslim Brothers and Politics in Egypt), Cairo, Markaz Al-Mahrusa.

———, 1996, *Al-Ikhwan al-muslimun wa al-ta'adudiyya al-hizbiyya: qira'a fi ru'iat hassan al-banna* (The Muslim Brotherhood and Multiparty: A Reading into the Stance of Hassan Al-Banna), Centre for Political Research and Studies, Cairo University, Egypt.

———, 1998, *Al-Nizam al-siysasi wa al-ikhwan al-muslimun fi misr: min al-tasamuh ala al-muwajha 1981–1996* (The Political System and The Muslim Bothers in Egypt: From Tolerance to Confrontation 1981–1996), Beirut, Dar Al-Tali'a.

———, 2000, *Al-Dawla wa al-tanmiyya fi misr* (The State and Development in Egypt), Centre for the Study of Developing Countries, Cairo University, Egypt.

Ibrahim, Sa'd Eddin, 1996a, "Islamic Activism and Political Opposition In Egypt", in Sa'd Eddin Ibrahim. *Egypt, Islam and Democracy: Twelve Critical Essays*, Cairo, American University in Cairo Press.

———, 1996b, "Islamic Alternative in Egypt: The Muslim Brotherhood and Sadat" in S. Ibrahim, *Egypt, Islam and Democracy: Twelve Critical Essays*, Cairo, American University in Cairo Press.

Imam, Abdullah, 1997, *Abdul al-nasser wa al-ikhwan al-muslimun* (Abdul Nasser and the Muslim Brothers), Cairo, Dar Al-Khayyal.

Al-Jamal, M., 1993, *Al-Nukhba al-siyasiyya fi misr* (The Political Elite in Egypt), Beirut, Markaz Dirasat Al-Wihda Al-Arabiyya.

Jami', Mahmud, 1999, *'Araft al-sadat* (I Knew Sadat), Cairo, Al-Maktab Al-Misri Al-Hadith.

Jensen, Michael, 1998, "Islamism and Civil Society in the Gaza Strip", in A. Moussalli (ed.), *Islamic Fundamentalism: Myths and Realities*, Reading, Ithaca Press.

Jum'a, Salwa, 1988, "Al-tagiur wa al-istimrariyya fi mu'sasat sl-riasa: halat misr" (Change and Continuity in the Presidential Institution: the Case of Egypt), A. Hilal (ed.), *Al-Nizam al-siyasi al-misri: al-tagiur wa al-istimrar* (The Egyptian Political Regime: Change and Continuity), Cairo University, Egypt.

Kepel, Gilles, 1985, *Muslim Extremism in Egypt: The Prophet and the Pharaoh*, Berkley, University of California Press.

Khalifa, Magdi, 1996, *Socioeconomic Aspects of the Economic Reform Policies in Egypt*, Cairo, Institute of National Planning.

Khalil, Abdullah, 1999. *Azmat niqabat al-muhamin* (The Crisis of Professional Syndicates), Cairo, Markaz Al-Qahira li Dirasat Huquq Al-Insan.

Kharbousch, M. (ed.), 1994, *Al-Tatawur al-siyasi fi misr 1982–1992* (Political development in Egypt 1982–1992), Centre for Political Research and Studies, Cairo University.

Khoury, Philip, 1983, "Islamic Revivalism and the Crisis of the Secular State in the Arab World", in Ibrahim, Ibrahim (ed.), *Arab Resources*, Washington DC, Georgetown University, Centre for Contemporary Arab Studies.

Kienle, Eberhard, 1998, "More Than a Response to Islam: The Political Deliberalization of Egypt in the 1990s", *Middle East Journal*, vol. 52, no. 2, Spring.

——, 2001, *A Grand Delusion: Democracy and Economic Reform in Egypt*, London, I.B.Tauris.

Korayem, Karima, 1991, *The Egyptian Economy and the Poor in the Eighties*, Cairo, The Institute of National Planning.

Korpi, Walter, 1985, "Power Resources Approach vs. Action and Conflict: On Casual and International Explanation in the Study of Power", *Sociological Theory*, vol. 3, no. 2.

Leenders, Reinoud, 1996, *The Struggle of State and Civil Society in Egypt: Professional Organisations and Egypt's Careful Steps Towards Democracy*, Amsterdam, Middle East Research Associates, Occasional Papers, no.26, April.

Lofgren, Hans, 1993, "Economic Policy in Egypt: A Breakdown in Reform Resistance", *International Journal of Middle East Studies*, vol. 25, no. 3.

Luciani, Giacomo, 1988, "Economic Foundations of Democracy and Authoritarianism: The Arab World in Comparative Perspective", *Arab Studies Quarterly*, vol. 10, no. 4.

Lubeck, P. and Britts, B., 2001, "Muslim Civil Society in Urban Spaces: Globalisation, Discursive Shifts and Social Movements", Working Papers Series, Centre for Global, International and Regional Studies (CGIRS), University of California, Santa Cruz.

Lynch, G. "The Legitimacy of Communism in Eastern Europe", cited from *http://members.tripod.com/index.html*, accessed March 2003.

McDermott, A., 1988, *Egypt From Nasser to Mubarak: A Flawed Revolution*, London, Croom Helm.

Martini, Jeffrey. Kaye, Dalia and York, Erin, 2012, *The Muslim Brotherhood Youth: Generational Divides and Implications for US Engagement*, RAND.

Mashhur, Mustafa, 1987, *Al-Taiyar al-islami wa dawruhu fi al-bina'* (The Islamic Trend and Its Role in Building), Cairo, Dar Al-Tawzi' wa Al-Nashr.

Meijer, Roel, 1997, *From Al-Da'wa to Hizbiyya: Mainstream Islamic Movements in Egypt, Jordan and Palastine in the 1990s*, Amsterdam, Middle East Research Associates, Occasional Papers, no.10, August.

Migdal, Joel, 1988, *Strong Societies and Weak States: State Relations and State Capabilities in the Third World*, New Jersey, Princeton University Press.

Al-Miligi, A, 1994, *Tarikh al-haraka al-islamiyya fi sahat al-ta'lim* (The History of the Islamic Movement in the Education Field), Cairo, Maktbat Wahba.

Minysi, A., 1997, "Rigal al-a'mal fi intikhabat 1995", (Businessmen in the 1995 Elections), in Mustafa, H. (ed.), *Al-Intikhabat al-barlamaniyya fi misr 1995*, (Parliamentary Elections in Egypt 1995), Cairo, Al-Ahram Centre for Political and Strategic Studies.

Al-Minufi, Kamal (ed.), 1996, *Intikhabat majlis al-Sha'b 1995*, (The Elections of the National Assembly 1995), Cairo, Cairo University.

Mitchell, R., 1969, *The Society of the Muslim Brothers*, Oxford, Oxford University Press.

Mitckis, Huda, 1989, "Al-Shar'iyya wa al-mu'arada al-dinniyya: dirasat halat kul min al-magrib wa misr" (Legitimacy and Religious Opposition: the Case of Morocco and Egypt) in Mustafa Al-Sayyid (ed.), *Al-Tahawlat al-siyasiyya al-haditha fi al-watan al-'arabi* (Modern Political Transformation in the Arab Country), Centre for Research and Political Studies, Cairo University, Egypt.

Mitwali, Abdul Hamid, 1966, *Mabadi' nizam al-hukm fi al-islam* (Principles of the Government System in Islam), Cairo, Dar Al-Ma'arif.

Moore, Clement Henry, 1990, "Islamic Banks and Competitive Politics in the Arab World and Turkey", *Middle East Journal*, vol. 44, no.2.

Moussalli, A. (ed.), 1999, *Moderate and Radical Islamic Fundamentalism: the Quest for Modernity, Legitimacy and the Islamic State*, Gainesville FL, University Press of Florida.

Mubarak, H., 1995, *Al-AIrhabiyun qadimun: dirasa muqarana bayna mawqif al-ikhwan al-muslimin wa jama'at al-jihad min qadiyat al-'unf* (The Terrorists are Coming: A Comparative Study of the Position of the Muslim Brotherhood and the Jihad Groups from the Question of Violence), Cairo, Dar Al-Mahrusa.

——, 1997, "What Does the Gama'a Islamiyya Want?", in Joel Beinin, and Joe Stork, eds., *Political Islam: Essays from Middle East Report*, London, I.B.Tauris.

Muhammad, Jamil, 1996, *Al-'Ilaqa bain al-nizam al-siyasi wa al-harakat al-islamiyya fi misr, 1970–1977*, (The Relation Between the Political Regime and the Islamic Movements in Egypt), unpublished MA Dissertation, Cairo University, Egypt.

Al-Munawi, Abdul-Latif, 2012, *Al-ayyam al-akhira li-nidham mubarak, 18 yawm* (The Final 18 Days of the Mubarak Regime), Cairo the Lebanese-Egyptian Publishing House.

Al-Munifi, K., and H. Ibrahim, *Al-Thaqafa al-siyasiyya fi misr* (Political Culture in Egypt), vol. 2, Cairo, Centre for Research and Political Studies, 1994.

Murphy, C., 1995, "The Business of Political Change in Egypt", *Current History*, vol. 94, no. 588, January.

Mustafa, Hala, 1995, "The Islamist Movements Under Mubarak", in Laura Guazzone (ed.), *The Islamist Dilemma*, Reading, Ithaca Press.

——, 1996, *Al-Dawula wa al-harakat al-islamiyya al-mu'arida bain al-muhadna wa al-muwajha fi ahdai al-sadat wa mubarak* (The State and the Oppositional Islamic Movements, between Accommodation and Confrontation), Cairo, Al-Mahrusa.

——, 1997 *Al-Intikhabat al-barlamaniyya fi misr 1995* (Parliamentary Elections in Egypt 1995), Cairo, Al-Ahram Centre for Political and Strategic Studies.

——, 2001. *Intikhabat Majlis al-Sha'b 2000.* (The 2000 People's Assembly Elections), Cairo, Al-Ahram Centre for Political and Strategic Studies .

Mustafa, Tamir, 2000, "Conflict and Cooperation Between the State and Religious Institutions in Contemporary Egypt", *International Journal of Middle East Studies,* vol. 32, no. 1, February.

Naf'a, Hassan, 1988, "Al-Nizam al-siyasi al-'arabi: halat misr", (The Political Arab Regime: the Case of Egypt), *Al-Mustaqbal Al-'Arabi*, no. 112, June.

Nijm, Ihab, 1996, *Al-Dawr al-siyasi li al-jam'iyyat al-ahliyya al-islamiyya fi misr, 1921–1992*, (The Political Role of the Islamic Informal Associations in Egypt, 1921–1992), unpublished MA dissertation, Cairo University, Egypt.

Nuwair, Abdul Salam, 1993, *Al-Hirak al-ijtima'i wa al-taghaiur al-siyasi fi misr* (Social Mobilisation and Political Change in Egypt), unpublished MA dissertation, Cairo University, Egypt.

Oweiss, Ibrahim, 1990, "Egypt's Economy: the Pressing Issues" in Ibrahim Oweiss (ed.), *The Political Economy of Contemporary Egypt*, Washington DC, Georgetown University, Centre for Contemporary Arab Studies.

Pargeter, Alison, 2010, *The Muslim Brotherhood: The Burden of Tradition*, London, Saqi Books.

Poggi, G., 1978, *The Development of the Modern State: A Sociological Introduction*, Palo Alto CA, Stanford University Press.

Posusney, Marsha, 1995, *The Political Environment of Economic Reform in Egypt: The Labour Movement vs. Privatisation Revisited*, Amsterdam, Research Centre for International Political Economy and Foreign Policy Analysis, University of Amsterdam.

——, 1997, *Labor and the State: Workers, Unions and Economic Restructuring*, New York, Columbia University Press.

Qandil, Amani, 1989, "Jama'at al-masalih wa al-siyasi al-kharijiyya: dirasa li dawr rigal al-'amal fi misr" (Interest Groups and Foreign Policy: A Study on the Role of Businessmen in Egypt), *Al-Mustaqbal Al-Arabi*, Issue 128, October, pp. 95–82.

——, 1992, "Al-Jama'at al-mihaniyya wa al-musharka al-siyasiyya" (Professional Groups and Political Participation), paper presented to the *Symposium for Political Participation in Egypt*, Cairo University, Egypt.

——, 1992, "Al-Niqabat al-mihaniyya fi misr wa azmat al-khalij" [Professional Syndicates in Egypt and the Gulf War], in Mustafa Al-Sayyid (ed.), *Hata la tanshb harbun 'arabiyya-'arabiyya ukhra* [So that No Other Arab-Arab War Erupts], Centre of Research and Political Studies, Cairo University, Egypt.

——, 1993, "Taqyeem ada' al-islamiyyin fi al-niqabat al-mihaniyya" (An Evaluation of the Performance of the Islamists in Professional Syndicates), paper presented to the Fifth Franco-Egyptian Symposium on *The Phenomenon of Political Violence*, (Published Proceedings), Cairo University, Egypt.

——, 1994, *Al-Jam'iyyat al-ahliya fi misr* (Informal Associations in Egypt) Al-Ahram Centre for Political and Strategic Studies, Cairo.

——, 1995, *"Amaliyyat al-tahawul al-dimuqrati fi misr 1981–1993"* (The Process of Democratic Transformation in Egypt 1981–1993), Cairo, Ibn Khaldun Centre.

——, 1996, *Al-Dawr al-siyasi li jama'at al-masalih fi misr: dirasat halat li niqabat al-atiba'a 1984–1995* (The Political Role of Interest Groups in Egypt: a Case Study of the Medical Syndicate 1984–95), Cairo, Al-Ahram Centre for Political and Strategic Studies.

Rabi', Majda, 1992, *Al-Dawr al-siyasi li al-azhar: 1952–1981* (The Political Role of Azhar: 1952–1981), Cairo University Centre for Research and Political Studies, Cairo.

Rabia, Amr Hashim, 2011a, *Al-ikhwan wa al-barlaman: dirasa fi al-fi kr wa al-suluk* (The Brothers and Parliament: A Study of Ideology and Behavior), Al-Ahram Centre for Political and Strategic Studies.

——, 2011b, *Thawra 25 yanayir: qira'a awaliya wa ru'iya mustaqilla* (The 25 January Revolution: An Initial Analysis and Independent Vision), Al-Ahram Centre for Political and Strategic Studies.

——, 2012, *Intikhabat majlis al-sha'b 2011–2012* (The 2011–2012 People's Assembly Elections), Al-Ahram Centre for Political and Strategic Studies.

Richards, Alan, 1990, *The Political Economy of Dilatory Reform: Egypt in the 1980s*, Amsterdam, Stichting, Middle East Research Associates, no. 7.

Robinson, Glenn, 1998, "Islamists Under Liberalization in Jordan", in A. Moussalli (ed.), *Islamic Fundamentalism: Myths and Realities*, Reading, Ithaca Press.

Rubin, Barry, 1990, *Islamic Fundamentalism in Egyptian Politics*, London, Macmillan.

Rumaih, Tala'at, 1997, *Al-Wasat wa al-ikhwan* [Al-Wasat and the Ikhwan], Cairo, Markaz Yafa.

Sadowski, Yahya, 1991. *Political Vegetables? Businessman and Bureaucrat in the Development of Egyptian Agriculture*, Washington DC, The Brookings Institution.

Al-Sa'id, Rif'at, 1984, *Hassan al-banna, mu'asis jamat al-ikhwan al-muslimin: mata, kaifa, wa limaza?*, (Hassan Al-Banna: the Founder of the Muslim Brothers, When, How and Why?), Cairo, Dar al Saqafa al Jadida.

Saleem, Mohammad Al-Sayyid, 1983, *Al-Tahlil al-siyasi al-nasiri* (The Nasserite Political Analysis), Beirut, Markaz Dirasat Al-Wihda Al-Arabiyya.

Samak, Najwa, 1999, *Al-Qita' al-ahli wa al-tanmiyya al-iqtisadiyya fi misr*, (The

Informal Sector and Economic Development in Egypt), Cairo, Centre for the Study of Developing Countries, Cairo University.

Samruh, Abdul Fattah, 1993, *Qanun al-muhamah al-muadil* [The Reformed Law of the Lawyers], Zaqaziq, n.p.

Al-Sayyid, Hassan, 1997, *Al-Tahawulat al-dimuqratiyya wa shar'iyyatt al-nizam al-siyasi fi misr 1981–1993* (Democratic Transformation and the Legitimacy of the Political Regime in Egypt 1981–1993), unpublished MA dissertation, Cairo University, Egypt.

Al-Sayyid, Huda, 1992, "Ather tahwilat al-'amilin bilkharij 'ala al-fi'at al-ijtima'iyya wa al-iqtisadiyya fi misr 1980–1991" (The Effect of Remittances form Workers Abroad on the Social and Economic Sectors in Egypt 1980–1991", *Misr Al-Mu'asira*, no. 429, July.

Al-Sayyid, Mustafa Kamel, 1988, *Intikhabat majlis al-sha'b fi ibril 1987: dilalat nata'ij al-intikhabat* (The Elections of the National Assembly in April 1987: Indications of the Elections Results), Cairo, Al-Ahram Centre for Political and Strategic Studies.

Al-Sayyid, Mustafa K., 1993, "A Civil Society in Egypt?", *Middle East Journal*, vol. 47, no. 2.

Shaar, John, 1981, *Legitimacy in the Modern State*, New Brunswick, Transaction Studies.

Shadi, Salah, 1981, *Safhat min al-tarikh: hasad al-'umr,* (Pages from History), vol.1, Kuwait, Sharikat Al-Shu'a' li Nashr.

Al-Shafi'i, Muamin, 2001, *Al-Dawla wa al-tabka al-wusta fi misr* (The State and the Middle Class in Egypt), Cairo, Dar Qiba'.

Sharaf, S., 1996, *Abdul Nasser: kaifa hakam misr?* (Nasser: How Did He rule Egypt?), Cairo, Madbuli Al-Sagir.

Sharaf Al-Din, N., 1998, *Umara' wa muwatinun* (Princes and Citizens), Cairo, Maktabat Madbuli.

Shihab Al-Din, Fathi, 2000, *Baya' al-qita'a al-'am,* (The Selling of the Public Sector), Tanta, Dar Al- Bashir.

Al-Shubki, A., 1997, "Al-Ma'raka al-intikhabiyya: zawahir jadida" (The Election Contest: New Phenomena), in H. Mustafa (ed.), *Al-Intikhabat al-barlamaniyya fi misr 1995* (Parliamentary Elections in Egypt 1995), Cairo, Al-Ahram Centre for Political and Strategic Studies.

Shukr, Abdul Ghafar (ed.), 2001, *Al-Jam'iyyat al-islamiyya al-ahliya fi misr* (Islamic Informal Associations in Egypt), Cairo, Markaz Al-Buhuth Al-'Arabiyya, Dar Al-Amin.

Sidiq, Mohammad, 1996, "Al-Siyasat al-iqtisadiyya wa al-qita' ghayr al-rasmi" (Economic Policies and the Informal Sector) in Al-Saiyyid Al-Hussaini (ed.), *Al-Qita' ghayr al-rasmi fi hadar misr* (The Informal Sector in Urban Egypt), Cairo, Markaz Al-Buhuth Al-Ijtima'iyya wa Al-Jina'iyya.

Singerman, Diane, 1995, *Avenues of Participation: Family, Politics, and Networks in Urban Quarters of Cairo*, Princeton NJ, Princeton University Press.

Skovgaard-Peterson, Jakob, 1997, *Defining Islam for the Egyptian State*, Leiden, Brill.

Springborg, R., 1989, *Mubarak's Egypt: Fragmentation of Political Order*, London and Boulder, Westview Press.

Stacher, J., 2002, "Post-Islamist Rumblings in Egypt: The Emergence of the Wasat Party", *Middle East Journal*, volume 56, no, 3, Summer.

Stinchcombe, A. L., 1968, *Constructing Social Theories*, New York, Brace and World.

Sullivan, D., 1994, *Private Voluntary Organisations in Egypt: Islamic Development, Private Initiative and State Control*, Gainesville FL, University Press of Florida.

Sullivan, D. and S. Abed-Kotob, 1999, *Islam In Contemporary Egypt: Civil Society vs. the State*, Boulder CO, Lynne Rienner Publishers Inc.

Sullivan, Denis, 1990, "The Political Economy of Reform in Egypt", *International Journal of Middle Eastern Studies*, vol. 22, no. 3.

Tammam, Hussam, 2012, *Al-ikhwan al-muslimun: sanawat maa qabla al-thawra* (The Muslim Brothers: The Years before the Revolution), Cairo, Dar Al-Shurouq.

Taneera, Bakr, 1979, *Tatwur al-nizam al-siyasi fi* misr 1952–1976 (The Development of the Political Regime in Egypt), unpublished PhD thesis, Cairo University, Egypt.

Tawfiq, Hassanain, 1998, *Al-Ikhwan al-muslimun wa al-nizam al-siyasi al-misri* (The Muslim Brothers and the Egyptian Political Regime), Beirut, Dar Al-Tali'a.

Al-Tawil, Mohammad, 1992, *Al-Ikhwan fi al-barlaman* (The Ikhwan in Parliament), ?Cairo, Al-Maktab Al-Misri Al-Hadith.

Tebeileh, Faisal Hassan, 1991, *The Political Economy of Legitimacy in Rentier States: A Comparative Study of Saudi Arabia And Libya*, unpublished PhD thesis, University of California, Los Angeles, USA.

Terterov, Marat, 2001, *Privatisation of the Public Enterprises in Egypt, 1994–2000: A New Strategy for the Management of the a Statist Economy*, unpublished PhD thesis, St. Anthony's College, Oxford University, UK.

Tilmesani, 'Umarn, 1984, *Ayyam ma'a al-sadat* (Days With Sadat), Cairo, Dar Al-I'tisam.

Tripp, C. and M. Wenner (eds.) , 1989, *Egypt Under Mubarak*, London, Routledge.

Tripp, C., 1996, "Islam and the Secular Logic of the State", in Abdul Salam Sidahmed and Anoushiravan Ehteshami (eds.), *Islamic Fundamentalism*, Boulder CO, Westview Press.

Tucker, Robert, 1968, "The Theory of Charismatic Leadership", *Daedalus*, vol. 97, no. 3, Summer.

'Uwaiss, Mustafa, 1997, *Al-Harb al-ahliyya fi niqabat al-muhamin* (The Civil War in the Lawyers' Syndicate), Cairo, Markaz Al-Dirasat wa Al-Ma'lumat Al-Qanuniyya li Huquq Al-Insan.

Vandewalle, Dirk, 1988, "Egypt and It Western Creditors", *Middle East Review*, no. 20, Spring.

Viorst, Milton, 1998, *In The Shadow of the Prophet: The struggle for the Soul of Islam*, New York, Anchor Studies.

Al-Wa'i, Tawfiq, 2001, *Al-Fikr al-siyasi al-mu'asir 'ind al-ikhwan al-muslimin* (The Contemporary Political Thought of the Muslim Brothers), Kuwait, Al-Manar Al-Islamiyya.

Waterbury, John, 1973, "Endemic and Planned Corruption in a Monarchical Regime", *World Politics*, vol. 4, no. 25, July.

——, 1985, "The 'Soft State' and the Open Door: Egypt's Experience with Economic Liberalization 1974–84", *Comparative Politics* vol. 18, no. 1. October.

Weatherford, Stephen, 1992, "Measuring Political Legitimacy", *American Political Science Review*, vol. 86, no. 1, March.

Weber, Max, 1947, *The Theory of Social and Economic Organisations*, trans. A. Henderson and T. Parsons, New York, Oxford University Press.

Wickham, Carri Rosefsky, 1996, *Political Mobilisation Under Authoritarian Rule: Explaining Islamic Activism in Mubarak's Egypt*, unpublished PhD thesis, Princeton University, New Jersey, USA.

——, 1997, "Islamic Mobilisation and Political Change: The Islamist Trend in Egypt's Professional Associations", in Joel Beinin and Joe Stork, *Political Islam: Essays from Middle East Report*, London, I.B.Tauris.

Wilensky, H., 1975, *The Welfare State and Equality: Structural Ideological Roots of Public Expenditure*, Berkley, California University Press.

Yakan, F., 1998, *Manhajiyat al-imam al-shahid hassan al-banna wa madaris al-ikhwan al-muslimin* (The Methodology of the Martyred Imam Hassan Al-Banna and the Schools of the Muslim Brotherhood), Beirut, Al-Risala Publishers.

Yahia Zoubir, 1998, "State, Civil Society and the Question of Radical Fundamentalism in Algeria", in A. Moussalli (ed.), *Islamic Fundamentalism: Myths and Realities*, Reading, Ithaca Press.

Youssif, Samir, 1994, "The Egyptian Private Sector and the Bureaucracy", *Middle Eastern Studies*, vol. 30, no. 2.

Zahran, Jamal, 1988, "Al-Dawr al-siyasi li al-qada' al-misri fi 'amaliyat sun' al-qarar" (The Political Role of the Judiciary in Decision-making), in A. Hilal (ed.), *Al-Nizam al-siyasi al-misri: al-tagiur wa al-Istimrar* (The Egyptian Political Regime: Change and Continuity), Cairo University, Egypt.

Zaki, Moheb, 1995, *Civil Society and Democratisation*, Ibn Khaldun Centre, Cairo.

——, 1999, *Egyptian Business Elites: Their Vision and Investment Behaviour*, Cairo, Arab Centre for Development and Future Research.

Zeghal, Malika, 1999, "Religion and Politics in Egypt: "ulama" of Al-Azhar, Radical Islam and the State, 1952–94", *International Journal of Middle East Studies*, vol. 31, no. 3, August.

Official Documents & Reports

Amnesty International, *Annual Report, 1983*, London.

Arab Republic of Egypt, Consultative Assembly (*majlis al-shura*) 1994, *Muwajhat al-irhab* [Confronting Terrorism], Report 14, Cairo, Government Printing Office.

Centre For Human Rights Legal Aid, n.d., *Military Courts in Egypt: Courts Without Safeguards, Judges Without Immunity, Defendants Without Rights*, Cairo, CHRLA, n.d.

Institute of National Planning, 1992, *In'ikasat azmat al-khalij 1990/1991 'ala al-iqtisad al-misri* (The Effects of the Gulf Crisis 1999/1991 on the Egyptian Economy), Cairo, INP.

Al-Taqrir al-istratiji al-'arabi, (The Arabic Strategic Report), Al-Ahram Centre for Strategic and Political Studies, Cairo, 1984, 1985, 1986, 1987, 1988, 1989, 1990, 1991, 1992, 1993, 1994 and 1995.

Taqrir al-hala al-diniyya fi misr 1995, (Report on the Religious Condition in Egypt, 1995)) Al-Ahram Centre for Political and Strategic Studies, Cairo, 1996.

Taqrir al-hala al-diniyya fi misr 1996, (Report on the Religious Condition in Egypt, 1996) Al-Ahram Centre for Political and Strategic Studies, Cairo, 1997.

Al-Umma fi a'am, (The Umma in a Year), The Centre for Civilisational Studies, Cairo, 1992–93.

Private & Internal Documents

Al-azma al-mumtada: 'ilaqat al-nizam al-misri bi al-ikhwan al-muslimin, al-mazahir, al-asbab, al-nata'ij (The Extended Crisis: The Relation of the Egyptian Regime with the Muslim Brotherhood, Aspects, Reasons, Results), n.d.

Barnamij hizb al-Amal (The Programme of *Al-Amal* Party), Cairo, November, 1994.

Barnamij hizb al- Islah (The Programme of the *Islah* Party), undated.

Barnamij hizb al-Shura, (The Programme of *Al-Shura* Party), undated.

Al-Ikhwan al-muslimun wa al-nizam al-misri: mu'adlat al-sira' wa al-bahs an masar, (The Muslim Brotherhood and the Egyptian Regime: The Formulae of the Struggle and the Search for a Path), 1996.

Al-Mashru'iyya al-disturiyya wa al-qanuniyya lil jama, (The Legal and Constitutional Legitimacy of the Group), undated.

Al-Qisa al-kamila Li ikhtiyyar al-ikhwan al-muslimin al-tarshih dimn qwa'im hizb al-wafd (The Complete Story for the Choosing of *Al-Ikhwan Al Muslimin* to Contest the Elections with the Wafd), undated.

Rapana taqabl mena [Oh Our Lord, Accept from Us], 1989, Alexandria University.

Al-Synariuhat al-mustaqbaliyya al-badila: muhawla li al-bahs an masar jadid fi daw' mu'adlat al-azma bain al-nnizam al-misri wa al-ikhwan al-muslimin (Alternative Future Scenarios: An Attempt to Explore a New Path in Light of the 'Formulae' of the Crisis between the Egyptian Regime and the Muslim Brotherhood), n.d.

Tagrubatina al-niqabiyya 1984–95, (Our Syndicates' Experience, 1984–95), no author, undated.

Welcome, (A Welcome Pack), 1988, Mansura University, the Student Union.

Wuduh al-ru'iyya, (A Clear Vision), undated. ?approx date available.

Newspapers

Al-Ahali, 20 October 1993.

Al-Ahram, 21 May 1971, 15 October 1981, 4 June 1982, 7 November 1983, 20 August 1993, 10 November 1986, 26 April 1986, 21 July 1986, 8 May 1987, 7 July 1987 and 4 May 1990.

Al-Ahrar, 10 January 1983.

Al-Akhbar, 15 July 1976.

Akhbar Al-Khalij, 27 April, 1982.

Arab Times, 29 and 30 December 1984.

Al-'Arabi, 27 September, 1993 and 9 November, 1995.

Cairo Times, 3 April 1997.

Al-Hayat, 16 November 1995, 18 November 1995, and 29 November 1995.

Al-Itihad, 14 June 1986.

Al-Masri Al-Youm, 14 February 2013

Al-Quds Al-Arabi, 22 March 2013

Al-Sha'b, 18 December 1992, 22 October 1993, 2 April 1993, 23 April 1993, 22 June 1993, 22 July 1993 and 20 May 1994.

Al-Sharq Al-Awsat, 22 and 23 January 1983, 2 February 2007

Al-Wafd, 4 October 1990, March 25, 1990 and 17 November 1993.

Magazines

Al-Ahram Al-Iqtisadi, January 1988 and 18 July 1988 and 23 December 1994.

'Akhir Sa'a, 25 November 1992 and 6 February 1985.

Arabia (English), July 1986.

Le Monde, 17 November 1995.

Liwa' Al-Islam, issue 168, September, 1988 and 12 September, 1990.

Middle East Times, 21 December 2001.

Al-Muhandisin, issue 417, 1990 and issue 469, 1995.

Al-Mujtama', 12 December 1993, 19 July 1994, 6 September 1994, and 15 August 1995.

Al-Mukhtar Al-Islami, issue 56, September 1987.

Al-Musawwar, May 1995.

Newsweek, 10 April 2001.

Al-Nida' Al-Jadid, 10 January 1996.

Ruz Al-Yusuf, 16 July 1984 and 11 December 1995.

Personal Interviews:

December 2000 – February 2001; June 2002 – August 2002; April 2007; September 2012

Abdul Fatah, Nabil, political analyst in Al-Ahram Centre for Political and Strategic Studies.

Abdul Fatah, Sayf, Lecturer in Political Science, Cairo University.

Abdullah, Ahmad, psychiatrist and former President of Student Union, Cairo University.

Abdul Majid, Hamid, Lecturer in Political Science, Cairo University.

Abdul Majeed, Wahid, editor of *Al-Nida'* magazine and an analyst in Al-Ahram Centre for Political and Strategic Studies.

Abdul Maqsud, Mahmoud, General Secretary, Pharmacists' Syndicate.

Abdul Maqsud, Salah, Ikhwan journalist and Director of *Al-Markaz Al-'Arabi* for Press Services.

Abdul Rahim, Ali, treasurer of the Asyut branch of the Engineers' Syndicate.

Abdul Raziq, Hussein, editor of *Al-Yasar* Magazine.

Abu Al-Futuh, Abdul Mun'em, member of *maktab al-irshad* and Former Secretary General, Medical Syndicate.

Abu Khalil, 'Amr, psychiatrist and former President of the National Union of Egyptian Universities.

Abu Al-Majd, Kamal, independent Islamist intellectual and former Minster of Information.

Ahmad, Makram Mohammad, Editor of *Al-Musawwar* Magazine.

'Akif, Mahdi, the former *murshid* of the Muslim Brothers.

'Alam, Fu'ad, former assistant to the Director of Security Services in Cairo.

Amin, Jalal, Lecturer in Economics, American University in Cairo.

Al-'Aryan, 'Esam, member of *maktab al-irshad* and former Assistant Secretary General of the Medical Syndicate.

'Auda, Khalid, Lecturer in Geology, Asyut University, and businessman.

Badr, Mohammad Badr, Ikhwan journalist and editor of *Afaq Arabiyya* newspaper.

Al-Bishri, Tariq, independent Islamic intellectual and former Judge in the Supreme Constitutional Court.

Al-Fiqi, Mustafa, Member of Parliament and former Secretary of Information of President Mubarak.

Fu'ad, Mohammad, Ikhwan veteran.

Ghazi, Badr, Lecturer in Chemistry and former President of the Teachers' faculty Club, Cairo University.

Al-Ghazali, Abdul Hamid, Lecturer in Economics, Cairo University.

Habib, Mohammad, former Brothers leader.

Hashish, 'Esam, member of the Engineers' Syndicate.

Hilal, Ali Eddin, Minister of Youth and Sport, and former Dean of Political Science, Cairo University.

Al-Hudaybi, Ma'mun, Former *murshid* of the Muslim Brothers.

Hussein, Mahmoud, Lecturer in Engineering, Asyut University.

Huwaidi, Fahmi, Journalist and independent Islamic writer.

Ibrahim, Sa'd Eddin, Professor of Sociology, American University in Cairo.

Jabara, Abdul Mun'em, Ikhwan veteran and member of *maktab al-irshad*.

Al-Jazzar, Hilmi, Ikhwan activist and former Assistant Secretary General, Medical Syndicate, Giza Branch.

Lutfi, Ahmad, Lecturer in Economics, Cairo University.

Madi, Abu al 'Ila, founder of *Hizb Al-Wasat* and former Assistant Secretary General, Engineers Syndicate.

Mahmoud, Abdel Moneim, journalist and former Brothers Member.

Mashhur, Mustafa, former *murshid* of the Muslim Brothers.

Mohammad, Jamal, medical doctor and former student leader, Cairo University.

Munir, Ibrahim, Ikhwan veteran.

Munir, Khalid, journalist for *Al-Hayat* newspaper, Cairo.

Naf'a, Hassan, Lecturer in Political Science, Cairo University.

Al-Nahas, Ahmad, engineer, and former student leader, Alexandria University.

Qandil-Amani, independent political scientist.

Al-Qassas, Mohammad, former activist.

Rajab, Mohammad, Leader of the Consultative Assembly.

Rami, Ahmad, mid-ranking Brothers leader.

Rashwan, Diaa, expert on Islamist movements.

Al-Sa'id, Rif'at, General Secretary of *Al-Tajammu'* Party.

Al-Samman, Mohammad, engineer, and founder of *Hizb Al-Amal*.

Shalabi, 'Asim, Ikhwan activist and businessman.

Shalabi, Mohammad, businessman.

Al-Shatir, Khairat, owner of *Salsabil*, and member of *maktab al-irshad*.

Shihata, Anwar, Treasurer, Medical Syndicate.

Shihata, Hassanain, Ikhwan veteran and accountant.

Wilson, Rodney, Professor of Economics, University of Durham, UK.

INDEX

Note: References to annotated text are indicated as '89 (n43)', references to chapter notes as '108 n42'.